Sport Business Analytics

Using Data to Increase Revenue and Improve Operational Efficiency

Data Analytics Applications

Series Editor: Jay Liebowitz

PUBLISHED

Sport Business Analytics: Using Data to Increase Revenue and Improve Operational Efficiency

by C. Keith Harrison, Scott Bukstein

ISBN: 978-1-4987-6126-0

FORTHCOMING

Data Analytics Applications in Law

by Edward J. Walters

ISBN: 978-1-4987-6665-4

Data Analytics for Marketing and CRM

by Jie Cheng

ISBN: 978-1-4987-6424-7

Data Analytics in Institutional Trading

by Henri Waelbroeck

ISBN: 978-1-4987-7138-2

Sport Business Analytics

Using Data to Increase Revenue and Improve Operational Efficiency

C. Keith Harrison

University of Central Florida, Orlando, USA

Scott Bukstein

University of Central Florida, Orlando, USA

CRC Press
Taylor & Francis Group
Boca Raton London New York

CRC Press is an imprint of the
Taylor & Francis Group, an **informa** business

AN AUERBACH BOOK

CRC Press
Taylor & Francis Group
6000 Broken Sound Parkway NW, Suite 300
Boca Raton, FL 33487-2742

© 2017 by Taylor & Francis Group, LLC
CRC Press is an imprint of Taylor & Francis Group, an Informa business

No claim to original U.S. Government works

ISBN-13: 978-1-4987-6126-0 (hbk)

Library of Congress Cataloging-in-Publication Data

Names: Harrison, C. Keith, editor. | Bukstein, Scott, editor.
Title: Sport business analytics : using data to increase revenue and improve
operational efficiency / editors, C. Keith Harrison and Scott Bukstein.
Description: Boca Raton : Taylor & Francis, a CRC title, part of the Taylor &
Francis imprint, a member of the Taylor & Francis Group, the academic
division of T&F Informa, plc, [2017] | Series: Data analytics applications
; 1 | Includes bibliographical references and index.
Identifiers: LCCN 2016026176 | ISBN 9781498761260 (alk. paper)
Subjects: LCSH: Sports administration--Data processing. | Sports
administration--Decision making. | Sports--Economic aspects. |
Sports--Marketing. | Business planning. | Strategic planning.
Classification: LCC GV713 .S6736 2017 | DDC 796.06/9--dc23
LC record available at https://lccn.loc.gov/2016026176

Visit the Taylor & Francis Web site at
http://www.taylorandfrancis.com

and the CRC Press Web site at
http://www.crcpress.com

I would like to thank my two heroes, my parents, Claude and Maxine Harrison. My folks have provided unconditional love and support as I pursue my dreams in life. They also taught me how to work hard and help others.

C. Keith Harrison

Mom, you have taught me the importance of humility, authenticity, positivity, and kindness. You inspire me daily. Dad, thank you for teaching me how to play tennis and dish out assists on the basketball court. You introduced me to sports. Trevor, you are an incredible human being. Pure genius with an unparalleled work ethic. You see the ocean beyond the horizon. The best twin brother, ever. Shine up, smile thru. Ryan, your guidance and perpetual support mean everything. Thank you for always believing in your little brothers. Kevin, you continue to amaze me with the selfless work you do as a paramedic and firefighter. I love each of you. Just choose to feel good. Why choose otherwise?

Scott Bukstein

Contents

FOREWORD ix

PREFACE: A WELCOME FROM THE EDITORS xi

ACKNOWLEDGMENTS xiii

EDITORS xv

CONTRIBUTORS xvii

CHAPTER 1 EVOLUTION AND IMPACT OF BUSINESS ANALYTICS IN SPORT 1

SCOTT BUKSTEIN

CHAPTER 2 ANALYTICS AND TICKETING INNOVATIONS AT THE ORLANDO MAGIC 23

JAY RIOLA

CHAPTER 3 TICKET MARKETS IN SPORT: IS THE SECONDARY MARKET BECOMING THE PRIMARY MARKET? 35

TROY KIRBY

CHAPTER 4 CUSTOMER RELATIONSHIP MANAGEMENT AND FAN ENGAGEMENT ANALYTICS 53

RAY MATHEW

CHAPTER 5 THE ASPIRE GROUP'S TICKET MARKETING, SALES, AND SERVICE PHILOSOPHY 69

MICHAEL FARRIS

CHAPTER 6 EMPIRICAL RESEARCH METHODS: SEASON TICKET HOLDER MANAGEMENT AND FAN ENGAGEMENT 89

MICHAEL LEWIS, MANISH TRIPATHI, AND MICHAEL BYMAN

CHAPTER 7 DEVELOPING AND MEASURING THE EFFECTIVENESS OF DATA-DRIVEN DIRECT MARKETING INITIATIVES 107

JOHN BREEDLOVE

CHAPTER 8 FAN ENGAGEMENT, SOCIAL MEDIA, AND DIGITAL MARKETING ANALYTICS AT DUKE UNIVERSITY 131

RYAN CRAIG

CHAPTER 9 LEVERAGING DIGITAL MARKETING TO ENGAGE CONSUMERS AND DRIVE REVENUE 145

MICHAL LORENC AND ALEXANDRA GONZALEZ

CHAPTER 10 COMMUNICATING THE VALUE OF SPORTS SPONSORSHIP 157

ADAM GROSSMAN AND IRVING REIN

CHAPTER 11 MARKET RESEARCH ANALYTICS AND DATA-DRIVEN INNOVATION 173

C. KEITH HARRISON AND SUZANNE MALIA LAWRENCE

CHAPTER 12 TALENT ANALYTICS: UTILIZING ANALYTICS TO EVALUATE EMPLOYEE PERFORMANCE 187

BRANDON MOYER

CHAPTER 13 DATA VISUALIZATION AND DATA-DRIVEN STORYTELLING 201

RYAN SLEEPER

CHAPTER 14 TEACHING A SPORT BUSINESS ANALYTICS COURSE 219

MICHAEL MONDELLO

INDEX 229

Foreword

In 2012, when I left the University of Central Florida (UCF) to become the founding director of the Sport & Entertainment Graduate Program at the University of South Florida (USF), the first issue I needed to address was the proposed graduate curriculum. Based upon my industry experience with the NBA and my consulting background, I felt there were two glaring weaknesses in graduate sport business education programs. The weaknesses I identified and immediately addressed were a lack of coursework in digital marketing and social media strategy and in the area of sport business analytics—also referred to as data-driven decision-making. In my work with the Orlando Magic, I saw the benefits and impact of a truly integrated business strategy unit that was able to integrate their research and analyses across departmental units to demonstrate how data could be used to help make strategic decisions. Initially, the Magic began analyzing data to determine ticket pricing and the content of ticket plans to be offered for sale. Later, applications of analytics included projecting renewals, analyzing ROI in corporate partner agreements and also examining merchandise sales and food and beverage issues. I was also able to see first hand the benefits of having employees trained in analytics and the value they brought to the Magic. It also became clear to me that there was an emerging job market for graduates with these skills.

We immediately added the Sport Business Analytics course and budgeted for interested students to attend the Sloan Sports Analytics Conference at MIT. The next growth in this area was initiated under the leadership of my esteemed colleague, Dr. Mike Mondello, who developed and added our own Sport and Entertainment Analytics Conference powered by Ticketmaster, which we have hosted for the past two years. These efforts bore fruit immediately, as with only two years of graduates we currently have five USF alums employed in the analytics area.

When I left UCF in 2012, I also left behind two excellent colleagues—Dr. C. Keith Harrison and Professor Scott Bukstein—who have seen fit to develop what I believe to be the first text/reader devoted to sport business analytics and classroom use. I am excited about this book, which is edited by two outstanding classroom teachers and researchers who have secured the contributions of a number of leading practitioners—some of whom were my students at UCF and among the early employees in the sport business analytics area.

I am excited that such an academic resource now exists, and I am very confident that the efforts of the editors and contributing authors based on their own first-hand experiences in the area of sport business analytics will prove invaluable to the next wave of students interested in pursuing this career path. I am also hopeful that, now that this resource exists, more sport business programs will see fit to add such a course to their curriculums. As my colleague at the NBA and now CEO of the Philadelphia 76ers and New Jersey Devils, Scott O'Neil, would say, "we must understand both the art and the science of marketing and sales if we hope to be truly successful and maximize our revenue producing capabilities."

Dr. William A. "Bill" Sutton
Founding Director and Professor of Marketing
Sport & Entertainment Management MBA/MS Program
University of South Florida
Tampa, Florida

Preface: A Welcome from the Editors

We are excited about our sport business analytics book and the potential contribution this book will hopefully make with researchers and practitioners. This year (2016) marked the 100th anniversary of the American Educational Research Association (AERA), which is an organization dedicated to the dissemination of new knowledge and policy based on data-driven insights. The theme of the 2016 AERA conference, which was held in Washington, DC, was "Public Scholarship to Educate Diverse Societies." The theme of the AERA conference represents the field of higher education celebrating a century of creating new knowledge and making decisions based on evidence and data. This conference theme is important because just a decade ago the sport business industry did not commonly brand data analytics as a viable career lane for aspiring sport business professionals. However, researchers, academics, and scientists have been collecting and analyzing data for many years. In a sense, our book brings higher education to the industry.

Our goal was to create a book that was both timely and relevant. This book aims to provide students and industry leaders with practical strategies to collect data and then convert that data into meaningful, value-added information and actionable insights. Developing and implementing a systematic analytics strategy can result in a sustainable competitive advantage within the sport business industry. A primary objective of this book is to help sport business organizations utilize data-driven decision making to optimize revenue generation in areas such as ticket sales and corporate partnerships. Readers will learn more about the role of big data and analytics in areas such as ticket pricing, season ticket member retention, fan engagement, sponsorship valuation, customer relationship management, digital marketing, market research, and data visualization.

We hope you enjoy reading this book as much as we enjoyed writing/editing it.

Let's continue to innovate with data and analytics together.

C. Keith Harrison

Scott Bukstein

Acknowledgments

We would like to thank our publisher Taylor & Francis Group (CRC Press). John Wyzalek, senior acquisitions editor with CRC Press, was a joy to work with throughout the writing and publishing process. We would also like to thank Todd Perry, Project Editor at CRC Press, and S. Valantina Jessie, Project Manager at SPi Global, for their tremendous help during the book editing process. A very special thank you to Dr. Jay Liebowitz, who invited us to be the lead authors and coeditors of this book. We were (and remain) honored by Jay's invitation to write the first practical book on business analytics in sports. Jay is the series editor for the entire CRC Press data analytics applications book series. A personal thank you to each contributing author. We appreciate you. It was a joy to work on this project with five of our former graduate students. This book is the result of a true collaborative and collective effort. We also thank all of our colleagues and students who reviewed chapter drafts and provided helpful feedback.

Our families were instrumental throughout the book writing process. Much love and infinite gratitude for our parents, brothers, and other family members who provided endless support and encouragement as we worked together on this book project. We will continue to work hard every day to make you proud.

Finally, a thank you to everyone who reads the book—especially those of you who actually read all of these acknowledgments.

Editors

C. Keith Harrison is a tenured associate professor within the College of Business Administration at the University of Central Florida (UCF), Orlando, Florida, as well as an associate program director of the DeVos Sport Business Management Graduate Program. Dr. Harrison, a former NCAA scholar-athlete who played center on the West Texas A&M University football team, has over two decades of university teaching and research experience at the community college level (Cerritos, Fullerton, and Cypress) and university level (Washington State University, Indiana University, University of Michigan, Arizona State University, and UCF). Harrison has published many peer-reviewed journal articles and book chapters. Harrison's career and research focus is on student-athlete and professional athlete identity constructs, diversity/inclusion issues related to gender and race relations, data-driven cultural innovation in sport, and the marketing of emerging multicultural demographics. In 2015, Harrison was named editor of the *Journal of Higher Education Athletics & Innovation*. Harrison's brief list of clients and partnerships (past and present) include the NFL, Minnesota Vikings, Oakland Raiders, Miami Dolphins, Jordan Brand, EA Sports, Paragon, Florida Citrus Sports, Boise State University, UCLA's School of Education, University of Colorado–Boulder, Wharton Sports Business Academy, and Emory University's Goizueta Business School. In addition,

Harrison is the president, chief innovation officer, and cofounder of scholarballer.org.

Scott Bukstein has been a faculty member at the University of Central Florida (UCF), Orlando, Florida, since 2010. Bukstein currently serves as the director of the Sport Business Management Undergraduate Program within the College of Business Administration at UCF. Bukstein is also an associate director of the DeVos Sport Business Management Graduate Program at UCF. In addition, Bukstein is an adjunct instructor within the College of Business at the University of South Florida, Tampa, Florida. Bukstein also served as an adjunct assistant professor within the Goizueta Business School at Emory University, Atlanta, Georgia, from 2013 to 2015. Bukstein has developed and taught several sport business analytics courses at the graduate and undergraduate levels. Bukstein's research focus is on business analytics in sport, the intersection of sport and the law, collective bargaining in professional sport, the business of collegiate athletics and professional sport, the perceptions and academic performance of college student-athletes, mobility patterns and career paths of coaches and other executives, and leadership and diversity/inclusion issues in sport. Bukstein also collaborates with his colleague, C. Keith Harrison, on a variety of sport business consulting projects. Prior to becoming a college professor and administrator, Bukstein worked as a corporate attorney at Faegre Baker Daniels in Minneapolis, where he represented clients in a wide variety of transactional matters, including public and private mergers and acquisitions, corporate finance and securities, venture capital financings, and general corporate counseling. Bukstein also provided legal counsel to several sport organizations.

Contributors

John Breedlove joined the Tampa Bay Buccaneers in 2012 as the manager of insights and strategy. In this role, Breedlove is responsible for producing insights, analysis, and tools that aid in improving the effectiveness and efficiency of all business units. Breedlove's internal clients include sales, marketing, guest and member relations, partnership sales/activation, ticket operations, finance, and legal. His duties include maintaining and developing the CRM and e-mail systems, managing e-mail marketing efforts, conducting and analyzing research (both proprietary and syndicated), managing search engine marketing and retargeting, analyzing website metrics, exploring new systems/tools, and conducting ad hoc data analyses as needed. In his time prior to the Buccaneers, Breedlove spent almost seven years as the director of database and analytics for Madison Square Garden.

Michael Byman is a marketing PhD student at Emory University's Laney Graduate School, Atlanta, Georgia, with a focus on sports analytics.

Ryan Craig joined Duke University Athletics, Durham, North Carolina, in March of 2011 and serves as the executive director of digital media. In his role, Craig leads a team that is responsible for editorial, creative, and strategic decisions regarding the department's mobile apps, social media platforms, and official website, GoDuke. com. Before arriving at Duke, Craig worked at WRAL-TV in Raleigh, North Carolina, for seven years, serving as a news production assistant, producer, photographer, reporter, radio host, and sports web editor. A native of Setauket, New York, Craig graduated from Duke University in 2005 with degrees in history and psychology. He currently resides in Raleigh, North Carolina, with his wife, Blair, and daughter, Austen.

Michael Farris creates innovative research solutions that lead to actionable strategies for partners of The Aspire Group. Since joining Aspire, Michael has led the Strategic Consulting and Research team in conducting services for over 50 best-of-brand partners in seven countries across three continents. Under his leadership, the department conducts fan research, constructs ticket packaging and pricing models, and develops ticket marketing, sales, and service plans to drive revenue for partners throughout the sport and entertainment industry. Michael's experiences include engagements with Aushorse, Georgia Tech Athletics, Lancashire County Cricket Club, the National Rugby League, The Royal and Ancient/The Open, Tijuana Xolos, and West Ham United.

Alexandra Gonzalez is currently a digital marketing account manager at Google, helping CPG brands pivot to digital and refine their online marketing strategies. She previously worked with professional sports leagues and Broadway clients in Google's Media & Entertainment sector, after two years of focusing on small businesses' digital marketing initiatives. Alex leads internal trainings at Google on presentation skills and energy management. She often travels as a public speaker and spends her time outside of work volunteering as a guest teacher at Chicago Public Schools. She graduated from the University of Florida, Gainesville, Florida, with a BS in journalism.

Adam Grossman is president/founder of the sports sponsorship and analytics firm Block Six Analytics. He is a lecturer for Northwestern University's Masters of Sports Administration Program, Evanston, Illinois, where he developed the course "Entrepreneurship in Sports" and codeveloped "Sports Management Analytics." He is the coauthor of *The Sports Strategist: Developing Leaders for a High-Performance*

Industry, which was the featured book at the 2015 Sloan Sports Analytics Conference. His work has been featured in publications including *Forbes*, *The Washington Post*, *The Chicago Tribune*, *Comcast SportsNet Chicago*, and *Oxford University Press*.

Troy Kirby is currently the director of Ticket Operations at the University of California-Davis. Previously, he hosted and owned the "Tao of Sports Podcast" where he interviewed sports executives throughout the world, focusing on sales, revenue streams, marketing strategies, communication plans, training of staff, and compliance from the amateur and professional ranks. Troy has also held various ticketing manager roles at Eastern Washington University, Cheney, Washington, and Seattle University, Seattle, Washington.

Suzanne Malia Lawrence is a graduate of the University of Tennessee's applied sport psychology program (Knoxville, Tennessee). Currently, Dr. Lawrence is a professor in the Kinesiology Department at California State University, Fullerton. She works as a dissertation mentor for psychology doctoral candidates. Her research interests include female football fans' preferences, stereotypes surrounding athleticism, career transition of college athletes, athletes' experiences of concussions, and Whiteness in sport. Lawrence has been awarded seven different research rewards including the Dean's Accomplished Scholar Award. Lawrence has a passion for mentoring junior scholars and she encourages self-confidence, teamwork, and leadership with her mentees/students.

Michael Lewis is an associate professor at the Goizueta School of Business at Emory University, Atlanta, Georgia. In addition to sports topics, Dr. Lewis specializes on marketing issues such as dynamic pricing, customer relationship management, and brand equity. Lewis has published in academic journals such as *Marketing Science*, the *Journal of Marketing* and the *Journal of Marketing Research*. He also publishes original sports-related research at the Emory University Sports Analytics Research Blog.

Michal Lorenc is a 14-year veteran of Google who has held multiple leadership roles on the revenue-generating side of the business. Mike is currently heading up Google's Ticketing & Live Events Group where he oversees a team responsible for fostering strategic relationships with key partners in the sports, music, and ticketing industries. Mike also recently became a co-owner of AFC Ann Arbor, a minor league soccer team in Ann Arbor, Michigan. Mike is a marketing and international business graduate of Loyola University of Chicago, Illinois. Mike currently resides in Ann Arbor, Michigan, and considers himself extremely lucky to work in the cross section of the sports and online marketing worlds.

Ray Mathew's first experience in the sports business world came when he decided to attend graduate school at the University of Central Florida, Orlando, Florida. He completed a Master of Sport Business Management and a Master of Business Administration in 2009. He then took a role helping to start up a new NBA Development League team (the Maine Red Claws) primarily in a sales capacity, but his role also included sponsorship sales and numerous other operational duties. Two years later, he joined the Tampa Bay Buccaneers, initially as a sales representative and then as a CRM coordinator soon after. Ray was responsible for managing the CRM efforts for the entire sales department. After a few years in that role, he accepted a position with Fan Interactive Marketing as a Sports CRM Analyst, running the day-to-day CRM systems for multiple sports and entertainment clients. Ray grew up in North Carolina, where he attended the University of North Carolina at Chapel Hill receiving business administration and economics undergraduate degrees in 2004.

Michael Mondello, PhD, is a professor in the Department of Marketing and the associate director of the MBA sport and entertainment management program at The University of South Florida, Tampa, Florida. Mondello teaches finance and analytics. His research interests focus on financial/analytical issues related to sports organizations, including competitive balance, economic impact analysis, contingent valuation, ticket pricing, and stadium financing. He has published research in both business and sport management peer-reviewed publications, including the *Journal of Sports Economics*, *Sport Marketing Quarterly*, *Economic Development Quarterly*, the *Journal of Sport Management*, *Management Decision*, and the *International*

Journal of Sport Finance. He was recognized as a NASSM research fellow in 2007.

Brandon Moyer works with The Aspire Group, Inc., as a Database Marketing and Analytics Coordinator at Colorado State University, Fort Collins, Colorado. Brandon graduated from West Virginia University, Morgantown, West Virginia, in 2013 with a bachelor of science degree in business administration, where he was also a four-year member of the West Virginia University men's swimming and diving team. After he graduated, Brandon worked for a dewatering company as an inventory coordinator. After a year, Brandon decided to attend the University of Central Florida, Orlando, Florida, as a part of the DeVos Sport Business Management Graduate Program where he earned an MBA and MSBM before joining The Aspire Group in January 2016.

Irving Rein, PhD, is a professor of communication studies at Northwestern's School of Communication, Evanston, Illinois. Dr. Rein is an internationally known expert in public communication and popular culture and was a recipient of the National Communication Association's Outstanding Professor of the Year Award for 1999–2000. He is the coauthor of *The Sports Strategist: Developing Leaders for a High Performance Industry, The Elusive Fan: Reinventing Sports in a Crowded Marketplace,* and *High Visibility: Transforming Your Personal and Professional Brand.* Rein has been a communication consultant to many corporations, including Major League Baseball, the United States Olympic Committee, and NASA.

Jay Riola is in his tenth season with the Orlando Magic. Jay oversees the Orlando Magic's business strategy efforts, including strategic planning and the use of data and analytics to improve business performance. Jay began as an intern for the Magic in 2006 working for the department overseeing the design and construction of the new Amway Center in downtown Orlando, Florida. Riola received his bachelor's degree in finance and marketing from Trinity University in San Antonio, Texas, in 2006, and an MBA from the University of Florida, Gainesville, Florida, in 2011. He currently resides in Orlando, Florida, with his wife, Julia.

Ryan Sleeper is director of data visualization and analysis at Evolytics, where he has worked with data-driven brands, including the Atlanta Hawks, Kansas City Chiefs, NAIA, and many others. Ryan enjoys creating innovative data visualizations that have led to several notable Tableau recognitions including four-time Top 25 Tableau Public Viz of the Year, 2014 Tableau Public Viz of the Year Runner-Up, 2014 Elite 8 Sports Viz Finalist, 2013 Elite 8 Champion, 2013 Tableau Iron Viz Champion, and 2015 Tableau Public Viz of the Year. His work has garnered attention from popular websites including The Guardian, ESPN, and U.S. News & World Report.

Dr. William A. "Bill" Sutton is founding director and professor of the Sport and Entertainment Business Management Graduate Program in the Management Department at the University of South Florida, Tampa, Florida. He is the founder and principal of Bill Sutton & Associates, a consulting firm specializing in strategic marketing and revenue enhancement. His consulting clients cover a veritable who's who of professional athletics: the NBA, WNBA, NHL, the Orlando Magic, the Phoenix Suns, MSG Sports, and the New York Mets. Sutton served as vice president, Team Marketing and Business Operations, for the National Basketball Association (NBA), where he helped establish the TMBO approach to team services. In this capacity, Sutton assisted NBA teams with marketing-related functions such as sales, promotional activities, market research, advertising, customer service, strategic planning, and staffing. Dr. Sutton has gained national recognition for his ability to meld practical experience in professional sports with academic analysis and interpretation. He holds three degrees (BA, 1972; MS, 1980; and ED.D, 1983) from Oklahoma State University, Stillwater, Oklahoma, where he was inducted into the College of Education Hall of Fame in 2003. A native of Pittsburgh, Pennsylvania, Sutton and his wife Sharon currently reside in Tampa and Clearwater Beach, Florida.

Manish Tripathi joined the Goizueta Business School faculty in 2008 after completing a PhD in marketing at the Kellogg School of Management, Northwestern University, Evanston, Illinois. Tripathi earned a BA in economics from Stanford University, Stanford, California, and, prior to his doctoral studies, worked for four years as a marketing and business development manager at Homestead Technologies, a software company in Menlo Park, California. Manish also worked as a financial analyst for the investment bank, Hambrecht & Quist, conducting valuation, financial advisory, and transaction execution for technology and emerging growth companies. His research interests include multichannel strategies, market structure and entry, structural models, and Bayesian statistics.

EVOLUTION AND IMPACT OF BUSINESS ANALYTICS IN SPORT

SCOTT BUKSTEIN

Contents

Overview of Analytics and Data-Driven Business Strategy 1
  Data and Analytics Defined 2
  Overview of the Sport Business Analytics Process 4
Evolution of Analytics in the Sport Business Industry 6
Business Analytics Application Areas in the Sport
Business Industry 7
  Ticket Pricing and Sales Inventory 7
  Customer Relationship Management and Fan Engagement 11
  Social Media and Digital Marketing Analytics 14
  Corporate Partnership Acquisition, Valuation, and Evaluation 15
  Market Research 17
Obstacles to Adoption and Successful Use of Analytics in
the Sport Business Industry: The Importance of Strategy,
Communication, and Collaboration 18
References 20

Overview of Analytics and Data-Driven Business Strategy

During the 2014–2015 National Basketball Association (NBA) season, Atlanta Hawks weekday home games at Philips Arena started at 7:30 p.m. The starting time for similar weekday home games for the 2015–2016 NBA season changed to 8:00 p.m. As explained by Atlanta Hawks chief executive officer Steve Koonin, the organization tries "to make every decision data based" (Vivlamore, 2015). The 30 minute change to the starting time of select home games resulted directly from collecting and analyzing relevant data. For example, the Atlanta Hawks analyzed data with respect to ticket holder arrival at games based on the exact time each ticket was scanned when fans entered Philips Arena. The organization also analyzed local traffic patterns to determine whether pushing back the game start time would result in a more efficient fan commute to Philips Arena. This data-driven business decision aligned with customer input, and the change resulted in an increased number of fans in arena seats at game tip-off time. The Hawks now will likely collect data on how the variation of game start time impacts game-day revenue categories such as individual game and season ticket sales in addition to merchandise and food and beverage sales.

Data and Analytics Defined

A primary objective of this book is to help sport business managers utilize *data* and *analytics* in order to optimize revenue by making more informed, strategic business decisions. "Data" are generally defined as either "facts or information used to calculate, analyze or plan something" or "information that is produced or stored by a computer" (Merriam-Webster, 2016). Stated differently, "data" refer to the identification, aggregation, storage, and management of relevant information. Author and data expert Bernard Marr explains, "the basic idea behind the phrase 'big data' is that everything we do in our lives is or soon will leave a digital trace (or data), which can be used and analyzed" (Marr, 2015, p. 9).* Analytics describes any data-driven process as well as any actionable insights derived from data (see Liebowitz, 2014). Analytics involve the analysis/evaluation and application/presentation of data (i.e., transforming data into

---

* The terms "data" and "big data" are used interchangeably throughout this book. Big data describes the aggregation of large volumes of structured and unstructured information (e.g., text, audio, visual, and image). As explained by Mayer-Schönberger and Cukier (2013), although "[t]here is no rigorous definition of big data…big data refers to things one can do at a large scale that cannot be done at a smaller one" (p. 6). The phrase "sport business analytics" refers to data-driven, analytical decision-making within the sport business industry.

reliable and actionable intelligence). Ransbotham et al. (2015a) describe analytics as "the use of data and related business insights developed through applied analytical disciplines (for example, statistical, contextual, quantitative, predictive, cognitive, and other models) to drive fact-based planning, decisions, execution, management, measurement, and learning" (p. 63). As applied to the sport business industry, analytics function as "tools to find, interpret, and use data to make better decisions…[and to add] valuable objectivity to the decision-making process" (Rein et al., 2015, p. 103).

The core purpose of "sport business analytics" is to convert raw data into meaningful, value-added, and actionable information that enables sport business professionals to make strategic business decisions, which then result in improved company financial performance and a measurable and sustainable competitive advantage. Ben Alamar, director of production analytics at ESPN, suggests a primary objective of sport business analytics should be to save decision-makers' time by making relevant information efficiently available so that these decision-makers can analyze information rather than spend time gathering information; in addition, the data-driven analytics process should also provide decision-makers with novel insight (Alamar, 2013). An effective sport business analytics system should result in increased incremental revenue, reduced costs, managed risk, more effective utilization of human resources (i.e., "talent analytics"), optimized product and service development (e.g., data-driven innovation), improved customer marketing and service (e.g., fan engagement), and overall more informed strategic decision-making (see Troilo et al., 2016; see also SAS, 2016). For example, sport business analytics enable sport organizations to better understand and market to current and prospective customers via targeted customer relationship management (CRM) initiatives. Sport business analytics also improve and optimize business processes (and resultant incremental revenue) with respect to ticket pricing, corporate partnership prospecting and activation, and food and beverage offerings. In a recent empirical study on the adoption of analytics by professional sport organizations, the use of analytics correlated with revenue growth of 7.2% in the year following adoption of a business analytics strategy as compared with general sport business industry expectations of 3% annual increases in revenue (Troilo et al., 2016).*

Overview of the Sport Business Analytics Process

The sport business analytics process generally involves data collection, management, visualization, implementation, and evaluation. Sport business organizations are encouraged to focus first on clearly defining business strategies, goals, and objectives before developing a data-driven initiative or staffing an analytics department (see Marr, 2015). Next, organizations need to identify the data systems that will be used to collect and capture data. For example, a sport team could leverage ticketing and point-of-sale software systems to monitor season ticket holder accounts (e.g., frequency of ticket utilization and most recent game attendance) and concessions sales (e.g., track food and beverage inventory along with corresponding revenue at each sales area).

In addition to determining the "right" system(s) for data collection, it is imperative for organizations to access and assess the "right" data based on business strategy. For example, if a sport team plans to utilize intercept surveys to determine the probability of season ticket holder renewals, the team could focus on collecting the following information from current season ticket holders: (1) amount spent on season ticket(s) and personal seat license (if applicable); (2) years of season ticket membership; (3) number of games attended during the current season; (4) whether season ticket holder is an individual or business; (5) distance of season ticket holder commute to each home game; (6) number of times season ticket holder attempted to resell tickets; (7) success rate with respect to season ticket holder attempts to resell tickets; and (8) attendance/engagement at ancillary team events with exclusive access for season ticket holders.

---

* Troilo et al. (2016) also found that sport business managers "perceive a benefit from the adoption of analytics" with respect to reducing costs, but "this benefit is illusory" (p. 82). Results from this empirical study also indicated when sport business organizations "realize benefits from the adoption of analytics, it is almost entirely with regard to revenues" (p. 82). Future research should analyze the extent to which sport organizations (e.g., professional sport teams and college athletics programs) prioritize generating revenues as compared with managing expenses.

An effective and efficient data management system (i.e., "data warehouse") will enable a company to organize, standardize, centralize, integrate, interconnect, and streamline the collected data. An organization will then be able to quickly mine the data and create an analytic model that transforms the raw data into practical, actionable insight.* For example, a sport team could use Microsoft Excel or statistical software such as SAS to pinpoint all first-year season ticket holders who purchased the least expensive season ticket package, lived over 40 miles from the arena, have resold over 50% of their tickets through the team's official season ticket exchange program, and have not personally attended a game in over 2 months. The team would likely flag these season ticket holder accounts as "most likely not to renew," which could directly impact the renewal prioritization strategy of team sales and service representatives responsible for renewing season ticket accounts.

Data presentation and visualization will then empower analytics team members to communicate results so that data are accessible, understandable, and usable with respect to developing operational strategies.† After an organization implements the data-driven recommendations, key decision-makers should consistently monitor and evaluate initiative effectiveness so that the organization can adjust both business operations and future analytics processes. Sport business organization leaders should also continuously track best practices with respect to data-based opportunities for collaboration and innovation. When companies "use analytics to improve their ability to innovate, they also tend to collaborate more through their use of analytics…organizations that innovate with analytics don't merely increase their use of analytics in decision making; they also change the way they behave as organizations" (Kiron et al., 2014, p. 33). The following section provides an overview of the evolution and integration of business analytics within the sport business industry.

---

* Jay Liebowitz, series editor for the Taylor & Francis Group (CRC Press) data analytics applications book series, defines "insight" as "gain[ing] an understanding of a business situation that allows a manager to make the best possible decision where *best* refers to a numerically measurable business outcome that is consistent with the goals and objectives of the organization in question" (Liebowitz, 2014, p. 30).

† In Chapter 13, Ryan Sleeper discusses the significance of data visualization and data-driven storytelling.

Evolution of Analytics in the Sport Business Industry

Sport teams have applied analytic models to assist with decision-making for over 50 years. However, until recently, much of the advanced analytics application related solely to player and team strategies on the playing field. For example, in one of the first sport analytics studies, Lindsey (1959) analyzed baseball player and team strategies such as the importance of batting average, pitcher selection, strategic lineup adjustments, and overall team defensive strategy (see also Alamar and Mehrotra, 2011). Lindsey (1963) also analyzed historical team and player statistics to determine situations in which an intentional walk, a double play allowing a run to score, a sacrifice fly, and an attempted steal are advisable game management strategies. As explained by Lindsey (1963), "in order to judge the advisability of any particular strategy, it is necessary to take into account not only the immediate situation on the bases, but also the inning and the score" (p. 499). Lindsey (1959) forecasted that, with respect to "the interpretation of data on past performance in order to influence decisions regarding future situations, there may be some thoughts still worth developing" (p. 197).

Sport organizations continue to develop Lindsey's thoughts and utilize data to influence player personnel and team strategy decisions. In addition, throughout the past 10 years, many sport organizations have integrated data-driven decision-making into core business functions such as ticket pricing, database management, corporate partnership valuation, fan engagement, and CRM (see Troilo et al., 2016). Sport business organizations have emulated "revenue management" and "yield management" strategies previously developed in other industries.

For example, since the 1990s, the airline and hotel industries have implemented variable and dynamic ticket/room pricing models based on consumer demand and product/service availability in addition to creating customer loyalty and rewards programs (e.g., frequent-flyer miles) along with developing customer experience "upgrades" (e.g., opportunity for consumers to increase spend for a premium hotel room or for more legroom on an airplane) (see Davenport, 2014; Drayer et al., 2012; Stein, 2014). Data-driven strategies in the sport business industry also differ from operational strategies common to the airline and hotel industries. For example, as explained by Diehl et al. (2016), "The availability of a legal resale market for sporting event tickets stands in stark contrast to other fixed-supply industries like the airlines, which strictly prohibit the resale of tickets" (p. 83).

Sport organizations also collaborate with and learn best practices from innovators in several other industries in order to consistently develop and integrate analytics strategies. For instance, Davenport (2014) explained, "The [Orlando] Magic organization has also learned a great deal from its partnership with the Walt Disney Co.—which has a strong analytics group in Orlando—for joint promotions to residents and visitors in the area" (p. 12). Similarly, sport organizations have adopted digital marketing tactics (e.g., targeted e-mail campaigns and optimized website designs) as well as consumer brand loyalty strategies (e.g., product recommendations, bundling, and subscriptions) from e-commerce companies such as Amazon in order to develop personalized data-driven strategies based on the particular preferences and purchasing patterns of sport consumers. Innovators in other industries continue to create an analytics blueprint and establish key performance indicators (KPIs) for sport organizations.

The next section of this chapter spotlights some of the key sport business analytics application areas, including ticketing systems, consumer prospecting and retention, social media and digital marketing, corporate partnerships, and market research. The following section also provides a preview of the other chapters within this sport business analytics book.

Business Analytics Application Areas in the Sport Business Industry

Examples of business analytics application areas

Ticket pricing and sales inventory	Customer relationship management	Fan engagement and sport event experience	Social media and digital marketing	Corporate partnership ROI

Ticket Pricing and Sales Inventory

Sport business organizations utilize analytics to inform the ticket inventory and pricing decision-making process. Most sport teams focus on a combination of "attendance maximization" and "revenue optimization" (see Drayer et al., 2012). Teams also focus on creating customer value (e.g., fan event experience) in addition to understanding the importance of "customer lifetime value" (e.g., cumulative amount of total business derived from a current or prospective ticket holder). Ticket demand models combined with direct feedback from customers assist sport organizations in developing ticket pricing strategies and customized ticket promotions.*

For example, the Cleveland Indians identified that season ticket sales had declined in certain premium areas of Progressive Field. Organization leaders understood the importance of improving the fan experience in the club section of the ballpark in order to increase ticket sales and other game-day revenue streams. The team subsequently collected survey data from more than 700 current season ticket and single game ticket holders to better understand customer priorities and preferences with respect to variables such as ticket price, seat location, and food and beverage offerings. Members of the team's analytics department collaborated with other front office executives to quantify ticket holder preferences in order to determine the combination of ticket offerings and pricing that would maximize value for both the club and consumers and would ultimately lead to new product/service development (e.g., new ticket options for fans) (Gershenfeld, 2015). As a result of this ticket pricing, seat location, and food and beverage analytics initiative, "[a]ctual revenue for the club section increased 6% in 2012. The increased net revenue came as a result of improved price segmentation, providing overall lower prices with an anticipated increase in attendance" (Gershenfeld, 2015, p. 171). Alex King, vice president of marketing and brand management at the Cleveland Indians, explained that ongoing season ticket holder and single game pricing analyses are "the two largest components of revenue growth in our entire ticketing business" (Gershenfeld, 2015, p. 174). The sport business industry "continues to seek ways to redefine the season ticket holder relationship" in part by focusing on data-driven ticketing innovations involving

---

* Ticket sales models used to generate potential new sales (i.e., lead generation models) will typically significantly differ from ticket retention models used to calculate the likelihood of season ticket holder renewals.

"seat concepts, price structures, ticket policies, and amenity packages" (PwC, 2015, p. 2).

"Dynamic pricing" refers to a ticket sales approach in which sport teams make "real-time" adjustments to ticket prices based on factors such as actual consumer/market demand, win/loss record for home team and opponent, injuries to star player(s), day of week of the game, other local entertainment options on game day, and anticipated weather conditions. A current challenge (and opportunity) for many sport teams relates to understanding how to leverage data and analytics to effectively design and implement dynamic ticket pricing strategies (see Xu et al., 2015; see also Diehl et al., 2016). A primary goal of dynamic pricing is to simultaneously increase season ticket sales (e.g., by offering season tickets at lower prices than dynamically priced single game tickets), ticket utilization rates (i.e., rate at which ticket holders attend games), and ticket yield for single game tickets (i.e., average amount paid for ticket).

In 2015, approximately 45% of all NBA, Major League Baseball (MLB), National Hockey League (NHL), and Major League Soccer (MLS) teams utilized a dynamic pricing model for single game tickets. Sport teams within these leagues have also expanded dynamic pricing to include season ticket trade ("buyback") programs (PwC, 2015). National Football League (NFL) teams were not permitted to dynamically price tickets until the 2015 NFL season; approximately 25% of NFL teams adopted a dynamic ticket pricing model during the 2015 NFL season (Kaplan, 2015). Stein (2014) opined that reluctance by some sport teams to adopt dynamic ticket pricing "may reflect the fact that airline tickets are nontransferable, while most event tickets can easily be resold…the box office, unlike the airlines, faces unpredictable amounts of competition from early purchasers who are reselling their own seats" (p. 17). The secondary market (i.e., ticket reselling) directly impacts ticket pricing strategies adopted by sport teams. Some analysts suggest that dynamic pricing exclusively addresses the recapture of lost ticket value from the secondary market (PwC, 2015).*

---

* PwC analysts assert that reasons for team reluctance in adopting dynamic pricing include "limited single game inventory, administrative costs, and the use of alternate strategies to secondary markets, including direct participation in official ticket exchanges…and more aggressive season ticket holder policies such as delayed ticket delivery, ticket resale restrictions, and ticket transfer fees" (PwC, 2015, p. 3).

Ticketing analytics can assist teams that want to more effectively control the secondary ticket market. For example, in March 2016, the Boston Bruins analyzed the team's "season-ticket population" and discovered that the team had a higher than projected number of ticket resellers; team analysts monitored the number of games each season ticket holder attended as well as the number of secondary marketplaces in which tickets were listed for resale to determine which season ticket accounts belonged to ticket agencies. As a result of this internal data collection, the team cancelled the accounts of high-volume resellers so as to increase the number of tickets available for individuals who purchase season tickets for personal use; in addition, the team announced that high-volume resellers would be subject to paying a premium of 9% or more in the future for season tickets (Adams, 2016).

Secondary ticket marketplaces such as Ticketmaster and StubHub also utilize data to inform ticket pricing strategies. For example, in 2013, based in part on consumer complaints about ticket service charges, StubHub implemented an "all-in" pricing structure in which all service fees were included in the total price viewed by prospective ticket purchasers. Scott Cutler, president of StubHub, explained, "the hope was that the industry would follow and that would yield greater transparency" (Smith, 2015a). However, by late 2015, StubHub decided to return to its former approach of including a 10% transaction fee for buyers; this major decision was based on decreases in overall company ticket sales revenue in addition to data collected via A/B (split) testing with prospective ticket buyers. In the StubHub A/B testing, one group of prospective ticket buyers viewed the "all-in" prices, whereas the other group of prospective ticket buyers in the study viewed a listed price with the transaction fee added at transaction completion. Cutler noticed a common theme in consumer responses "within the first hour of the data starting to come in" (Smith, 2015a). Findings from this consumer study indicated higher sales completion rates and total sales amounts associated with the old "price plus service fee" model.

Sport organizations must continue to evolve and innovate in order to avoid becoming extinct.

In Chapter 2, Jay Riola details ticketing innovations and data-driven season ticket member strategies recently developed by leaders at the Orlando Magic. In Chapter 3, Troy Kirby provides an in-depth analysis on ticket pricing, ticket reselling, and the impact of ticket brokers.

Customer Relationship Management and Fan Engagement

Sport organizations develop CRM systems both to create fan profiles and to structure ticket sales strategies. The CRM data warehouse functions as a centralized, integrated database for information related to customer demographics in addition to customer ticketing, merchandise, and food and beverage purchase patterns (Smith, 2015b). Organizations can then analyze these data to develop customized messages for specific season ticket holders (or other categories of customers). For example, a college athletics department could mine the CRM data to identify that a particular season ticket holder typically purchases nachos and a soft pretzel at the same concession stand at the end of the first quarter of every home football game. The analytics team would also have access to customer background information such as the birthdate of each season ticket holder. Equipped with these data, a team representative could be waiting at the concession stand at the end of the first quarter during the football game that is closest to the ticket holder's birthday in order to provide the ticket holder with a personalized thank you—and free nachos, soft pretzels, and soft drinks for the entire family. An effective CRM data warehouse can also help sport organizations identify—and subsequently create "pitch packages" for—prequalified sales prospects (Smith, 2015b).

Analytics initiatives also assist sport organizations with respect to improving the overall fan experience. For example, in 2014, the New York Mets partnered with SAS to apply a "data-driven approach to discover what fans want and how they behave so the team can design experiences that appeal to them on a personal level" (SAS, 2014). SAS software was utilized to analyze data regarding fan arrival time, seat location, food and beverage purchases, merchandise sales, and engagement with in-game promotions, with the ultimate end goal of improving the overall fan experience—and increasing season ticket sales (SAS, 2014).

Many sport organizations have partnered with companies such as Experience to increase game-day revenue via seat upgrades and

"VIP experiences." For example, the Experience App might create the opportunity for a fan who had originally purchased a $40 ticket to sit in section 322 to now pay $10 during the second quarter to upgrade to a premium area seat in section 112 or 122. Sport teams utilize analytics to determine which seats will likely remain unsold/open; seat upgrades function as both an incremental revenue opportunity and an opportunity to collect additional fan data. The Experience App could also create an opportunity for this same fan to pay $20 for the opportunity to "high-five" players and then shoot baskets on the court after a game. Two weeks after this event, a sales representative might follow up with the fan to offer a customized "eight-game flex-plan" ticket package with seats in section 122 and with special VIP experiences similar to high-fiving players and shooting hoops on the court. Fan engagement analytics also provide tremendous value during the season ticket holder renewal process. For instance, in 2014, the Atlanta Falcons achieved early season ticket renewals from 85% of season ticket holders who participated in a customer loyalty rewards program via the Experience App that allowed season ticket holders to redeem points for VIP experiences.

In addition, data-driven storytelling and insight-based event content improve the fan experience. For instance, for the 2016 Australian Open, Tennis Australia collaborated with IBM to develop an immersive, automated, and comprehensive mobile content delivery strategy in order to enhance the at-event experience and provide event organizers with a competitive edge against broadcasters. Data-driven content included tennis match statistics along with related tournament notifications and updates. Event organizers leveraged each fan's personal opt-in preferences and could customize digital content and push notifications via the event app. Kim Trengove, Tennis Australia's manager of digital and publishing, explained that Tennis Australia aimed "to use the data and analytics to tell the story to enrich the customer experience through our various applications...what we're trying to do is get the fan to engage at whatever level they want" (Cameron, 2016; see also Stockwell, 2015).

Emerging technological innovations provide consumers with a unique opportunity to create and control digital and other in-venue content while also simultaneously providing sport organizations with an opportunity to collect valuable data. For example, during the 2016 NHL season, the Tampa Bay Lightning collaborated with the innovative fan engagement company Enthrall Sports to develop an app that involves fans in "game presentation, delivery and evaluation of the experience" (Sutton, 2016). For example, the Tampa Bay Lightning could use the FanCap app to conduct real-time fan polling during the game to determine fan preferences on items such as in-game promotions. The team could then utilize Enthrall's facial recognition capabilities to analyze and evaluate fan responses and reactions to specific sponsor activations (see Sutton, 2016). Likewise, fans could create customized video content via the FanCap app that might then be posted on the arena scoreboard to share with others in attendance. Fans could also influence the music played in the arena during the games. The FanCap app would receive fan permission to access the fan's music library on his or her smartphone (see Sutton, 2016). In addition to improving the event experience by curating self-created fan videos and music recommendations, the team could leverage the collected data into future revenue-generating campaigns. For instance, if the Lightning captured data indicating that a specific fan repeatedly recommended songs by musical artist Beyoncé at five games in the previous month, the team could then incorporate complimentary tickets to an upcoming Beyoncé concert at Amalie Arena (or other Beyoncé-related memorabilia) in its season ticket renewal proposal to this fan.

New technologies also expand the capabilities of sport organizations with respect to personalized messaging, customized content, and individualized special access; sport organizations are then able to accumulate valuable customer data from these targeted fan engagement initiatives. For example, in August 2015, all MLS teams collaborated with technology company Playing2 to print the images of thousands of season ticket holders on the back of player jerseys. Selected season ticket holders for each MLS team used a web-based portal to upload a personal photo. Fans could also order customized jerseys and additional merchandise with the "fan-infused" numbers at each team's official stadium store (Major League Soccer, 2015). Fans who attended Orlando City Soccer Club home games could pay $30 to have the number containing their photo pressed onto an already-owned jersey. Orlando City founder and president Phil Rawlins explained, "This innovative program will literally bring fans onto our backs and onto the pitch in support of our Club. We're thrilled to participate in this program to build an even closer connection between our fans and their club" (Orlando City SC, 2015). By providing fans with an authentic, meaningful connection to the team, Orlando City and other MLS teams were able to generate incremental revenue from merchandise sales while gathering insight on fan preferences and purchasing patterns. For example, Orlando City would be able to include data-driven, customized fan experience upgrades and purchase incentives in the club's season ticket renewal proposals (e.g., offering a team soccer scarf signed by the player whose jersey contained the photo of a season ticket holder who had not yet renewed his or her tickets for the following soccer season).*

In Chapter 4, Ray Mathew discusses consumer prospecting, CRM, and fan engagement. In Chapter 5, Michael Farris discusses The Aspire Group's innovative approach to ticket marketing, sales, and service analytics. In Chapter 6, Michael Lewis, Manish Tripathi, and Michael Byman analyze key metrics and empirical strategies for improving season ticket holder management and increasing fan engagement and brand loyalty. In Chapter 7, John Breedlove writes about developing and measuring the effectiveness of data-driven direct marketing initiatives.

Social Media and Digital Marketing Analytics

Gauging the value of social and digital media marketing campaigns "has become a large concern across the industry" (Spanberg, 2016). Sport organizations attempt to analyze both impression-based metrics (e.g., website page views, number of Twitter "followers," and similar KPIs) and attention-based metrics (e.g., measuring the authenticity, quality, and extensiveness of consumer engagement) to determine the overall effectiveness of social and digital media marketing campaigns. Sport business industry leaders such as Bob Bowman, MLB president of business and media, understand that

---

* In 2011, Spanish club Sevilla FC became the first soccer team to utilize the Playing2 jersey photo technology. Playing2 estimated that approximately 3000 photos could fit into each jersey number. Fans paid approximately $30 per each 2 × 2 mm photo. This initiative provided Sevilla FC with an opportunity to generate over $2 million in incremental revenue.

corporate sponsors "have gotten smarter about understanding that more subtle, immersive experiences on social media get better results" (Spanberg, 2016). For example, time spent watching video content on a website and relevant comments in response to a social media post are likely more reliable indicators of consumer engagement as compared with merely "liking" a Facebook post or visiting a website. Likewise, visual analytics applied to consumer Twitter posts of sport team or corporate partner logos/images might provide superior insight on the reach of (and consumer engagement with) a team or sponsor brand as compared with basic Twitter retweets and consumer use of hashtags (see Jensen et al., 2015).

In addition to using social and digital media platforms to produce (and evaluate) marketing content, sport organizations can leverage these platforms to drive ticket sales. Sales representatives with the Sacramento Kings utilized LinkedIn Sales Navigator to strengthen relationships with existing ticket holders, which then resulted in a higher than usual rate of season ticket renewals. The sales team also utilized LinkedIn Sales Navigator to connect and converse with existing leads already identified as quality ticket holder prospects within the team's internal CRM database, which resulted in approximately 6% of the team's overall new business surfacing from deals sourced from LinkedIn Sales Navigator. Sport business industry pioneer Bill Sutton emphasizes the importance of embracing technological innovations in the sales process: "The reach and breadth of social media, with its built-in referral and connecting mentality, can achieve much greater exposure than solely calling via telephone" (Sutton, 2014).

In Chapter 8, Ryan Craig spotlights the development and implementation of several social and digital media marketing initiatives within the athletics department at Duke University. In Chapter 9, Michal Lorenc and Alexandra Gonzalez explain how sport businesses can effectively leverage digital marketing platforms to engage consumers and grow incremental revenue.

Corporate Partnership Acquisition, Valuation, and Evaluation

As explained by Mondello and Kamke (2014), "One area of sport business research that continues to remain elusive centers on how to accurately quantify the expected return on investment (ROI) involving corporate sponsorships" (p. 4).* Industry research indicates "about one-third to one-half of [United States] companies don't have a system in place to measure sponsorship ROI comprehensively...many companies still do not effectively quantify the impact of these expenditures" (Jacobs et al., 2014). Although sponsorships in the sport industry typically involve large financial investments, sponsors are "often at a loss in coming up with a viable means for measuring the ROI of these investments" (Wolfe, 2016).

Results from a 2015 report published by IEG, a company that assists sport and entertainment organizations with corporate partnership valuation, indicated that sponsors identified assistance in measuring ROI and return on objectives (ROO) as the most valuable service provided by properties (e.g., rights holders such as professional sport teams). However, almost 75% of sponsors commented that properties failed to meet corporate partner expectations with respect to measuring ROI and ROO. IEG concluded, "Despite the fact that measurement help is now the top service sponsors want from rights holders, their partners are not very good at delivering it" (Ukman, 2015, p. 26).

Common sponsor objectives include the following: (1) improve brand reach, awareness, and visibility via experiential marketing; (2) increase consumer brand loyalty and community goodwill; (3) drive retail traffic and showcase/sell product; (4) personalize client entertainment and prospecting; and (5) leverage the right to use a sport organization's marks and logos (i.e., monetize intangible sponsorship assets). Evolving corporate partnership ROI and ROO metrics include the following measurement categories: (1) sponsor recall; (2) brand awareness, perception, and affinity; (3) sponsor cost per consumer dollar spent (i.e., direct revenue from sponsor activation); (4) media impressions; (5) social media engagement; and (6) lead

---

* Kim et al. (2015) similarly commented that "managers and researchers lack of systematic and integrative understanding of key factors that influence sponsorship outcomes...executives remain skeptical about the value of sponsorship to their organizations" (pp. 408, 421).

generation for future sales (see Kim et al., 2015, for a detailed analysis of factors that influence sport sponsorship effectiveness).

In Chapter 10, Adam Grossman and Irving Rein provide additional insight on key corporate partnership ROI and ROO metrics and also examine how sport organizations can leverage data to develop an informed sponsorship platform and activation strategy.

Market Research

Market research provides insight into many core business functions of a sport organization, resulting in enhanced revenue generation, targeted branding efforts, and amplified fan engagement and satisfaction. Results from market research data collection can inform planned new business initiatives while simultaneously helping an organization evaluate current approaches to key business areas such as ticket sales, food and beverage offerings, and the overall fan event experience.

Concessionaire Delaware North Sportservice organized a series of consumer focus groups with the goal of improving the fan experience at sport facilities managed by the company. The insights gained from the focus group led to Sportservice testing a kiosk at the 2015 NHL All-Star Game at which fans could self-order merchandise to be delivered to the fan's home address (Muret, 2015). Similarly, in 2016, the Orlando Magic developed targeted fan intercept surveys to gain insights into the effectiveness of sponsor activation strategies, which then allowed the team to identify corporate partners who would be strong candidates for sponsorship renewal based on utilization of existing sponsor entitlement spaces within the arena. These examples illustrate the impact and importance of collecting quantitative and qualitative data from sport consumers in order to guide business strategy development.

In Chapter 11, C. Keith Harrison and Suzanne Malia Lawrence provide a series of practical examples related to how market research can improve decision-making in areas such as marketing to female sport fans, in addition to optimizing concessions and retail offerings.

**Obstacles to Adoption and Successful Use of Analytics
in the Sport Business Industry: The Importance of
Strategy, Communication, and Collaboration**

The role of analytics should function as one component of a broader interconnected company strategy so that a sport organization can manage its analytic investment to maximize revenue (see Alamar, 2013). An extensive survey of more than 2000 corporate managers, which was conducted by *MIT Sloan Management Review* and *SAS Institute* revealed, "Achieving competitive advantage with analytics requires resolve and a sustained commitment to changing the role of data in decision making.... Companies that are successful with analytics are much more likely to have a strategic plan for analytics... [that is] aligned with the organization's overall corporate strategy" (Ransbotham et al., 2016, p. 4). For instance, in 2014, 77% of the survey respondents reported an increase in access to useful data since the previous year, yet only 52% of corporate managers reported that they had been using insights effectively to further guide business strategy (Ransbotham et al., 2015b).

As explained by Liebowitz (2014), "Analytics helps extract insight from data. Without action, however, this insight rarely leads to economic return" (p. 8). A core challenge for sport organizations relates to translating analytics insight into action (i.e., making business decisions based on the results of the analytics process) (Stein and Greenland, 2014). Ransbotham et al. (2015a,b, 2016) found there is "often a gap between an organization's capacity to produce analytical results and its ability to apply them effectively to business issues... many companies still struggle to figure out how to use analytics to take advantage of their data" (pp. 3, 63).

Numerous sport organizations hire analytics personnel and create analytics departments based on the perceived business imperative of making data-driven decisions.* However, some of these organizations have failed to "start with strategy" (Marr, 2015, p. 21). Mondello and Kamke (2014) noted, "Teams continue to increase their analytic capabilities. While this growth has largely produced positive results,

---

* In Chapter 12, Brandon Moyer explains how sport business organizations can utilize analytics to evaluate job candidate potential as well as employee performance for all positions within the company (including analytics-related positions).

it has also resulted in many teams possessing technology systems with highly complex architecture loosely stitched together" (p. 10). Alamar and Mehrotra (2011) opined that "Despite the remarkable growth in the amount and variety of data available [for] examination and analysis, the world of sports analytics still faces the same ubiquitous challenge: How to get meaningful information into the hands—and minds—of the people who are in a position to make effective use of the data and corresponding analysis" (p. 37).

Communication gaps between the analytics team (and sales team) and other key decision-makers can also produce implementation obstacles. For example, Snyder et al. (2016) examined the interactions between sales and marketing departments at sport organizations. Findings from this empirical study reiterated the importance of interdepartmental alignment and integration; cooperation and collaboration can help alleviate the "mistrust and conflict that result from an unfamiliarity with the other department's role and lack of overall communication" (Snyder et al., 2016, p. 4). Similarly, Alamar and Mehrotra (2012) suggested, "Many team executives have little or no formal experience with statistical modeling, and as such have a natural discomfort with and distrust for what these tools may have to offer.... This type of distrust is often exacerbated by the general communication barrier between analysts and professionals in sports" (p. 23). For example, Troilo et al. (2016) found that all components of the analytics process (e.g., collection, analysis, and planning) correlate with actual revenue increases; however, managers in the empirical study associated only strong analysis with perceived increases in revenue. Gershenfeld (2015) explained, "Tools and methods must be simultaneously accessible to executives who do not have deep expertise in the analytic techniques; however, [analysts] must also maintain the rigor and fidelity of the analysis" (p. 169). Sport organizations can further improve at building "communication bridges" so that recommendations from members of the analytics team are "more consumable by managers" (Ransbotham et al., 2015a, p. 64).* Executives leading sport organizations can likewise work to become more

---

* Snyder et al. (2016) recommend hiring "experts in business analytics who are able to bridge the gap and create a more common language between marketing and sales executives" (p. 11).

knowledgeable about interpreting data-driven results as well as increasing their own involvement in the overall analytics process.

Collaboration and consistent communication are vital during all phases of the sport business analytics process. Basketball analyst Dean Oliver commented that "The 'old school' people who are sometimes portrayed as out of touch—many of them are very smart about the sports they work with, and their feedback into analytics is one of the most important ways to improve analytical methods" (Alamar, 2013, p. xi). Glass and Callahan (2015) believe "the companies that create a culture that has intense focus on the customer through data, that values analyzing data, that is open to the truths data analysis reveals, and that has the guts to act on those conclusions will be the companies that prevail" (p. 12).

The remaining chapters in this book expand on the overview of sport business analytics provided in this chapter.

References

Adams, D. (2016). Bruins battle high-volume ticket resellers. *Boston Globe*.

Alamar, B. (2013). *Sports Analytics: A Guide for Coaches, Managers, and Other Decision Makers*. New York: Columbia University Press.

Alamar, B. and Mehrotra, V. (2011). The rapidly evolving world of sports analytics. *Analytics Magazine*, 33–37.

Alamar, B. and Mehrotra, V. (2012). Analytics and sports. *Analytics Magazine*, 22–26.

Cameron, N. (2016). Australian Open details data analytics improvements driving digital engagement. Retrieved from http://www.cmo.com.

Data (2016). *Merriam Webster Online*. Retrieved from http://www.merriam-webster.com.

Davenport, T. (2014). What businesses can learn from sports analytics. *MIT Sloan Management Review*, 10–13.

Diehl, M. A., Drayer, J., and Maxcy, J. (2016). On the demand for live sport contests: Insights from the secondary market for National Football League tickets. *Journal of Sport Management*, 30(1), 82–94.

Drayer, J., Shapiro, S. L., and Lee, S. (2012). Dynamic ticket pricing in sport: An agenda for research and practice. *Sport Marketing Quarterly*, 21, 184–194.

Gershenfeld, G. (2015). Conjoint analysis for ticket offerings at the Cleveland Indians. *Interfaces*, 45(2), 166–174.

Glass, R. and Callahan, S. (2015). *The Big Data-Driven Business: How to Use Big Data to Win Customers, Beat Competitors, and Boost Profits*. Hoboken, NJ: John Wiley & Sons.

Jacobs, J., Jain, P., and Surana, K. (2014). Is sports sponsorship worth it? Retrieved from http://www.mckinsey.com.

Jensen, R. W., Limbu, Y. B., and Spong, Y. (2015). Visual analytics of Twitter conversations about corporate sponsors of FC Barcelona and Juventus at the 2015 UEFA final. *International Journal of Sports Marketing and Sponsorship*, *16*(4), 3–9.

Kaplan, D. (2015). Dynamic ticket pricing makes successful debut in NFL. *SportsBusiness Journal*.

Kim, Y., Lee, H. W., Magnusen, M., and Kim, M. (2015). Factors influencing sponsorship effectiveness: A meta-analytic review and research synthesis. *Journal of Sport Management*, *29*(4), 408–425.

Kiron, D., Prentice, P. K., and Ferguson, R. B. (2014). Raising the bar with analytics. *MIT Sloan Management Review*, 29–33.

Liebowitz, J. (2014). *Business Analytics: An Introduction*. Boca Raton, FL: Taylor & Francis Group, LLC/CRC Press.

Lindsey, G. (1959). Statistical data useful for the operation of a baseball team. *Operations Research*, *7*(2), 197–207.

Lindsey, G. (1963). An investigation of strategies in baseball. *Operations Research*, *11*, 477–501.

Major League Soccer. (2015). MLS clubs honor fans by printing their pictures on jersey numbers during league games in August. Retrieved from http://www.mlssoccer.com.

Marr, B. (2015). *Big Data: Using SMART Big Data Analytics and Metrics to Make Better Decisions and Improve Performance*. Oxford, U.K.: John Wiley & Sons.

Mayer-Schönberger, V. and Cukier, K. (2013). *Big Data*. New York: Houghton Mifflin Harcourt.

Mondello, M. and Kamke, C. (2014). The introduction and application of sports analytics in professional sport organizations. *Journal of Applied Sport Management*, *6*(2), 1–12.

Muret, D. (2015). Concessions go deep with analytics. *SportsBusiness Journal*.

Orlando City Soccer Club. (2015). MLS fan-faced jerseys to feature in August 2015. Retrieved from http://www.orlandocitysc.com.

PwC (2015). At the gate and beyond: Outlook for the sports market in North America through 2019. PwC, New York.

Ransbotham, S., Kiron, D., and Prentice, P. K. (2015a). Minding the analytics gap. *MIT Sloan Management Review*, *56*(3), 63–68.

Ransbotham, S., Kiron, D., and Prentice, P. K. (2015b). The talent dividend. *MIT Sloan Management Review*, 1–12.

Ransbotham, S., Kiron, D., and Prentice, P. K. (2016). Beyond the hype: The hard work behind analytics success. *MIT Sloan Management Review*, 1–16.

Rein, I., Shields, B., and Grossman, A. (2015). *The Sports Strategist: Developing Leaders for a High-Performance Industry*. New York: Oxford University Press.

SAS. (2014). New York Mets sign SAS to lead off their analytics lineup. Retrieved from http://www. http://www.sas.com.

SAS Institute, Inc. (2016). Big data. Retrieved from http://www.sas.com.

Smith, E. (2015a). StubHub gets out of 'all-in' pricing. *Wall Street Journal*.

Smith, M. (2015b). Fan analytics movement reaching more colleges. *SportsBusiness Journal*.

Snyder, K., McKelvey, S., and Sutton, W. (2016). All together now? Exploring sales and marketing integration. *Sport, Business and Management: An International Journal*, 6(1), 2–18.

Spanberg, E. (2016). Placing values on social media engagement. *SportsBusiness Journal*.

Stein, F. and Greenland, A. (2014). Producing insights from information through analytics. In J. Liebowitz (Ed.), *Business Analytics: An Introduction*. Boca Raton, FL: Taylor & Francis Group, LLC/CRC Press, pp. 29–54.

Stein, G. (2014). Will ticket scalpers meet the same fate as spinal tap drummers? The sale and resale of concert and sport tickets. *Pepperdine Law Review*, 42, 1–52.

Stockwell, S. (2015). Using live data and social amplification to drive fan engagement. *Journal of Direct, Data & Digital Marketing Practice*, 16(4), 275–277.

Sutton, W. (2014). Beyond the telephone: Rethinking sales training, strategies. *SportsBusiness Journal*.

Sutton, W. (2016). How technology puts fans in the game, measures enjoyment. *SportsBusiness Journal*.

Troilo, M., Bouchet, B., Urban, T. L., and Sutton, W. A. (2016). Perception, reality, and the adoption of business analytics: Evidence from North American professional sport organizations. *Omega*, 59, 72–83.

Ukman, L. (2015). *IEG's Guide to Sponsorship*. Chicago, IL: IEG, LLC.

Vivlamore, C. (2015). Atlanta Hawks' 8 p.m. start—A ticket scan shows a lot. *The Atlanta Journal—Constitution*.

Wolfe, M. (2016). The elusive measurement dilemma of sports sponsorship ROI. Retrieved from http://www.bottomlineanalytics.com.

Xu, J., Fader, P., and Veeraraghavan, S. (2015). Evaluating the effectiveness of dynamic pricing strategies on MLB single-game ticket revenue. In *MIT Sloan Sports Analytics Conference*, Cambridge, MA.

2

ANALYTICS AND TICKETING INNOVATIONS AT THE ORLANDO MAGIC

JAY RIOLA

Contents

Ticketing Marketplace Changes 24
Ticketing Innovation No. 1: Fast Break Pass...................................25
    Casual Fan Research Insights...25
Ticketing Innovation No. 2: Season Ticket Member Benefits 29
    Loyal Blue Research Insights 29
    Orlando Magic App Changes...31
    Orlando Magic Mobile App Benefits 31
    An Evolving Success Story...32
Acknowledgments 33

Innovation and business strategy are core tenets of the Orlando Magic. The team is one of the firsts in the National Basketball Association (NBA) to build an enterprise data warehouse and establish a department dedicated to analytics. Leaders at the Orlando Magic continually strive to innovate, improve business performance, and deliver legendary moments and experiences to fans. As the sports ticketing marketplace evolves from growing disruption and technological advancements, the Orlando Magic works to develop innovative solutions that allow fans more options and flexibility.

Two of the team's latest ticketing innovations—the Fast Break Pass and Mobile Season Ticket Member Benefits—are the result of insights gleaned from extensive research and the ability to leverage new technologies. This chapter outlines the journey the team took to launch these new solutions and details the early adoption that led to the mobile revolution of the Orlando Magic App.

Ticketing Marketplace Changes

As technological improvements and other disruptive forces infiltrate sports and entertainment, fans are constantly introduced to new ticket purchase options. On account of these changes, teams like the Orlando Magic no longer have complete control over how tickets are priced. Resell marketplaces like StubHub and SeatGeek allow for resellers to buy and sell tickets at prices determined by the resellers.

In 2006, most NBA teams priced every game equally with no price differences to account for the attractiveness (or unattractiveness) of the opponent or date of the game. Therefore, sophisticated resellers could exploit arbitrage opportunities and more accurately price and resell tickets on the secondary market. This loss of control over the secondary market forced teams to strategically optimize ticket pricing. Eventually, most NBA teams (and many members of other sports leagues) began to both variably and dynamically price tickets to more accurately account for, and capitalize on, pricing opportunities.

Similar to the secondary market, mobile technology has also had a profound impact on the sports ticketing marketplace. In years past, sports fans had to either call or visit a team's box office in person to purchase single-game tickets. With the proliferation of smartphones and the advancement of mobile app technologies and venue Wi-Fi systems, sports teams have become more capable and progressive in offering fans and attendees mobile ticketing solutions such as digital ticketing.

Digital ticketing allows buyers the ability to manage tickets entirely online. This often includes printing PDF tickets at home, digitally forwarding tickets to friends or family, reselling the tickets on the secondary market, or registering the tickets with a mobile app and accessing the game using a smartphone. Additionally, a number of technology vendors now offer complete integration into a sports team's mobile app. This allows fans to make purchases at the venue, such as seat upgrades or unique experiences (such as an in-game visit from a team mascot or access to the head coach's postgame press conference), directly from their smartphone while attending the game.

In light of these and other key changes to the ticketing marketplace, the Orlando Magic needed to look for ways to combine flexibility, more sophisticated pricing, and mobile technology to enhance the fan experience while also helping to boost business performance.

Ticketing Innovation No. 1: Fast Break Pass

Fans are the core of the Orlando Magic business. The team dedicates significant time and energy to research fans and game attendees. This includes the use of online and arena intercept surveys, focus groups, and one-on-one interviews.

In 2012, the Magic began additional research efforts to better understand the team's "casual fans," or consumers that reside in Central Florida, who occasionally buy single-game tickets and attend only one or two games every few seasons. By tracking customer data, the Magic noticed a considerable amount of casual fans were not buying tickets for multiple games in the same season or even for games across multiple seasons. The goal of the team's research was to pinpoint the factors that drove casual fans to purchase Magic tickets.

What impediments exist that prevent repeat purchases? How could the team encourage more frequent game attendance? The research uncovered the following findings:

Casual Fan Research Insights

Price sensitive: Casual fans have interest in attending games, but ticket affordability and personal schedules are major barriers to purchasing.

Discount shoppers: Casual fans are more likely to actively shop around for tickets in an effort to find the best deal.

Moderate fans: Casual fans are much less likely to consider themselves "huge fans," as compared with Magic season ticket members.

Additional costs: Casual fans are more likely to attend games with family or friends and make additional in-arena purchases on concessions and retail merchandise. Both factors contribute to higher "all-in" game expenses for casual fans.

Interest in NBA schedule: A majority of casual fans are aware that the NBA season begins in October, though they pay little attention to the NBA until after Christmas. The Magic also identified a key business need to drive early-season sales, as preseason and early regular season games offer softer purchase demand.

With these issues in mind, the Orlando Magic turned to mobile app technology to address the soft demand of early season and other less attractive games, while also cultivating and developing casual consumers into more frequent attendees.

In 2013, the Orlando Magic began offering in-game seat upgrades using the technology developed by a company called Experience, one of the team's mobile app partners. Experience provides real-time communication between the Magic's ticketing system and its mobile app. The Magic began offering attendees the ability to purchase seat upgrades using their mobile app. Attendees could browse available seats and make a purchase directly from their smartphone. As fans became accustomed to fluidly moving between seats throughout the arena with this technology, the Magic began conceptualizing a new and unique ticket product.

Adopting the same practice used by many of the Magic's neighboring Central Florida theme parks (including Walt Disney World, Universal Orlando, and SeaWorld), the Magic launched a new "pass" product for the 2014–2015 NBA season that resided exclusively within the team's mobile app and leveraged the Experience seat upgrade technology. Marketed as the "Fall Fast Break Pass," the product was a mobile-only group of tickets sold exclusively online to Florida residents. The Magic offered two versions of the pass:

1. *Fall Fast Break Pass*: A $49 pass that included access to the team's first eight games (four preseason and four regular season games)
2. *Fall Fast Break Plus Pass*: A $79 pass that included access to the team's first 11 games (four preseason and seven regular season games)

Purchasers bought their pass online at OrlandoMagic.com and then registered it within the Magic's mobile app. Pass holders were guaranteed general admission to Amway Center for all Magic home games included in their pass package, scanning into the arena's entrances using a QR code in the app. Then, randomized seat assignments were delivered digitally to customers through the app 15 minutes prior to game time. This randomness allowed the Magic to continue optimizing single-game ticket sales on the team's primary market, Ticketmaster.com, while also ensuring that a targeted attendance level was reached. Because no specific seat location was assigned to pass buyers, the Magic were able to offer the product at a deeply discounted price point—one specifically targeted to the casual Magic fan.

For roughly the same price it would cost a single-game ticket buyer to purchase seats to one October or November game, a fan could buy the Fast Break Pass and attend multiple games with the possibility of receiving lower bowl seats through the random seat assignment logic. However, unlike a season ticket member, partial plan, or single-game ticket buyer, Fast Break Pass buyers did not technically own a ticket. No physical or digital tickets were distributed and thus could not be printed, forwarded, or resold on the secondary ticket market. This guaranteed that Fast Break Pass purchasers were attending the game, as their personal smartphone represented their ticket. This differentiated the pass from any other ticket product.

Results for the Fast Break Pass during the 2014–2015 season were incredibly positive. Between the Fall and Fall Plus pass, the Magic sold more than 1500 passes to 700 unique customers. Eighty percent of accounts purchasing the Fast Break Pass were new customers to the Magic's database, 15% were stagnant customers reactivated through their Fast Break Pass purchase, and only 5% were existing customers who had purchased tickets to a recent Magic game. Across all games, 15,000 seats were assigned to Fast Break Pass buyers yielding a 70% attendance rate. The objective was achieved: provide casual fans an affordable and convenient product that results in more frequent game attendance (Figures 2.1 and 2.2).

Based on the results from the inaugural Fast Break Pass season in 2014–2015, the Magic made the strategic decision to expand the product line and include a wider variety of pass types in 2015–2016. This allowed more options for customers and helped drive sales and attendance to more games throughout the entire season. During the

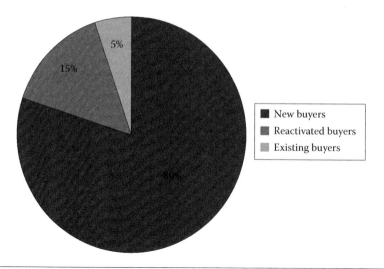

Figure 2.1   2014–2015 Fast Break Pass buyers.

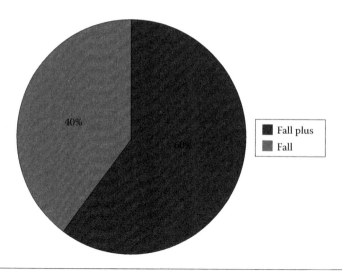

Figure 2.2   2014–2015 Fast Break Pass products.

2015–2016 season, the Magic offered the following Fast Break Pass options:

- *Season Pass*: Includes 34 games throughout the entire season
- *Half-Season Pass*: Includes games from mid-December onward
- *Weekday Pass*: Includes games on Monday to Thursday
- *Weekend Pass*: Includes Friday and Saturday games

- *Fall Plus Pass*: Includes 14 games during October and November
- *Fall Pass*: Includes 12 games during October and November
- *All-Star Pass*: Includes games during January and early February
- *Slam Dunk Pass*: Includes games during late February and March
- *Buzzer Beater Pass*: Single-game passes for select games

The Magic sold more than 5000 passes to approximately 2000 customers during the 2015–2016 season. Fast Break Pass sales have resulted in more than 30,000 seat assignments across all games with a 70% attendance rate. The majority of buyers continued to be new to the Magic's database, followed closely by customers whose engagement with the team had grown stagnant and was reactivated via purchase of the pass. Additionally, Fast Break Pass buyers proved to be terrific sales prospects, as numerous purchasers upgraded their investment to season ticket or partial plan products.

Ticketing Innovation No. 2: Season Ticket Member Benefits

In addition to introducing new fans to the Orlando Magic brand and cultivating the team's relationship with casual fans, the organization looked into mobile app technology to improve satisfaction and increase season ticket member loyalty. For the Orlando Magic, season ticket members—branded as the Loyal Blue—are the lifeblood of the organization's customer base. The Magic have administered countless research initiatives to achieve a better understanding of Loyal Blue members and their needs. Over the last few seasons, a number of feedback areas stood out, as outlined in the following.

Loyal Blue Research Insights

> *Ticket upgrades*: Season ticket members consistently ranked ticket upgrades as the most preferable way to improve the game day experience.
>
> *Resale challenges*: Despite efforts from the Magic to educate season ticket members on how to most effectively resell their

seats on the secondary market, successful ticket resales continued to be a challenge for many fans due to the changing nature of the ticket marketplace.

Schedule conflicts: Even for the most avid season ticket members, the intensity of the NBA schedule can be a challenge. Loyal Blue members have tickets to all 45 Magic home games between October and April. Given these schedule demands, it can be hard for season ticket members to use all their tickets. Even those planning to come to games often encounter last-minute conflicts that prevent them from attending. In focus groups, season ticket members often vocalized this challenge and were concerned about losing value from their investment when unable to attend games.

Similar to the development of the Fast Break Pass, the Magic looked for ways to use their new mobile platform as a solution to remedy key challenges uncovered by the team's season ticket member research. Predictive modeling efforts also identified that overall ticket usage was one of the most predictive variables in determining the season ticket member's likelihood to renew. Therefore, the Magic had to alleviate the burden of the demanding NBA schedule while also allowing members a way to customize and improve their experience through seat upgrades and other unique experiences.

Beginning in 2014, the Magic unveiled new benefits within the Orlando Magic App exclusively for season ticket members. Members could now use a feature within their app called "Not Going" to return tickets for Magic games they were unable to attend. Fans would then receive a credit for the face value dollar amount of the returned tickets. This credit, called "Magic Money," became a digital currency stored within the app that could be used to upgrade seats at future games.

In its first season, 50% of season ticket members used the "Not Going" feature and used Magic Money to customize their game day experience. During the 2015–2016 season, the team's second season providing mobile benefits, the percentage of members using Magic Money to customize their experience rose to 80% as the team expanded the number of offerings made available to fans within the app. Members can now use their Magic Money to upgrade seats, add additional tickets to future games, purchase concessions and merchandise items, and access team events such as press conferences and player autograph sessions. Users also can transfer their Magic Money funds to non–season ticket holders. The team also plans to add more experiences in the future, such as locker-room tours, dinner at arena restaurants, personalized messages on the arena video board, valet parking, and being a ball boy for a game.

Orlando Magic App Changes

Based on the strong initial success of more technologically advanced functions, the Magic aimed to expand its mobile app capabilities via a new partnership with VenueNext. A technology company on a mission to transform the way people around the world experience venues, VenueNext's platform provides venue owners and users with a suite of sophisticated software tools and services that enhance business performance. VenueNext also develops context-aware smartphone apps that seamlessly connect guests with everything a venue has to offer.

Starting with the 2015–2016 season, Orlando Magic fans experienced a brand new version of the team's mobile app, powered by VenueNext's platform. The new adaptation seamlessly integrated services including mobile tickets, parking, wayfinding, enhanced loyalty services for members, and the ability to order food, drinks, and merchandise for express pickup or in-seat delivery.

As an added benefit, season ticket members had even more options and flexibility to customize their membership by using Magic Money not only on seat upgrades and experiences but also on food, beverage, and retail merchandise.

Orlando Magic Mobile App Benefits

Mobile ticket management: Fans can access tickets on game day through the app and scan tickets on their phone to enter Amway Center. Fans can also transfer, resell, or upgrade tickets through the app.

Not Going: Mobile ticket exchange allows season ticket members to return tickets for games they are unable to attend and receive credit for use on purchases at future games.

Bring friends: Fans can add additional seats for any game, allowing them to bring family, friends, or clients to the arena.

Parking: Parking passes purchased for the Magic's garage can be accessed in the app and scanned at the parking entrance.

Mobile food and beverage ordering: Fans can browse, order, and pay for food directly through the app and place orders for express pickup or in-seat delivery.

Mobile retail shopping: Fans can browse Magic gear in the app and place orders. Items are available for pickup at locations throughout the arena.

Magic marketplace: Fans can buy unique experiences including
  • Postgame press conference featuring the Magic head coach
  • High-five line on the court during player introductions
  • Dinner in the Fields Ultimate Lounge located near the Magic locker room

Magic Money: Magic Money allows fans to customize their game day experience by purchasing unique activities, sitting closer to the action, or indulging in game day fare. Members receive Magic Money when exchanging tickets to games they cannot attend.

An Evolving Success Story

The Orlando Magic's 2015–2016 season was the year of the app. Success metrics have exceeded the organization's expectations, but more importantly, the behavior of fans is beginning to significantly change. More than 20,000 fans have downloaded the Orlando Magic App and mobile ticketing to home games is at an all-time high.

Orlando Magic CEO Alex Martins explains, "In continuing the Orlando Magic's commitment to our fans and their experiences at Amway Center, we are turning our patron's mobile devices into remote controls for the live experience."

Whether a casual fan looking to attend a few games per year or a passionate Loyal Blue member, the Magic have used research and technology to create innovative solutions that improve the overall consumer experience.

Orlando Magic COO Charles Freeman reaffirms this position: "What's so special about the technology is it provides us the ability to target the next generation Magic fan, which is becoming more important for the future growth of our fan base. In addition, we are able to offer our loyal season ticket members flexibility and personalization around their Magic experience."

Looking forward, the team aims to further customize and individualize each fan's experience. Critical data gleaned from the app shed tremendous light on spending patterns and preferences that can be used to make individual-level recommendations. Using the technology located throughout the arena to determine a fan's location, the Magic will also look to deliver customized push notifications, mobile coupons, and distinct messages uniquely tailored to each consumer. With the technology permeating deeper into sports and entertainment, the Magic are positioned at the forefront of innovation with a constant focus on developing data-driven solutions that improve the consumer experience. As each Orlando Magic fan enters Amway Center, the question is no longer what can be done to make this game day better—the question is what cannot be done to make this experience unforgettable.

Acknowledgments

The author of this chapter, Jay Riola, would like to thank his colleagues at the Orlando Magic for their support. A special thank you to Stefanie Mattos, Ryan Pierce, and Trish Wingerson for their invaluable assistance and insight.

3

TICKET MARKETS IN SPORT

Is the Secondary Market Becoming the Primary Market?

TROY KIRBY

Contents

Primary Market vs. Secondary Market 35
    Ticket Reselling 38
        Key Secondary Market Concepts 41
        Los Angeles Dodgers Case Study on Ticket Flooding. 41
    Ticket Pricing Strategies, Consumer Demand, and
    the Impact of Ticket Brokers 43
        "The Fight of the Century" Case Study 45
        Tom Brady and Ticket Markets Case Study 47
Conclusion 50
References 51

Primary Market vs. Secondary Market

Google, Inc., has altered the consumer perception between the primary market and secondary market for ticket sales. Access to wider ticket distribution channels is set in two distinct periods of time—before and after search engine optimization (SEO). Prior to SEO, a franchise's tickets were distributed to customers through direct contact sales or minimally through mid-level, family-run reselling businesses with a set book for clients. A key component was street-level, night-of-event sales near the venue, where brokers would haggle with foot-traffic prospects for last-minute returns on their investment. That model was dominant until Google's birth in 2000; this old model has now been rendered a marginal player in the high-stakes, data-focused ticket resale world of today.

Ticket resale is now a billion dollar enterprise, showcasing a vast network of digital advertising resources, with the goal of geotargeting prospective consumers throughout their entire online experience. The majority of professional sports teams and college athletics departments do not participate in the secondary ticket market. These sports teams and athletics programs hold a product that is purchased, by brokers, and resold continually for a profit yet resist becoming active players themselves. The boom of the secondary market is one that sport business industry leaders have not yet adapted to and instead have forcefully attempted to negate without much success. Reselling tickets online is a technological disruption creating massive revenue streams against the wishes of sport business executives, many of whom instead focus on outdated inside sales telemarketing models from the 1990s.

Sport sales fundamentals have become a relic, unequipped for the modern, digital age. Dozens of young prospective hires are recruited for minimal base salary plus commission, with training directed at developing phone skills and scripted conversations. This creates a sawmill employment structure for revenue generation management. Each young account executive is generally required to make 100 outbound phone calls per day or spend 5 hours of quality talk time with prospective customers. It is a top-down indoctrination process that denies modern innovation as well as thwarts creative sales thinking.

The current, stagnant inside sales model structure implemented by the majority of sport organizations disregards the billions of dollars generated by Amazon or other e-retailing sites, because teams maintain the position that purchasing tickets is a different experience. The phone-heavy structure pushed by sport organizations is forced upon groups of young sales representatives, the majority of whom never answer cold calls or buy anything over the phone as consumers. The phone-heavy, digital-avoidance emphasis of sport sales diminishes the value of the young sales representatives to target their fellow generational consumers, eliminating potential revenue streams for dying ones. And this is how the secondary ticket market beats the majority of franchises that are selling their own product, reaping the rewards of a high profit margin, with lower overhead costs, daily.

Systematic market disruption is a frightening piece of technological genius for an entire vertical monopoly created by franchises, ticket platforms, and venues over the past 100 years. By choosing not to focus on digital investments, such as retargeting, social media reach, and SEO, the franchise executive has lost ground to the ticket broker who has embraced these mediums of advertisement. The only option left is one of reactionary indignation by the franchise executive, accusing the ticket broker of fraud, because the broker found a way to resale the ticket product at three times the price that the franchise originally sold to them.

Despite tighter controls by franchise executives on the ticket product, in an effort to eliminate digital ticket availability options on their primary site, the prospective consumer finds alternative avenues through the secondary market. The sales barometer for franchises has traditionally been season tickets, a product that yields a steady revenue stream regardless of consumer use. Brokers and corporations tend to make up the majority of season ticket accounts for each major league franchise. Brokers do not utilize season tickets as one-off usage roles; each seat is separated out into individual ticket sales, priced according to their demand value, and placed on the secondary ticket market for resale. Secondary ticket inventory moves at a higher volume and faster rate and with an increased profit yield than its franchise's ticket counterparts on the primary market.

Season ticket holders require an abundant amount of home game usage to receive an annual value per year to recoup a ticket investment. It is a required commitment that consumers are unwilling to partake in, over individual ticket purchases for one-off events. That is why consumers will pay a higher premium for fewer tickets, rather than the alternative of a discounted group of multiple tickets spread throughout the season. Major League Baseball's (MLB) teams have 81 home games per season. Each year, every National Basketball Association (NBA) and National Hockey League (NHL) team has 41 home dates on its schedule. The National Football League's (NFL) 32 teams each have 10 regular season dates at their home stadium, including 2 preseason games. Spread out as a commitment for MLB per customer, from April to September, there can be 15 Monday, 10 Tuesday, 13 Wednesday, 18 Thursday, 19 Friday, 19 Saturday, and 16 Sunday home games, including 10 consecutive days with a home date during selected periods of the season. Some of these games are scheduled at noon or 7 p.m., as day–night doubleheaders, during all types of weather. While franchises have identified customer expectations of purchasing season tickets, or small segmented plans to reserve specific seating locations, consumers use the secondary market in order to achieve greater choice and freedom in their purchasing decision.

Ticket Reselling

Franchises end up dissuading investment in long-term ticket buys when they reduce value through the capping or elimination of resale options. By implementing a ticket barcode cancellation policy on resold tickets to unsanctioned markets, the franchise harms the buyer's strategic investment incentive to purchase the season tickets, as well as the seller's customer experience with the ticket product. When a franchise permits its tickets to be resold, yet limited to select secondary ticket platforms, it harms the seller's ability to recoup or yield a profit off of the initial investment by reducing the potential buying customers. Franchises sanction specific secondary market platforms over others, thereby generating a cut of service fees on resale transactions.

Ticket resale giant StubHub, Inc., filed a lawsuit in March 2015 against the Golden State Warriors of the NBA and Ticketmaster, alleging collusion over secondary market practices. Golden State and Ticketmaster enforced a binding agreement that required all Golden State ticket holders who chose to resell to list their tickets on the Ticketmaster secondary market only. In StubHub's lawsuit, which was later dismissed by a judge, the secondary platform accused Ticketmaster and Golden State of double-dipping as both organizations received service fees from both the primary and secondary sale of tickets.

Ticket regulation has been such a staple of state politics in Florida that the state's media outlets have nicknamed it "The Ticket Wars." A 2013 Zogby poll of Florida residents found that 76% of Floridians believe that once someone buys the ticket, they have the right to do what they want with it. Ticketmaster disagrees strongly with that sentiment (Dean, 2015). Ticketmaster has lobbied Florida legislators to eliminate all non-Ticketmaster resale options, suggesting that the company can act as a regulator, as well as seller, of the ticket product. This structure is not good for the consumer, as it eliminates aspects of choice and the ability to gain the best deal price for the product. It reinforces a vertical monopoly that restricts commerce and the capitalist marketplace competition by eliminating price differentials. Ticketmaster's "protect the consumer" mantra does not elicit a guarantee that consumers will not receive falsified tickets or have ticket barcodes cancelled by the box office. Therefore, it would create market restrictions without improving consumer experience.

The ticket product has a notorious ambiguity in legal terms. Franchises, venues, and platforms have determined that a ticket is a revocable license. The consumer treats it as a material good (Foer, 2012). When a material good is purchased, the owner has the right to resell it to whomever they wish, without having to inform the original maker of the transaction, let alone give them a cut of resale proceeds. But according to those in the anti-resale primary market, the consumer does not own the ticket, merely leasing a seat for that moment, at that event. In a 2013 U.S. Supreme Court decision of *Kirtsaeng v. John Wiley & Sons*, the rights of resellers were supported through the first-sale doctrine. Student Supap Kirtsaeng was fined $600,000 for importing Wiley textbooks from his native Thailand, where they were less expensive, and reselling them in the United States. The first-sale doctrine giving owners of published books and recordings the right to sell them to whomever they want was held to apply to imported works and U.S. publications (*Kirtsaeng v. John Wiley & Sons*, 2013).

While the U.S. court system has never conclusively determined that a ticket is a revocable license, the legal language continues to persist within the vertical monopolies of ticket platforms, venues, and sport franchises. A revocable license only benefits the seller, not the buyer, who cannot revoke their end of the purchase at any time. It is undetermined if this legal definition is what the public is agreeing to when it is purchasing the ticket product. Yet the vertical monopoly of venue, ticket platform, and franchise has not been challenged in court on these legal claims on whether the organizations can end their license, cancelling out a customer's ticket, if it is resold through digital distribution channels that the originating primary market did not monetarily benefit from.

The buying public is often at odds with franchises over their ticket purchasing and resale rights. During the 2015 NHL Finals, the Tampa Bay Lightning created a media firestorm of controversy over cancelling a season ticket holder's two tickets behind the team bench (Contorno, 2015). The Tampa Bay Army Captain, a 2-year season ticket holder, had been honored on the ice by the Lightning in 2013 for his service. His required duty to be stationed in Fort Knox, Kentucky, for 5 weeks of Army training conflicted with the NHL Stanley Cup schedule; therefore, he chose to resell the tickets to games he could not attend. The Lightning threatened to cancel his tickets because they were listed on StubHub. After widespread city scrutiny, Lightning CEO Tod Leiweke apologized and allowed the Army Captain to resell (Peters, 2015). Franchise executives often fail to recognize the legitimate patterns of a ticket holder selling half of their unwanted seat inventory. A robust secondary market eliminates several risks for the ticket holder, gaining value for games that the sellers are unable to attend, while the buyer gains temporary access to an improved seat location that they cannot afford for an entire season.

The primary market has taken an aggressive stance against digital sales beyond just the resale aspects of the marketplace. The Tampa Bay Rays baseball team shut down online availability of attractive ballpark seating locations in 2015 in an effort to force consumers to order by phone, using their service representatives. As many as 1000 tickets per game were withheld in an effort to make inventory appear more "scarce" (Romano, 2015). This forced-channel mantra is an ineffective sales technique of "upselling" customers, by restricting product options, which can end up frustrating previously interested buyers. Black Friday sales dropped for retailers in 2015 as more shoppers chose to buy online than ever before. Yet franchise executives are continually mystified by digital channels of ticket sales or reject it in favor of outbound phone sales.

While some franchises have avoided embracing the secondary market or its technology, ticket brokers have become more innovative. Reselling platforms such as StubHub, Vivid Seats, or TicketNetwork have less staff, move more ticket inventory, and utilize the latest technological and digital distribution methods to access prospective customers. While professional teams own the initial ticket product, they lack the innovative standard to yield the maximum profit from it. Standard franchise practices for hiring have not improved either. The majority of franchises sell their tickets on one or two online marketplaces, specifically team websites. Ticket brokers list their tickets on 2000 or more platforms, reaching a wider audience.

When franchise executives have utilized the secondary market or brokers, it has been at a substandard level of disinterest—primarily only as financial aid and never with a specific secondary market strategic plan in place. When the team is down in the league standings or has little ticket movement, franchise executives instruct their representatives to clear individual seat inventory through brokers. Even when the team has an improved on-field record but is unable to move tickets through the primary market through outbound sales efforts or discounts, brokers are utilized.

The secondary ticket market works as any true marketplace does—on consumer demand. Yet franchise executives who move an abundance of tickets to the secondary market through brokers do not factor the overall lack of demand for their product. The secondary market has the ability to show a franchise exactly what its ticket product is worth and what consumers are truly willing to pay for it. And that may not yield to the franchise's expectations.

Key Secondary Market Concepts   Table 3.1 provides an overview of key secondary market terms that are covered in more detail later in this chapter.

Los Angeles Dodgers Case Study on Ticket Flooding   The Los Angeles Dodgers (from 2013 to 2015) are an interesting case study in ticket flooding, where too many tickets are on the secondary marketplace, without the demand to purchase those tickets. Each Dodgers home game had a seat listing average (SVG) of 6938 on the secondary market at a $40 average resale price (ARP). Overall, the 30 MLB team home games from 2013 to 2015 had a 7216 SVG against a $57 ARP. The $17 ARP gap between the Dodgers and MLB home teams is significant (see Figure 3.1). The secondary market is reactionary to consumer demand. It actually shows what a product is worth, which many times is less than what franchise executives are willing to sell those tickets for on the primary market.

Table 3.1　Secondary Market Glossary

TERM	DEFINITION
Average resale price (ARP)	This is the actual average price that resellers sold their tickets at. These data actually show what the average sale on the secondary market is, making it much more valuable data as it proves out what the true average asking price was for the ticket product, because it is what the secondary market customers were willing to pay to access the event, on average.
Median listing price (MLP)	This is the average listing asking price that brokers are desiring to sell their tickets at. The media often confuse prices at which inventory is sold on the secondary market with prices at which resellers are attempting to sell inventory. Typically, media outlets will write up a story referring to the median listing price (i.e., asking price) as how the "secondary market is skyrocketing" for a specific event. This is nonsense, as it merely shows the collective *ask*, not the *actual* sale, of the ticket product. If people are collectively asked for a $1.4 billion price tag on a 1985 Yugo GV, that doesn't mean that the actual value is anywhere close.
Get-in price (GIP)	This is the average rock-bottom listing price that brokers are willing to sell their tickets at.
Seat listing average (SVG)/total inventory	This is the amount of seat listings that are available on the marketplace at any one time. Please keep in mind that some may be duplicate seat listings, as brokers have the ability to list on multiple platforms and typically do not actually list the exact seat (beyond section and row) in order to avoid ticket deactivation by teams.

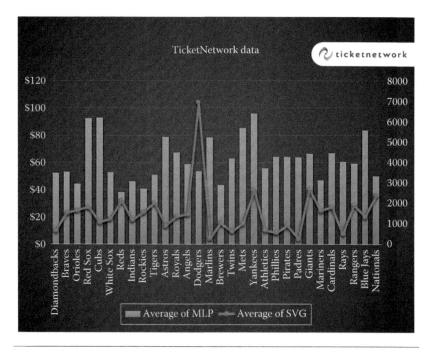

Figure 3.1　MLB home game median listing price vs. total inventory (seat listing average) (2013–2015).

Ticket Pricing Strategies, Consumer Demand, and the Impact of Ticket Brokers

There is a stark contrast between the ARP on the secondary market and the general acceptance by franchise executives of dynamic pricing on the primary market. Dynamic ticket pricing purports to reveal a consumer's perception of demand against the limited inventory available. It has made measurement of revenues less equal, as high-demand game incomes are covering for the bad returns of low-demand events.

Franchise executives do not want to lose a perceived value on ticket prices to the worst games, yet they admit that all games do not hold the same value. This contradiction supposes that the base static price originally decided upon by the franchise was invariably closer to the lower end of consumer demand, rather than at the top of it. A fundamental flaw in dynamic pricing for tickets is that it measures against the false demand structure of season tickets, taking tickets purchased by brokers in massive blocks to be resold on the secondary market and then judged against those new listings on the resale market, which creates a double-false factor of pricing measurement.

Secondary market data have the ability to reveal not only customer interest but also broker demand for the ticket product. When a broker does not invest in a league or team ticket product, it should be concerning for those franchise executives. The Ultimate Fighting Championship (UFC), NASCAR, and Major League Soccer (MLS) each have severe issues concerning a lack of secondary market demand for their ticket product. While all of the ticket product can be sold on the primary market, it is the secondary market where indicators of consumer demand exist. For the UFC, NASCAR, and MLS, each league's ARP has been stagnant or fallen over the past 3 years. Another indicator is from brokers, who are investing less in these sports' ticket product inventory, providing a lower SVG (300–500 listing average per event). These two factors suggest that the investment risk is higher than the reward of reselling those products.

Ticket brokers are no different than Wall Street traders when it comes to the commodity of goods that they sell. The secondary ticket market is reactionary to a news sphere, where perceived value can be assessed, minus regulatory oversight with a maximum amount of temporary investors. The marketplace for tickets exists despite the vertical monopoly against it, which hinders price displacement, allowing the product's price to be determined by the seller not the buyer. The secondary market initiates a true commerce between buyers and sellers that promotes overall capitalism within its non-governance system of operation. The majority of brokers do have a code of ethics within the secondary market, as well as organized associations—reselling the ticket product at a higher profit margin with fixed costs.

During the 2015–2016 NHL season, the Winnipeg Jets were considered a hot secondary market due to their high ARP per tickets resold for each of their home games. It is the highest ARP achieved for any NHL home game average over the last three seasons. Winnipeg benefits from multiple factors and may be a soft, untested marketplace overall. Only 20 SVG per 10-day average prior to a Jet's home game make it to the secondary market. Winnipeg also plays in a 15,294-seat arena, which holds 4,000–5,000 seats less than the Jets' NHL counterparts have at their home arenas. This case study presents the ultimate question of determining consumer demand. If the Jets played their home games in a similar NHL arena with a higher seating capacity, would the ARP for their ticket product be as high on the secondary market? This is where the ticket broker must make various determinations, similar to that of Wall Street, on the weight of consumer demand against potential soft market indicators in order to calculate both the median listing price (MLP) and get-in price (GIP), in order to achieve a higher ARP.

The price of the ticket product is subject to constant volatility amid an expiration date that eliminates value once the event is started. Investments are lost if the ticket inventory is not sold prior to the event, and market fluctuation depends on variable factors such as consumer demand, weather, player injury, and giveaways such as bobbleheads. This is why brokers parlay their actions across the secondary market. Resellers purchase season tickets to multiple teams, events, and entertainment acts. When the Yankees are down, the Giants may be up, or Taylor Swift may have just launched a new national tour. Brokers purchase their inventory across various venues, in multiple regions, in order to protect their overall investment strategy.

Part of this investment strategy is reacting to real-time breaking news that can affect the overall secondary market. While sports tickets have the highest grossing resale components of the ticket product, it is due to annual guaranteed events, amid high consumer demand, which dictate pricing and revenue.

"The Fight of the Century" Case Study Professional boxer Manny Pacquiao sent one tweet on December 31, 2014, directly to his rival champion boxer Floyd Mayweather Jr. requesting a fight between the two. Less than 100 characters in length, Pacquiao's social media message ignited consumer demand overnight in interest over what was billed as "The Fight of the Century." Since 2009, match logistics had been negotiated between the two boxers yet had continually stalled. When, in February 2015, Mayweather Jr. publicly announced the fight would take place at the MGM Grand in Las Vegas on May 2, 2015, primary ticket prices were set at $3,500–$250,000.

The secondary ticket market reacted immediately, with 160 listings on February 21, 2015, with an $8119 MLP and a $3500 GIP. The ARP is the middle ground between both ends of the spectrum of the broker's ask for each listing. This means that a $5809 ARP would have been expected as a yield from ticket profits sold at that point. However, that does not mean that all tickets listed are sold at the price. The Pacquiao vs. Mayweather Jr. ticket product on the secondary market is all about the details. Despite inventory being listed on February 21, 2015, none of the brokers had tickets "in hand" until April 24, 2015. Boxing promoter Bob Arum did not release ticket inventory to the secondary market until 2 weeks prior to the actual match date of May 2, 2015. Only 500 tickets went on the primary market as a general release to the public (Badenhausen, 2015). This limited ticket availability on the primary market helped feed and drive the reactionary consumer demand through "short sale" listings.

The practice of short selling ticket inventory is a controversial aspect of the secondary market. Wall Street allows short selling of stocks by its traders because it is an overall insurance over actual hard goods held. When short selling occurs on the secondary market, brokers are doing so on a guarantee from their wholesale ticket inventory supplier that they will receive those tickets to make good on each sale to the public. This was why so few tickets were listed on the secondary prior to the last 2 weeks leading up to the Pacquiao vs. Mayweather Jr. fight night. Low supply against higher consumer demand caused a skyrocketing asking MLP in the process.

In the 64 days leading up to the Pacquiao vs. Mayweather Jr. fight, there were 320 SVG on the secondary. Brokers may have practiced caution, due to resale issues at Super Bowl XLIX a few months prior. The Pacquiao vs. Mayweather Jr. fight's limited secondary offerings against astronomical consumer interest drove it to a $10,094 MLP and $5,154 GIP, hitting a $7,624 ARP during that time frame. When tickets on the primary were released on April 25, 2015, Ticketmaster had only 500 tickets for sale to the general public. Secondary inventory listings expanded by three times their average, going from 320 SVG to 985 SVG in the 8-day period leading up to the Pacquiao vs. Mayweather Jr. fight. The increased supply actually pushed down the consumer demand, dropping the MLP by $1336 to $8758, the GIP by $1796 to $3358, and the ARP by $1655

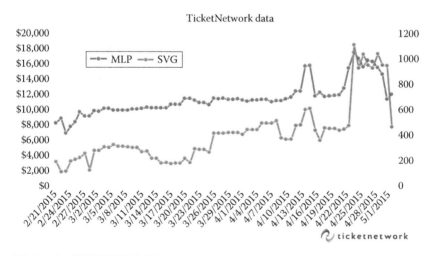

Figure 3.2   Pacquiao vs. Mayweather Jr. seat listing average and median listing price from date of announcement to date of event.

to $5969, which was only $89 ARP below where a standard ARP would have normally been placed (see Figure 3.2).*

Tom Brady and Ticket Markets Case Study New England Patriots Quarterback Tom Brady caused an endless amount of stress in the lives of brokers for the 2015 calendar year. One involved a collapsed secondary system that bankrupted several small brokerages and also hurt large ones, amid lawsuits and government oversight. And the other was a judicial ruling that created a demand that even resellers had a hard time keeping up with. Both were significant events in the history of the secondary market, but for much different reasons.

Brady's first interaction with brokers in 2015 was right after the January 18th AFC Championship, where his Patriots defeated the Indianapolis Colts. By January 22, 2015, major news broke that accused Brady of directing the Patriot's game equipment staff to deflate NFL game balls from a required standard after NFL referees had approved them. The game ball advantage would make the ball easier to throw and catch for the Patriots. Much like the practice of short selling on the secondary market, accusations surrounding "Deflategate" had the potential to crash an entire financial system of selling tickets. In the case of Super Bowl XLIX, both nearly did.

The secondary market for an NFL Super Bowl has been a standard one with little movement. In the 2 weeks leading up to the event itself, the market tends to set up a stabilizing MLP and GIP, gradually reducing over that period of time as a Super Bowl kickoff gets closer. A major factor in Super Bowl attendance is the consumer's level of commitment to attend the game, including spending

---

* The median listing price (MLP) can cause media hysteria. Journalists wrote incendiary articles about a few tickets on the secondary listed at $20,000 MLP or higher for every event resold. What media outlets fail to focus on is that the secondary is driven by consumer demand and their willingness to pay for an optimum price. Therefore, the top MLP asks are outliers, not norms. Data measuring average resale price (ARP) on secondary market sales are fairly consistent with overall ARP measurements. Despite suggestion to the contrary by journalists, secondary market pricing is not out of whack with consumer demand or unfair, as it truly comes down to what the consumer is willing to pay for the product. The ARP is typically within the expected average range between the MLP and get-in price of each listed event.

resources on flight and hotel, as well as weather and site location factors. Purchasing a Super Bowl ticket on the secondary market is rarely a last-minute decision. From the period of January 19 to 25, 2015, as Brady defended himself against a hostile media investigating Deflategate, secondary trends for Super Bowl XLIX matched the last two Super Bowls in terms of consumer demand and pricing. It was during the second week leading up to Super Bowl XLIX (January 26 to February 3, 2015), where the entire resale turned ugly, almost collapsing under a sudden, unexpected demand against a diminishing supply.

The Super Bowl XLIX resale market's MLP skyrocketed during that second week leading up to the game, creating a widespread panic for brokers as well as consumers (Robinson, 2015). This comes back to the practice of short selling, which permeated throughout the Super Bowl XLIX resale. Founded by RazorGator CEO Doug Knittle, sporting event hospitality partner PrimeSport had official deals with both Super Bowl XLIX participants, the New England Patriots and the Seattle Seahawks, totaling 12,600 tickets to the game. The NFL delayed ticket distribution until 1 or 2 days prior to the game for players, coaches, sponsors, and franchise executives. This was in stark contrast to past Super Bowls where tickets were distributed 5–6 days prior. This differential hindered resale and caused an overall panic in the secondary marketplace (Brooks, 2015).

This withheld supply caused the Super Bowl XLIX ticket supplier, PrimeSport, to pull back inventory and price guarantees to their broker affiliates who listed the tickets on their sites for a commissioned sale. Several of these reneged offerings had already been sold to consumers who had purchased the Super Bowl XLIX tickets months in advance. Had brokers ended up with the original committed transactions, they would have lost income on the price guarantee (Baker, 2015a).

Several other factors also played into why the resale demand by consumers shot up drastically, not just because of few tickets available within the marketplace. First, Super Bowl XLIX had a unique matchup between the New England Patriots and the defending Super Bowl Champion Seattle Seahawks. While Brady was mired in the speculation of Deflategate, Seahawks fans were celebrating a narrowly won 28–22 overtime win against the Green Bay Packers.

Bandwagon fan interest usually does not translate into secondary market sales for Super Bowl tickets. However, in 2015, several factors, including proximity of location of the Super Bowl site in Glendale, Arizona, to Seattle, made it more plausible. The secondary market skyrocketed, causing short sellers to cancel their original sold orders purchased at lower prices. They did so in order to accommodate a fluctuation in demand, selling to new customers willing to purchase for higher sale prices. Super Bowl ticket claims by Washington residents exceeded $800,000 (Baker, 2015b). The Washington State attorney general's office was flooded with complaints over the resale collapse (Baker, 2015c).

The Super Bowl XLIX resale market exposed brokers as helpless middle persons in a temporary financial system that chooses not to fully recognize them. As the secondary market MLP for Super Bowl XLIX tickets rose, so did the PrimeSport primary price for ticket inventory that was bought by brokers to fill orders. TeamTix sold "options" for Super Bowl XLIX tickets to fans during the 2014 NFL season. TeamTix guaranteed to sell those tickets at the primary price. TeamTix could not fulfill the options sold to local fans as a result of the supply shortage (Baker, 2015d). This was a challenge across the board throughout the secondary market. If an affiliate broker short sold a Super Bowl XLIX ticket on the secondary market from January 19 to 25, the unfilled order would have been sold for less than what it would eventually cost the broker to purchase from PrimeSport. This caused a conundrum of a broker losing money on a commissioned sale by initiating the sale to begin with. One of the largest Super Bowl resellers, SBTickets.com was sued by an Arizona firm, alleging that the website had violated the state's Consumer Fraud Act and was in breach of contract for unfulfilled orders. StubHub reportedly paid $2.3 million to PrimeSport in order to fulfill bad short-sold orders to customers.

The next encounter that resellers had with the New England Patriots and the team's quarterback was on September 3, 2015. It was on that date that the NFL's four-game suspension of Brady for his role in Deflategate was thrown out by Judge Richard M. Berman on the grounds that the NFL had not provided Brady with a fair process before penalizing him. Brady's reinstatement would force brokers to determine whether they had enough inventory to hold against consumer demand and whether the secondary market would collapse again under the weight of short ticket supply.

The Pittsburgh Steelers vs. New England Patriots would have been a big AFC matchup no matter what. But it was on Thursday Night Football, before any other games to open up the 2015 NFL season, and now Tom Brady was able to play again. From September 5 to 6, 2015, all three lines—the ARP, MLP, and GIP—had jumped higher with renewed expectation and consumer demand. It was September 7, 2015, when the secondary got a shock to the system, where the ARP of $490 was much lower than the MLP of $634. This meant that consumers were outbidding broker estimations and paying more for the ticket product. Brokers leapfrogged the MLP on September 8 to a $531 asking price. This caused a fluctuation with the ARP, hitting $438.58 from September 4 to 10, throwing it $31.58 above the overall ARP in the marketplace. This is precisely why the MLP–GIP chasm was 103% and the APR–GIP divide was 153%.

The last time that the Steelers ventured to face the New England Patriots at Gillette Stadium in Boston was November 3, 2013, where a robust secondary boomed as well. That market hit at $308 ARP despite limited inventory on the marketplace being 1519 SVG, which showed off a $2,922,940 base. It leaves open the question of how many tickets were distributed through the resale market by brokers during the summer, when the NFL's suspension of Brady looked to be a solid case instead of a withering vine.

Conclusion

The earlier case studies illustrate how the primary and secondary markets have blurred. Consumers see availability through digital channels, not based on who is selling inventory or whether messages are accurate representations of the franchise itself. Professional sport organizations and athletics departments fail to see the revenue lost to third-party affiliates such as brokers by committing themselves to outdated channels of distribution such as telemarketing phone sales.

Instead of embracing the secondary market, franchises have either ignored or sought to hinder it, causing more headaches than revenue chains for their product. The secondary market is a $5 billion gold mine that professional sports teams and college athletics departments routinely deride, misunderstanding that customers already go to the secondary market prior to the primary market, thinking that the secondary will yield a better deal on seats, even if in actuality, the asking prices are higher. Until sport franchises and athletics departments decide to adopt the practices of the secondary market, teams and athletics departments will be losing out to smaller organizations that show agility while other organizations are slow to move.

References

Badenhausen, K. (2015). Mayweather vs. Pacquiao tickets finally go on sale today. Retrieved from http://www.forbes.com.

Baker, G. (2015a). Super Bowl ticket brokers reneged on orders even while selling nearby seats for far more. Retrieved from http://www.seattletimes.com.

Baker, G. (2015b). Super Bowl ticket claims by Washington residents reach $820,000. Retrieved from http://www.seattletimes.com.

Baker, G. (2015c). Fans still reeling from Super Bowl ticket nightmare. Retrieved from http://www.seattletimes.com.

Baker, G. (2015d). Super Bowl tickets disappeared in an imperfect storm. Retrieved from http://www.seattletimes.com.

Brooks, D. (2015). What was PrimeSport's involvement with the Super Bowl ticket shortage? Retrieved from http://www.ampthemag.com.

Contorno, S. (2015). Tampa Army captain complains Lightning 'strong-arming' him over his Stanley Cup tickets. Retrieved from http://www.tampabay.com.

Dean, E. (2015). Ticket wars heating up in Florida. Retrieved from http://www.sunshinestatenews.com.

Foer, A. (2012). Who owns my ticket? Retrieved from http://www.nytimes.com.

Kirtsaeng v. John Wiley & Sons. 568 U.S. 697. (2013).

Peters, C. (2015). Lightning CEO apologizes to Army captain over ticket policy mess. Retrieved from http://www.cbssports.com.

Robinson, C. (2015). Super Bowl tickets at extremely low inventory; cheap seats rise to $8,500. Retrieved from http://sports.yahoo.com.

Romano, J. (2015). Tampa Bay Rays employ curious strategy for selling tickets. Retrieved from http://www.tampabay.com.

4

CUSTOMER RELATIONSHIP MANAGEMENT AND FAN ENGAGEMENT ANALYTICS

RAY MATHEW

Contents

Introduction 53
What Are CRM and Database Management? 55
What Are Some Common CRM Tools? 56
What Information Should Sport Business Companies Track? 57
Growing the CRM Database 60
Catering to the Individual, Not the Masses 61
Targeted Campaigns 62
CRM Snapshot—Examples Utilizing Microsoft
Dynamics CRM 65
Practical Application Case Study 67
What Does CRM Help Teams to Achieve? 68
References 68

Introduction

A primary goal of every sales and marketing organization is to maximize revenue, customer retention, and the footprint of the company brand. This business objective is especially difficult to achieve in the sport business industry as teams fight for entertainment dollars and against high-definition television, which makes it more convenient for fans to consume professional sports from the comfort of their home and more difficult for teams to sell tickets to games. If you are the head of sales or marketing for any professional sport team or any other organization in the sport business industry, then it is imperative you use every tool at your disposal to learn as much as possible about the marketplace and the potential customers you are trying to sell to. Let me share a story of the first time I realized the importance of this lesson.

I began my career in the sport business industry as one of four ticket sales representatives for a brand new franchise in the National Basketball Association (NBA) Development League. Generally, when you start a sales position, you are given sales leads to call. At the very least, you are provided with some tool or software to track the sales leads you find on your own. Since we were a brand new organization, there were no sales leads provided to start with and there was no software in place to track the ones we did find on our own. With our sales organization charged with the goal of selling out the inaugural home game in roughly 10 months, we had many season tickets and group tickets to sell to help achieve our goal. Initially, each sales representative prospected for his or her own sales leads either by looking through phone books or searching business directories online. We were tracking each person we talked to or met with in a spreadsheet along with compiling and organizing the notes from each of those interactions. Essentially, each sales representative was creating his or her own personal database. That personal database oftentimes included a post-it note with barely legible notes on it if we were too rushed to enter the information into a computer spreadsheet.

The obvious problem with each sales representative tracking his or her own leads independently was that it did not take long to realize that there were instances of sales representatives duplicating efforts by contacting the same leads and the same companies. It is easy to imagine how irritated someone might get when two separate sales representatives call from the same company pitching the same product. We also encountered challenges related to tracking information and interactions with the customers to which we had sold tickets. The ticketing system we used to sell customers seats to a game or for a full season tracked only contact information and what the customer had purchased. There was no place in the ticketing system to store notes from phone calls or e-mails with each customer. Why was that an issue?

As any customer service representative for a professional sport team will tell you, each season ticket holder believes he or she is the most important customer to the team. Customers often have very specific requests such as where they like to sit or who they want their tickets left for if they cannot make it to a particular game. Additional season ticket holder related issues surface throughout the season, which requires constant customer service support. With our organization having such a small staff, challenges would arise when a season ticket holder would call in about an issue they had previously raised with their sales representative, but the sales representative was not in the office. Of course the representatives that were in the office did not have any notes from previous interactions to reference, which at times led to an upset customer.

Needless to say, at times it looked as though we were not organized and that we did not communicate with each other. There was an obvious need to create a centralized database where all leads and customers could be tracked. It was not long before our organization made the investment to purchase customer relationship management (CRM) software that would help to alleviate these issues. Imagine the resources and scale needed to manage the database for an organization in one of the five major professional sport leagues (NBA, National Football League [NFL], National Hockey League, Major League Baseball [MLB], and Major League Soccer), which have bigger stadiums and almost exponentially larger fan bases. In the current sport business climate, no professional team can afford to run an effective sales and marketing department without a CRM system.

Currently, I am a Sports CRM analyst for Fan Interactive Marketing, a company that provides consultation and support for over 65 sports and entertainment clients primarily in CRM and e-mail marketing. The following sections of this chapter will provide a practical overview of CRM and its applications in professional sports, particularly in ticket sales, based on my professional experience along with business results that Fan Interactive Marketing has helped its clients achieve.

What Are CRM and Database Management?

What is CRM? According to Jill Dyche, CRM is "the infrastructure that enables the delineation of and increase in customer value, and correct means by which to motivate valuable customers to remain loyal—indeed, to buy again" (Dyche, 2002, p. 4). As it relates to professional sport, CRM is the tool or tools in which you can begin to track individuals from the first time they interact with the team with the ultimate goal of utilizing the available information to help maximize the value received from that individual monetarily as well as optimize this individual's overall engagement with the team. More simply put, CRM "helps businesses enter, analyze, and track customer information. CRM systems also provide a methodology for storing, measuring, and managing customer interactions" (CRM Resource and Guide, 2015).

Another term you might see in relation to CRM is database management. A database is "a usually large collection of data organized especially for rapid search and retrieval (as by a computer)" (Merriam-Webster Dictionary, 2015). A database is a tool or component of CRM used to store information about the individuals that interact with your company. Most CRM software or products include the database in which information is stored. Being able to leverage the information in that database to increase brand awareness, sell more tickets and sponsorships, or connect with the team's fan base is what makes a database an effective CRM tool. Merely storing information is not sufficient to sell more effectively and efficiently.

What Are Some Common CRM Tools?

In today's business world, there is so much information available. As I have previously alluded to based on my prior experience, it is not effective to track your own information in a spreadsheet in Microsoft Excel. You need to be able to update a "living" database that the necessary users can update in real time and at the same time as other users. While it is possible to use Microsoft Access for small organizations, most organizations need a more robust platform that has the speed and functionality to handle the number of customers or records required for that business.

Based on my experience working at and with numerous professional teams, the two most common CRM tools used by these organizations are Microsoft Dynamics CRM and Salesforce.com. Both tools offer a cloud-based option, meaning these platforms can be accessed via the Internet, which often provides easier access because it does not necessarily require logging into a company's network. The server-based version of Microsoft Dynamics CRM generally requires access to the company's network to access the tool. Often through a third-party developer, these tools can both be customized to fit the specific needs of a sport business organization, often incorporating the specific assets available to be sold to customers (i.e., tickets, hospitality, and sponsorships).

Another popular CRM option for teams is to leverage the system used to sell tickets to customers. Archtics, the ticketing system offered by Ticketmaster, is the most common ticketing software utilized for CRM purposes. Archtics offers the option to not only sell and track ticket inventory, but also the ability to record "memos" or interactions with customers as well as other demographic information. Ticketing systems like Archtics are typically used with ticket-related transactions only and are then supplemented with a more robust CRM tool.

In addition to CRM tools that store customer information and interactions, many teams leverage a platform for sending e-mails to use with other CRM tools. There are a large number of available options. Some of the more common e-mail platforms include Oracle Eloqua, Marketo, and ExactTarget (now called Salesforce Marketing Cloud). These tools offer the ability to gather and store metrics associated with each e-mail an organization sends such as how many recipients were sent a particular e-mail and how many recipients opened each e-mail. Metrics are also available down to the individual recipient level.

What Information Should Sport Business Companies Track?

The overarching theme for why CRM is important is because CRM allows organizations to sift through a vast amount of information. What information should sport teams track? Some of the important items to track in a CRM system include the following items:

Individuals: Generally speaking, individuals can be anyone that interacts with a team or organization. It is important to keep a record of anyone that has ever bought tickets or any other product from your organization. However, it is just as important to also keep track of anyone that has shown interest in making a purchase or is just a fan of the team if you have access to that information. At a minimum, you will want to collect basic contact information such as name, mailing address, phone number, and e-mail address. Individuals are great targets for selling tickets, merchandise, and sending news updates about the team.

Companies: In today's sports world, professional sport organizations rely heavily on companies for the team's season ticket base as well as the majority of premium seating sales such as luxury suites. Sponsorship departments depend almost exclusively on companies as key target customers for opportunities such as naming rights to a stadium or presenting sponsor(s) of the team. The process to sell any product to a company often requires a longer sales cycle, numerous phone calls, and in-person meetings to complete a deal. For that reason it could take years to finally complete a sale to a company. Tracking information from every interaction along the way is crucial to the process. Some of this information can be recorded at the individual level, as your company will work with an individual (or small group of individuals) that works at a particular company.

Interactions: Aside from maintaining information related to the individuals and companies that comprise the core of the database, a CRM tool generally offers a way to track interactions with the members of the database. An interaction is any method in which a team representative communicates with a member of the database, whether in-person or by other means. Common examples of interactions include phone calls, e-mails, and meetings. Oftentimes the sales process from start to finish takes multiple interactions to complete. For example, as a ticket sales representative for an NFL team, I can remember going back and forth with a prospective customer that was looking for specific wheelchair accessible seats that were not available at the time. Once those seats were available months later, I reached out to that customer just before the season started. I referenced the seats we had previously discussed. I was able to make the sale because I took detailed notes from our previous phone calls. In addition to the common interactions, a number of teams go a step further depending on the e-mail marketing tool employed by the team. Many teams are able to use an e-mail system to track which prospective customers open specific e-mails as well as to track the specific web links consumers click on within that e-mail.

Demographics: In order to utilize the full potential of CRM, it is important to obtain more than just the name and contact information for each individual in your database. Some examples of important information include gender, birthday, marital status, anniversary, spouse name, ticket partner's name, number of children, names of children, hometown, college, employer, income, and favorite teams. This kind of information can usually be obtained via phone (e.g., sales representative talking with customer), survey, or purchased demographic lists obtained via a third-party company.

Purchase history: Most professional team's databases should at the very least contain customers that have purchased tickets or any other product (ideally for as long of a time period as possible). From a sales perspective, this information is typically the starting point for prospective customers to target. It is integral to know if a customer has previously purchased a season ticket plan from the team or purchased tickets to multiple individual games during the current or previous seasons. Past ticket purchases indicate some interest in the team and a propensity to buy tickets again in the future. After a list of past ticket buyers is compiled, then a team representative can further dissect the list based on how recent the customers purchased tickets and how much they spent. The team representative can infer that someone that has purchased tickets in the last few seasons has more recently shown interest in the team as compared to someone who purchased tickets 5 years ago. Also, someone who spends more on tickets on a ticket purchase compared to another customer may have interest in a premium (or more expensive) ticket in the future.

Attendance: From a customer retention standpoint, attendance (i.e., ticket utilization) can be a very useful statistic to track. Typically, most ticketing systems for professional teams offer the ability to pull a report of how often a customer's tickets were scanned at the gates for each game to determine the percent of games attended for that season. For example, if you are a customer service representative and you notice that one of your clients has only attended one game halfway through your team's season, you might infer that the customer either does not want to attend games or is not aware of the ways in which they can utilize their tickets. That might also lead you to believe that the customer may potentially be at risk of not renewing the season tickets for the following season because they are not utilizing their tickets. Therefore, it would make sense to reach out to that customer at the midway point of the season and let them know that they have the option to send their tickets to clients, employees, family, or friends online through the ticketing system. You might also find out that the customer has experienced an issue at one game. Organizations can offer an experience upgrade at a game (e.g., opportunity to take a photo on the court before the game) or incentive such as an autographed item to address a previous negative consumer experience.

Growing the CRM Database

It is imperative for every CRM administrator to not only maintain as detailed a database as possible, but also it is vital to grow the number of individuals and companies in that database. If a team has annual season ticket renewals around 90% every year, it will not take long before team realizes how hard it is to replace the 10% of season ticket holders lost every year if team representatives are reaching out to the same set number of customers each year. In order to remain sustainable and foster growth, teams must constantly add potential customers to the database. Depending on the team and its season ticket base, you might find thousands of people who attend a game that were given tickets by someone else or bought tickets at the box office on the day of the game. All of those game attendees could potentially be customers but are not in the CRM database. For that reason, many teams develop data collection tables in stadium concourses with the sole purpose of obtaining names of people attending the game in order to reach out to them at a later time during strategic sales efforts. This information is typically obtained in the form of a raffle or "enter to win" contest, where the attendee provides his or her contact information and indicates whether they would like to be contacted via e-mail or phone.

Along those same lines, most teams have a presence at community events and business tradeshows where there is a strong emphasis on identifying prospective customers to add to the database. Lists of companies with contact names and information are also available to be purchased through third-party vendors. Most teams have web pages that fans visit in which fans can provide contact information to be subsequently contacted by the organization for a particular product such as season tickets. Those individuals should also be added to the database. Finally, individual sales representatives are always searching for new potential customers, whether through referrals from current clients or just looking at a list of new businesses in the local business journal. Growing a database requires being proactive. In the world of professional sports, a team's performance can fluctuate and as such demand for tickets varies. A team must consistently search for new customers to prepare for a potential unexpected yet sudden downturn in team performance.

Catering to the Individual, Not the Masses

What is the point of gathering so much information about individuals and companies? The goal is to utilize that information in such a way that an organization is not approaching sales and marketing from a mass marketing standpoint. Instead, the point is to utilize information to target individuals: "Treating customers like cattle is the antithesis of CRM, the goal of which is to recognize and treat each customer as an individual" (Dyche, 2002, p. 7).

For example, imagine you are someone who works the night shift during the week but you are free during the weekends and are a dedicated fan of the local MLB team. Would it make sense for that MLB team to contact you with an offer for full season tickets knowing that a large portion of the 81 home games will conflict with your work schedule? Instead, it makes more sense to e-mail or call you with an offer for a weekend ticket plan. A good CRM system allows organizations to track the preferences of individuals and target for a specific product.

While many "CRM tools, applications, and third-party apps compete for market share, all designed to help businesses generate sales and maintain relationships with customers" (CRM Resource and Guide, 2015). CRM systems can store information such as birthdays and anniversaries, which allows a team to create a personal connection by sending an e-mail or making a phone call on those special occasions. CRM not only allows teams to focus sales efforts, but also helps these organizations build authentic and meaningful relationships that increase retention and consumer spending if implemented properly.

Targeted Campaigns

With all the information captured via a comprehensive CRM strategy, teams can focus on individuals with specific criteria in a targeted campaign. For example, a targeted campaign in the context of ticket sales is an initiative to reach out to a group of leads in order to sell as many tickets to as many leads as possible. A targeted campaign utilizes a subset of a bigger group of leads, narrowed down by specific criteria to focus on a smaller number of leads that the data indicate are more inclined to purchase. What are common criteria used to create targeted campaigns?

> *Transactional*: As mentioned previously, the best leads are usually the individuals that have previously purchased tickets to a single game or to multiple games. There are a couple of ways to segment the individuals that make individual game purchases on their own, typically done via the Internet. The first method would be to look at the individuals that have previously purchased tickets to multiple individual games. Sport teams have found that individuals that buy tickets to

multiple individual games would be more inclined to purchase a partial season ticket plan or even full season tickets as compared with someone who buys tickets to just one game. Therefore, a sales representative could prioritize leads by creating a targeted campaign of individuals that purchased tickets to multiple games. Then, this team representative could collaborate with colleagues in the sales department to concentrate team efforts on individuals that bought for just one game. This philosophy does not solely apply to single game buyers; it can apply to individuals that have previously purchased a ticket plan. In that scenario, a team might want to look at the CRM database and target those individuals who had previously purchased a ticket plan because they at one time showed a propensity for owning a ticket plan for that particular team. Another method for segmenting leads using previous purchase history is looking at the total spend on tickets in a season or for a particular game to determine which individuals might have disposable income to purchase a ticket plan. Along those lines, a sales representative could break out a subset of buyers based on the location of the seats they have purchased for a game or multiple games. For example, I hypothetically purchase a pair of tickets to an NBA game for a total of $100 in the very last row of an arena. Another individual purchases a pair of tickets to the same game, but they pay $5000 for courtside seats. It would make sense that the individual who purchased courtside seats would be looked at as potentially having higher disposable income and likely would purchase a more expensive ticket plan than I would if we both bought ticket plans. In this scenario, a sales team would develop a campaign targeting the higher spend buyers first.

Behavioral: With some of the advanced e-mail marketing systems that are available today, professional teams are utilizing behavioral data to see who is engaging with the team. For example, a team might send out an e-mail newsletter to their entire database containing 200,000 e-mail addresses. The newsletter was primarily sent to inform individuals within the database that season tickets were going on sale for the following season. In the e-mail, there were web links where individuals could go to the team web page that contained information about season ticket plans or go to the web page where individuals could purchase season tickets directly online. Most e-mail marketing platforms allow organizations to track who opens a particular e-mail and who clicks on specific links within an e-mail. If 1% of the 200,000 recipients open the e-mail regarding season tickets, that would give you 2000 leads to create a targeted campaign. Now if half of the 2000 that opened the e-mail also clicked on one of the two season ticket-related links, then we are left with 1000 leads who you might infer have even more interest in season tickets than the individuals that merely opened the e-mail. These leads are highly effective because most of us delete e-mails from companies or people we do not directly know. If someone not only opens an e-mail from a team but also clicks on a season ticket–related link, then it shows the individual has made an effort to learn more about the product and is a good potential lead. Other behavioral data to track are whether individuals visit specific web pages or engage in social media platforms depending on what tools an organization has available to track such data.

Demographic: Another way in which sport teams can target individuals is by using demographic data to further segment out a list of potential leads. For example, a company might target an individual that has a high disposable income, has a high propensity for attending sporting events, and has a family including a spouse and kids. Those indicators might lead you to believe that if a sales representative reached out to that individual and pitched a ticket plan, then the prospect would be more likely to purchase or make a bigger purchase as compared to an individual who is believed to have lower disposable income and a lower propensity to attend sport events. Again, the key is to target specific individuals in the database based on their demographic data as opposed to attempting to target everyone in the CRM database.

Geographic: Another method for segmenting leads is to focus on individuals in a certain area or radius of a sport venue.

Sport teams have generally found that a large percentage of a team's season ticket base lives within a close radius of the stadium or arena. If an individual lives 2–3 hours away from an arena, then they are less likely to want to make the trip to attend multiple games as opposed to an individual that lives within an hour drive of the stadium. For example, Fan Interactive has one client in which 88% of the team's season ticket base lives within 90 miles of the team's home stadium. Oftentimes a sport organization can target individuals geographically along with one or more of the other previously listed criteria.

CRM Snapshot—Examples Utilizing Microsoft Dynamics CRM

Figure 4.1 provides an example of a record for an individual in Microsoft Dynamics CRM.

Figure 4.2 spotlights the activity history for an individual, including completed activities and future scheduled activities.

Figure 4.3 provides additional information for the individual, including address, communication preferences, and demographic details.

Figure 4.4 illustrates how an organization can run a report based on demographic prospect data (i.e., target fans of a particular team).

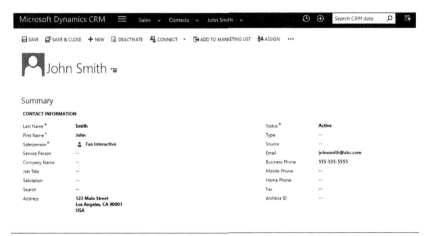

Figure 4.1 Microsoft Dynamics CRM summary.

Open Activities

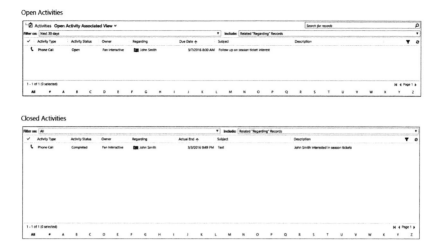

Figure 4.2   CRM activity history.

Address

Address Information

Street 1	123 Main Street		State/Province	CA
Street 2	--		ZIP/Postal Code	90001
City	Los Angeles		Country/Region	USA

Communication Information

Phone	Allow		Mail	Allow
Email	Allow		Bulk Email	Allow
Fax	Allow			

Demographic

Birthday	1/1/1975		Anniversary	8/1/2001
Gender	Male		Nickname	--
Marital Status	Married		Spouse/Partner Name	Jane
Household Income	$100,000		No. of Children	2
Hometown	Dallas, TX		Concert interests	Rock
Hobbies	--		Children's Names	Jack and Jill
College	UCLA		Classical music	☐
Sports interests	--		Country Music	☐
Favorite team	Dallas Mavericks		Pop music	☑
Favorite player	--		Rap music	☐
Favorite destination	--		Rock music	☑
Favorite restaurant	--		Family shows	☐
Other information	--			

Figure 4.3   Additional consumer data.

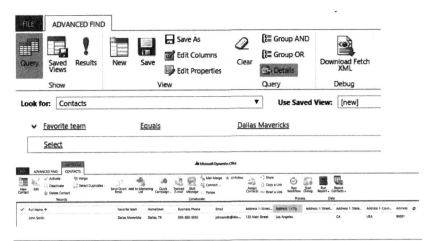

Figure 4.4   Sample prospect data report.

Practical Application Case Study

At Fan Interactive Marketing, we have a client that in a previous season targeted single game buyers by calling each customer the day after a game to pitch a ticket plan. However, the team felt they were not maximizing the revenue received for the effort sales representatives put into each phone call. Our client reached out to us to help consult and execute a plan that would allow them to increase revenue and work more efficiently. We proposed using transactional, behavioral, demographic, and geographic analysis to focus their sales efforts. First, we used the transactional data to pull the list of individuals that bought individual game tickets the previous season but that never purchased a ticket plan. Next, we used demographic and geographic analysis to segment out the buyers that fit different sets of criteria such as disposable income of over $100,000, married, kids under the age of 18, and lives within 30 miles of the arena (geographic analysis). If a single game buyer matched the different sets of criteria we defined, then we proposed sending one of two e-mails to those individuals offering a private locker room tour in one e-mail and an opportunity to play in the arena on a nongame day in the other e-mail. Finally, we pulled the list of individuals that opened the e-mails and had a sales representative reach out to them. This particular CRM initiative resulted in $7 more per lead despite making 3600 (62%) fewer phone calls (Table 4.1).

Table 4.1   Fan Interactive Case Study: CRM Results

PREVIOUS SEASON	NEXT SEASON
All buyers campaign	Targeted buyers campaign
5800 phone calls	2200 phone calls
$10 per lead in new sales	$17 per lead in new sales

What Does CRM Help Teams to Achieve?

In addition to creating targeted campaigns that lead to higher return on investment, CRM also helps bring a high level of accountability and efficiency to a sales department. Sales managers can use CRM to make sure sales representatives are meeting predefined goals for calling leads. Management can also make sure leads are being called and not being ignored. A CRM strategy allows teams to focus on specific leads rather than reaching out to everyone in the database. Marketing departments also use CRM to track consumer engagement with the team and what content the team is releasing that is getting the most impressions. Overall, an effective CRM system allows teams to utilize all the information available to the organization to not only work harder but also to work smarter.

References

Database. (2015). *Merriam Webster Online*. Retrieved from http://www.merriam-webster.com/dictionary/database.

Dyche, J. (2002). *The CRM Handbook: A Business Guide to Customer Relationship Management*. Boston, MA: Addison-Wesley.

The 2015 CRM resource and guide. (2015). *Avidian*. Retrieved from https://www.avidian.com/resources/crm.

5

THE ASPIRE GROUP'S TICKET MARKETING, SALES, AND SERVICE PHILOSOPHY

MICHAEL FARRIS

Contents

Ticket Sales: An Important Health Indicator for Every Sport Property 69
Introduction to The Aspire Group 70
Ticket Marketing, Sales, and Service Plan Analytics 71
    The Strategies 71
    The Tactics 73
Case Study: Georgia Tech Athletics Fan Relationship Management Center 73
    Research 74
    Retain 77
    Grow 79
    Acquire 81
    Capture 82
    Communicate 84
    Close 85
    Performance Analytics 87
Optimizing the TiMSS Plan for Success 87
References 88

Ticket Sales: An Important Health Indicator for Every Sport Property

At the core of every sport and entertainment property is the need to sell tickets. Since the beginning of professional sports, tickets have been the fundamental product for fans to purchase in order to interact with sport teams and build memories through the experience of watching their favorite teams live. Gate revenues (i.e., ticket sales) have long been noted as the catalyst for revenue and enterprise value

69

growth for a sport property (Mullin et al., 2014). In essence, tickets sold meant eyeballs in the venue for sponsorships, merchandise sales, and other related revenue streams.

The prominence of ticket sales may soon be ending as the growth of digital platforms increases the ease for fans to constantly connect and engage with their favorite teams. By 2018, media rights fees are projected to outpace tickets for the first time in the North America sports marketplace (PwC, 2015). Although industry indicators strongly push the growth of media rights, The Aspire Group continues to surpass expectations as a sport marketing agency concentrating on the niche of ticket marketing, sales, and service (TiMSS).

Introduction to The Aspire Group

The Aspire Group is a global sport and entertainment marketing company specializing in TiMSS^{SM}. Specifically, Aspire concentrates on four key capabilities:

1. *TiMSS*: Utilizing a mix between modern technology and personal relationship building, Aspire provides outsourced TiMSS support for partners across the globe.
2. *Strategic consulting and research*: To discover and execute on insights, Aspire conducts a full suite of research and consulting services focused on quantitative and qualitative fan research, ticket pricing models, and strategic planning.
3. *Marketing and revenue enhancement*: In conjunction with Aspire's ticketing capabilities, additional revenue-generating services are offered to assist partners with database marketing, sponsorships, and media negotiations.
4. *Sports investment optimization*: Leveraging the extensive years of experience within the sport business industry across Aspire, the company provides expertise regarding the disposition/acquisition or relocation of sport teams, facility renovation, and new venue development.

Although Aspire's 160+ partners incorporate multiple sports and levels within the industry, the company is widely known for its work within collegiate athletics. Since 2009, Aspire has innovated collegiate athletics ticket sales through their Fan Relationship Management Centers

(FRMCs) by implementing the first outsourced ticket sales operation, first outsourced database marketing and analytics position, and first outsourced specialized pro ticket sales operation model (i.e., positions dedicated to specific ticketed products and servicing accounts).

The genesis of Aspire's "firsts" in the industry is sourced from an innate nature to collect data, listen to the needs of partners, analyze received information, and prescribe customized solutions to solve critical business challenges. Each of Aspire's FRMCs is required to create an annual TiMSS plan outlining strategies and tactics to incrementally grow a partner's fan base. The TiMSS plan is built on an 8-point philosophy beginning and ending with data. The first step is research and the last step is performance analytics. Everything must be measured. This chapter provides an overview of, along with real-world case studies on, the complete TiMSS plan.

Ticket Marketing, Sales, and Service Plan Analytics

The purpose of a TiMSS plan is to produce a comprehensive road map designed to drive significant increases in attendance and revenue for a sport property using The Aspire Group's 8-point TiMSS philosophy. The philosophy is best described as an ecosystem. Although each point is separate from one another, all points are interconnected and at optimal performance when working together. The TiMSS plan identifies specific strategies and tactics that will be used to achieve outlined goals, as well as provides a definitive calendar for deployment of those strategies, tactics, and related initiatives based on the sport property's available resources. Market research (i.e., data collection and analysis) creates the foundation for the TiMSS plan through insight that guides the strategies and tactics. The following strategies and tactics comprise Aspire's 8-point philosophy (Figure 5.1).

The Strategies

Based on the attendance frequency escalator concept (Mullin et al., 2014), Aspire developed three core strategies to drive each ticket sales and service operation. These strategies require a dedicated focus to first bring back as many fans that have previously attended a sport event and increase overall attendance frequency. The TiMSS plan is

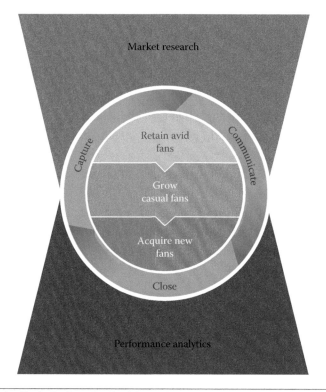

Figure 5.1   The Aspire Group 8-point ticket marketing, sales, and service philosophy.

weighted on the knowledge that attendance and revenue growth will primarily come from the ability of a sport team to increase the engagement frequency of current fans, rather than acquiring new fans.

1. *Retain avid fans*: Goal number one is to keep the fans that are currently attending the sport event(s). Aspire seeks to achieve an 85% renewal rate at every FRMC to protect against fan base erosion.
2. *Grow casual fans*: As ticket purchasers continually stay engaged, sport properties strive to move them up the proverbial sales escalator into more frequent and avid fans. There are multiple strategies to grow fans that focus on wallet share and consumption habits of the fan.
3. *Acquire new fans*: As the core fan base continues to grow, sport properties should seek broader exposure with new fans. The TiMSS plan focuses on targeting nonattendees who have the highest likelihood of attending in the future.

The Tactics

In order to execute the aforementioned strategies, Aspire utilizes the following tactics that involve consistent communication and relationship building with fans:

1. *Capture*: Aspire seeks to capture as much data about a fan as possible. Contact information for every fan that attends a game or engages within the team digitally should be captured. Additionally, data points detailing the "how" and "why" with each fan should be captured.

2. *Communicate*: With the numerous data points available on each fan, Aspire wants to communicate to each fan in the manner that they want to be communicated with. Creating highly targeted campaigns will yield higher open rates, click-through rates, and drive results via phone calls.

3. *Close*: After building the relationship with the fan through the other TiMSS elements, Aspire wants to consummate the sale. "Close" concentrates on delivering on fan expectations to ensure repeat purchase.

4. *Performance analytics*: Continual evaluation of the plan allows for improvisation and improvement. Aspire needs to know how each strategy and tactic performs within the ecosystem and evaluate their usage through the return on objectives (ROO) and return on investment (ROI) of implemented initiatives.

Within the TiMSS plan, a sport property will detail specific goals and objectives for each season. The plan will act as the road map for the cross-departmental team needed to fully execute on each element of the 8-point philosophy.

Case Study: Georgia Tech Athletics Fan Relationship Management Center

To illustrate the use of TiMSS plan analytics throughout Aspire's core business, this chapter will feature an array of strategies and tactics utilized at the company's Georgia Tech FRMC for football ticket sales. Georgia Tech was the first collegiate athletic program in the industry to outsource its TiMSS operation in 2009 through an innovative partnership with Aspire. After 6 years, the Georgia Tech FRMC has generated $18 million in ticket-related donation revenue since inception.

Currently, Aspire's Georgia Tech FRMC incorporates outbound and inbound sales and service, premium seating and service, related and stand-alone athletic donations, a specialized service and retention team, and a suite of consulting and research services. Within the past 2 years, Georgia Tech integrated Salesforce throughout its ticketing infrastructure (Paciolan) and implemented numerous automated processes to increase the efficiency of the sales process. This resulted in a school record of 5500 new football season tickets sold in 2015.

Research

The first step in building a TiMSS plan at Aspire's FRMCs is to conduct research to evaluate the fan environment and gain a firm understanding of historical and current sales strategies. In essence, Aspire wants to know the likes, dislikes, preferences, and behaviors of every fan who is a current or potential ticket purchaser. The goal is to have a 360° view of each fan through data available in the ticketing database, survey responses, and data appends available through secondary data vendors (e.g., Acxiom). The varying forms of data are stored within a customer relationship management (CRM) platform providing each sales consultant with instantaneous insight when connecting with fans.

Within Aspire's FRMCs, research is conducted every day. Each phone call provides an opportunity to ask questions, listen, and react to a fan and populate data points for strategic decision-making. From a call, a sales consultant can understand the motivations for a fan to purchase as well as barriers within the fan decision-making process; sales consultants can also assess fan preferences for available ticketed inventory. This data collection process is unstructured and allows the sales consultant to ask the second and third level questions in order to get to the true insight. When this type of research is aggregated over hundreds of calls a day and thousands of calls every week, significant data findings can be reported back to leadership.

The Georgia Tech FRMC extends its research practices through two different survey methodologies:

1. *Postgame surveys*: Following each home game, an automated survey is sent to ticket purchasers covering questions specific to attendance for that event. Data are received within 24–48 hours following the game, and all responses are uploaded to the CRM database. The feedback received from the surveys are used in the following ways:

   a. Respondents indicating a negative experience through either open-ended feedback questions or their satisfaction rating are flagged and prioritized for a follow-up call from a service consultant.

   b. An aggregated report is prepared incorporating every question on the survey and specific segments (e.g., season ticket holders vs. single game purchasers) are analyzed to pinpoint opportunities for improvement. Within 3 days after the event, a cross-functional game experience taskforce—involving ticket operations, sales, game operations, communications, marketing, and other departments—dissects the report and outlines strategies to improve the game day experience.

2. *Postseason surveys*: Following the conclusion of the season, Georgia Tech sends out a comprehensive survey to season ticket holders, which gathers input involving the entirety of the ticket purchase and game experience. This includes a significant question set geared toward understanding the importance placed on benefits offered and the potential opportunity to enhance the value of the season ticket package. For the 2014–2015 athletics season, Georgia Tech received over a 20% response rate from the athletic program's entire full season purchaser base. This insight provides the needed detail to improve satisfaction levels and renew season ticket accounts. From the survey, Georgia Tech concentrates on the following key metrics:

   a. *Net Promoter Score* (*NPS*): This is a standard benchmarking metric used to indicate the growth potential of a company through intention to recommend the experience (see Measuring Your Net Promoter Score[SM], 2016).

Consumers are segmented into three categories: promoters, passives, or detractors. A company with a higher percentage of promoters than detractors has a positive Net Promoter Score. For Georgia Tech, NPS is used to identify fans who are most likely to refer new accounts and flag accounts that are categorized as detractors.

b. *Value-weighted renewal rate*: Each season ticket holder is asked to rate how valued they feel as a season ticket holder and how likely they are to renew (both measured on a 7-point Likert scale). A correlation analysis between the two data points in the 2014–2015 season data revealed a significant positive relationship indicating that if a season ticket holder felt valued they were more likely to renew. This is an expected outcome. However, this analysis yields extensive value when the gap is identified. For example, Georgia Tech learned that season ticket holders who felt "Somewhat Valued" were 74% likely to renew, whereas those who felt "Valued" were 91% likely. Increasing a season ticket holder one point on the scale would result in a 17% increase in their likelihood to renew. This data point allows Georgia Tech to prioritize accounts for needed service touchpoints.

c. *Top box satisfaction rates*: These data are captured via a survey that includes over 30 elements measured on a 7-point Likert satisfaction scale. Each element is analyzed based on the percentage of season ticket holders who rate each element as "Satisfied" or "Very Satisfied," which are the sixth and seventh points on the scale. Ratings are categorized as "Exceeding Expectations" (90% and above), "Meeting Expectations" (70%–89%), and "Needs Improvement" (below 70%). Data are analyzed on the aggregated level as well as on the individual respondent level.

Although the Georgia Tech example primarily focuses on satisfaction surveying, a robust research strategy would incorporate topics such as motivations to purchase, price sensitivity, branding and fan engagement, ticket package attributes and benefits, and in-depth demographic assessments. To drive the most value with research for a TiMSS plan, it is important to keep in mind a "crawl, walk, run, sprint" progression for implementing market research strategies. Thus, even gathering the simplest of data points (e.g., demographics and satisfaction metrics) can provide exponential value as a sport property builds a foundation for data.

Retain

The retention of customers year-over-year is the number one priority for every sport and entertainment property—and for every business. Thus, it is vital that renewal rates for ticketed packages are tracked and dissected. Renewal rates are by far the most important indicators of a team's health and long-term stability due to the low cost to renew fans versus the higher costs of acquiring new fans (Maycotte, 2015). To incentivize renewal, sport properties focus on increasing fan satisfaction and providing unique experiences for loyal supporters.

On a foundational level, sport properties are tracking renewal rates through two perspectives: (1) percentage of ticket buyers who renew (e.g., seat-on-seat renewal rate) and (2) percentage of committed revenue renewed based on sales from the previous season (e.g., revenue renewal rate). Every sport team should strive to renew at least 85% of previous ticket purchasers to prevent erosion within the fan base. As illustrated in the example below (see Figure 5.2), even with an influx of new ticket purchasers, it will be challenging to grow the fan base if

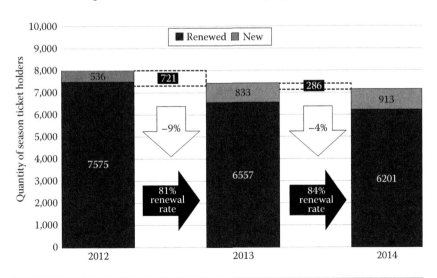

Figure 5.2   Season ticket holder attrition example.

the renewal rate is beneath benchmark. The example details the season ticket sales results by quantity sold for a mid-major collegiate athletic program. Although new sales increased from 2012 to 2013 by 55%, the overall season ticket base decreased by 9% due to a subpar renewal rate. Even though the fan base continued to decline going into the 2014 season, the erosion was slowed due to an emphasis on increasing the renewal rate. In the example, this particular sport property needed an average renewal rate of 89.2% over the course of the 2013 and 2014 seasons to maintain the sales total from the 2012 season.

To ensure that Georgia Tech is achieving the 85% renewal rate baseline, sales leaders track comprehensive renewal rates, utilize a specialized service and retention team, and leverage technology to track the full relationship of the season ticket base. For the football season ticket fan base, Georgia Tech tracks renewal rates by tenure of accounts, seat location, price category, and donation level. As the metrics are tracked, Georgia Tech is able to audible its focus on the varying segments to drive success through the aggregated renewal rate.

In tandem with a fully specialized service and retention team that concentrates solely on renewing accounts and generating new business from current customers, Georgia Tech utilizes personalized technology that customizes the experience for every season ticket holder. The epitome of the technology is exhibited through the use of personalized URLs (PURLs) for each account holder for a renewal microsite. The links are customized with the name and account details of each season ticket holder. As shown in Figure 5.3, Georgia Tech sends out team-based graphics that invite each season ticket holder to be a part

Figure 5.3   Georgia Tech personalized renewal graphic.

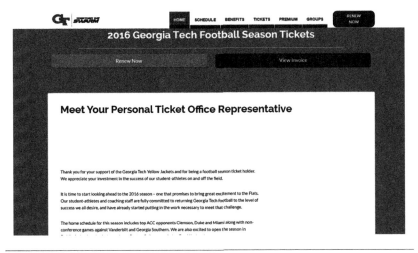

Figure 5.4   Georgia Tech personalized renewal letter.

of the team. Designing the graphic with the season ticket holder's name displays the emphasis placed on providing individual attention to each account holder. In addition to adaptable graphics, Georgia Tech is able to alter messaging through the PURL that addresses specific scenarios of the account holder such as seating location, quantity of seats, and possible avenues for upgrades (see Figure 5.4). An account holder's interaction through the PURL is tracked, and the service and retention team is able to monitor the quantity of pages viewed on the renewal microsite and the time spent during each visit. These data provide substantial insight to the service and retention team to investigate methods for increasing renewal intention.

Grow

Once a sport property is renewing ticket purchasers at a high level, the second priority is to move fans up the proverbial attendance frequency escalator. There are three core objectives for growing fans through ticketed products:

1. Increase the number of games a fan attends
2. Increase the quantity of tickets a fan purchases
3. Increase the level of spend by upgrading the fan to better seating locations and/or amenities

Each objective is achieved by offering stepped ticketing products that allow the fan to move to more desirable locations and/or add more games to the package through equally paced steps to individual lifestyle changes. Thus, Aspire works with partners to create packages that fit fans throughout a variety of needs. For the 2014 football season, Rutgers Athletics was interested in implementing a new miniplan package to provide a new step in the "attendance frequency escalator" (previously, Rutgers only offered season tickets, single game tickets, and group tickets). Aspire conducted a survey at the conclusion of the 2013 season to test the feasibility of new package leveraging potential opponents with the planned move to the Big Ten Conference. Survey results indicated that the more games that the fan attended, the more likely fans were to be interested in the package and the more likely fans were to buy (results from the survey are highlighted in Figure 5.5). The new miniplan package generated $400,000 in incremental revenue for the 2014 season.

This result might be common sense, but it is a perfect example of the "grow" strategy within the TiMSS plan. A sport property needs to be able to identify the most engaged fans and deliver products that suit the needs of these fans. Priority should be placed on growing current season ticket holders through upselling and add-ons. For the 2015 season, 21% of Georgia Tech's football new season ticket holder revenue was attributed to add-ons or upgrades for current season ticket accounts. Following season ticket holders, the next step would

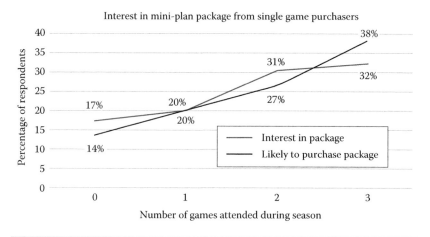

Figure 5.5   Rutgers 2013 football ticket package survey results.

be to "move up" multigame packages to full seasons and then single game purchasers to multigame packages. In essence, a well-oiled sales team will be backfilling churn from the season ticket holder base from existing customers within other facets of the organization.

Acquire

The last strategy of the Aspire TiMSS plan is to acquire new fans. In line with the first two strategies, Aspire analyzes data related to current ticket purchasers to find opportunities for revenue growth. Thus, the sales operation seeks to understand the demographic and psychographic profile of fans including knowing the key segments of purchasers. This allows Aspire personnel to concentrate on acquiring fans who are most like current purchasers instead of spending time on "Nonattending, Nonaware" (NANA).

Often acquisition strategies incorporate group ticket sales, unique game-specific promotions, discount ticket bundles, sampling programs (e.g., school vouchers to attend game), and referral programs. For Georgia Tech, referrals are the second largest lead source for new season ticket accounts with 15% of 2015 new season tickets sourced from a referral. To boost the efficiency of Georgia Tech's acquisition strategy, sales consultants generate detailed heat maps depicting the zip codes that drive the highest quantity of ticket purchasers (see Figure 5.6).

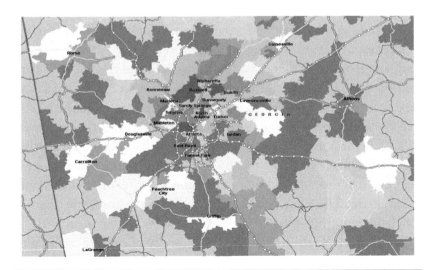

Figure 5.6   Georgia Tech season ticket holder heat map.

By interweaving a number of heat maps, Georgia Tech is able to identify trends in living and working locations throughout the local region. This includes understanding the location of university and athletic donors, season ticket holders, single game purchasers, and lapsed season ticket holders, among a number of other key segments. The heat maps provide the intelligence to Georgia Tech's marketing team to place advertising dollars throughout the Atlanta metropolitan area to best serve the population interested in Georgia Tech athletics. Additionally, the FRMC develops a community event calendar based on the heat spots on the maps. The goal is to "fish where the fish are" to best optimize a limited marketing budget.

Capture

To activate each of the *Retain, Grow,* and *Acquire* strategies, Aspire incorporates a myriad of methods to capture data from fans. These data provide critical insight for sales team representatives to build relationships and best align partners' products to fit the needs of fans. Aspire data capture techniques aim to achieve one of two goals:

1. Gather data on *new* fans who are likely to purchase in the future.
2. Expand the existing knowledge set for *current* fans to better serve their needs.

Throughout Aspire's network, the company conducts data capture techniques at a variety of technology levels based on the budget, staff, and scope of a partner's athletic program and the FRMC operated on-site. This ranges from simple capture techniques, such as paper contact forms, to extensive, sophisticated techniques, such as web tracking, social listening, and data appending. At a base level, each of Aspire's FRMCs concentrates the TiMSS plans on capturing vital contact details—name, e-mail, and phone number—for each fan that attends and/or watches the sport team. The accumulation of the data tactics used at each FRMC is known as the fan contact data capture plan.

The Georgia Tech FRMC utilizes a variety of capture techniques to expand the fan data universe, but has quickly transitioned from relying on concourse intercept surveys and other basic data collection methods to incorporating technology to capture data in-venue and online. Every source that brings in new data to the FRMC is tracked for tickets sold and revenue, allowing the FRMC leadership to evaluate time and monetary investment in each capture tactic.

Over the past two seasons, Georgia Tech invested in innovative web tracking and analytics technology with integrations through Salesforce CRM and Paciolan's FanOne. One of the key segments captured via the new technology is new fans visiting high-value website pages. The high-value pages categorized by Georgia Tech include eVenue links to buy tickets online, team schedules, and visiting sport-specific microsites (e.g., togetherweswarm.com). Each of these pages is tagged with specific codes to understand what page the fan is visiting and for what length. The FRMC is able to access the data through Salesforce and receive hyperlinks to view all the pages visited by the fan (see Figure 5.7 for an example of the high-value dashboard used at Georgia Tech). These leads are typically hot leads due to the high incidence rate of abandoned cart visitors within the data set. Thus, the sales team can review the fan's online process and gather intel on the

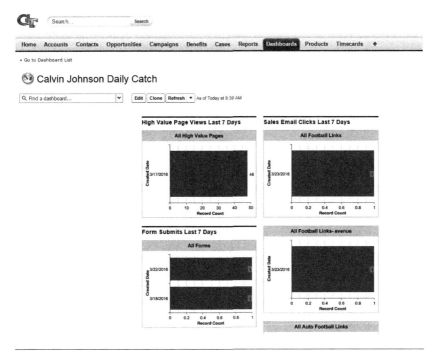

Figure 5.7   Georgia Tech high-value page visitor dashboard.

messaging points to influence their purchase after they know that the fan is already interested.

Communicate

Once Aspire captures the necessary data to learn about the fan, a personalized communication strategy needs to be developed. The FRMCs communication back to the fan is highly targeted with segmented content based on existing individualized fan data. Communication channels should directly fit with the preferred channel for the fan whether that is e-mail, text, social media, phone calls, direct mail, or other formats. Within Aspire's fan research initiatives, the company has learned that fans predominately prefer to be contacted by e-mail. With these data, Aspire seeks to send targeted e-mail messages rather than general or mass e-mails to the broad fan base. When e-mails are targeted, Aspire has seen increases of over 260% for open rates and 100% for click-through rates from previous general e-mails. E-mails are followed by phone calls to provide immediate touchpoints to the fan and walk them through the offer.

E-mails are not only the preferred method of contact but also provide an array of data back to the sales team. The e-mail provides an opportunity for the fan to engage. The fan could open the e-mail. The fan could click-through to different links in the e-mail. The fan could call the sales team to inquire about the offer. Or the fan could ignore the e-mail. Each of the actions provides a binary matrix of information to prioritize leads. With the "did or did not" data, the sales team operates at better efficiency than just following up with each fan by making a phone call. When Aspire sends out e-mail campaigns, the company uses the following priority order for follow-up calls:

1. Incoming e-mails and/or phone calls
2. Fans who opened and clicked on the offer link
3. Fans who only opened the e-mail
4. Fan who did not open the e-mail

For Aspire's FRMCs that do not have the technology support onsite like Georgia Tech, Aspire provides e-mail marketing support through its corporate office and the company's Manager of Client Partner Marketing, Madison Southerlin. During the 2014 athletic season, Madison worked with Tulane Athletics to execute a campaign to increase the men's basketball season ticket holder base by targeting current and past buyers. In line with the on-sale date for tickets, Madison curated an exclusive offer to cross-sell men's basketball tickets to highly engaged football fans with a base of over 2000 accounts. Madison Southerlin explained, "Rather than directing the current football season ticket holders to the website to purchase their own season tickets and redeem their incentives, they were directed back to their current personal sales representative located on-site in the Tulane FRMC, where they specialize in customer service." The digital touchpoint warmed the fans up for the phone call and led to significant growth in men's basketball ticket sales. The following data spotlight key marketing campaign details and results:

- *Audience*: Tulane football season ticket holders
- *Subject line*: Season ticket holder exclusive
- *Average open rate* (*across seven individual sales rep e-mails sent*): 64.76%
- *ROI*: 8136.36%
- *Improvements to efficiency on sales efforts*:
  - *Average number of calls per lead before close prior to sending e-mail*: 10
  - *Average number of calls per lead before close following e-mail*: 2

Close

The last tactic with the Aspire TiMSS plan is to confirm the sale and provide an outstanding level of customer and fan experience back to the purchaser. If a property conducts extensive research, details specific strategies (retain, grow, acquire) to increase revenue, and uses the tactics of data capture and communication, then the property has developed the needed framework to deliver the optimal package and experience for the fan. The close should be a seamless process.

For a successful close, a sales consultant is going to build a long-term relationship with the fan by seeking to understand why the fan is buying and what the fan wants from his or her experience. The sales consultant will then recommend the best ticketed products available to suit fan needs. Within the close tactic, all interactions with fans are tracked through CRM and the ticketing system. This allows for measurement across all steps of the process from knowing the quantity of calls prior to closing or the time of engagement with the fan (e.g., talk time).

At Georgia Tech, the sales team tracks the close tactic by aligning sales success to lead sources. Every lead that comes into the CRM whether through referrals, the website, or personal prospecting is coded and tracked. Each phone call with a fan is measured according to the lead source to calculate close rate efficiency, revenue per tickets sold, and percentage of revenue generated by lead source. Tracking at this level of detail brings the capture, communicate, and close tactics from Aspire to life (see Table 5.1).

Table 5.1 details 11 key lead categories tracked by Georgia Tech. Overall, the FRMC monitors the outcomes of 37 different types of leads. Season ticket holders are the heart of every fan base, which is illustrated by 50% of 2015 new football season ticket revenue being attributed to current and/or previous season ticket holders. Season ticket holders also contribute the highest revenue per ticket sold by over 15% compared to the average ticket sold for the 2015 season. Although the second lowest source of revenue within the categories in Table 5.1, previous purchasers contribute 17% more revenue per ticket sold than the average sell. This type of data provides insight for Ryan Gottlieb and the leaders at Georgia Tech to curate new sources of leads and provide focus to the sales operation.

Table 5.1   Georgia Tech Lead Sources by Contribution to 2015 New Season Ticket Revenue

LEAD SOURCE	PERCENTAGE OF 2015 FOOTBALL NEW SEASON TICKET REVENUE
Season ticket holder add-ons and upgrades	20.9
Referrals	15.2
Lapsed season ticket holders	14.2
Inbound phone purchases	11.4
2014 multigame purchasers	7.9
2014 single game purchasers	7.2
Prospecting	4.4
Web traffic	3.6
Men's basketball ticket purchasers	3.1
Previous purchasers (nonseason ticket holders)	2.5
Faculty/staff	1.7

Performance Analytics

The last step of the TiMSS plan is to continually evaluate. During and after conducting the strategies and tactics, Aspire needs to know what works and what does not work. Ultimately, each element of the TiMSS plan is tied back to either a ROI or ROO. Understanding the impact of the strategies and tactics within the TiMSS plan allows a sales operation to amend and adapt the plan for following seasons. Thus, each annual planning strategy is not a process of recreating the wheel—instead, the operation evolves.

Internal measurement of resources is also critical to the process of performance analytics. Aspire tracks daily, weekly, monthly, and annual performance metrics on each sales and service consultant. During onboarding, each employee of Aspire is told that their seat is a business and they are the entrepreneurs dictating their own career success. In turn, Aspire motivates the employee to achieve a 3:1 return on their cost to the partner through revenue output. To evaluate the performance of each employee, the leadership at Aspire's FRMC correlates sales success to positive behavior. This is referred to as measuring the "root" (i.e., the actions taken to achieve goals) and the "fruit" (i.e., the outcome of those efforts). Utilizing Aspire's seven key characteristics for leadership, sales and service consultants are evaluated on a four-category matrix (see Figure 5.8). Their characteristic rating tied with their revenue output provides an analytic perspective to identify top performers, employees that need extra development, and employees that may need to be managed out. Overall, this analytic approach allows the TiMSS plan to be optimized by ensuring that the staff is held to the same analytical approach as the strategies and tactics used every day. Chapter 12 provides additional details on employee performance analytics developed and implemented at The Aspire Group.

Optimizing the TiMSS Plan for Success

The TiMSS plan provides a structured data-driven strategy for any size or structure TiMSS operation with a multitude of applications even outside of the sport and entertainment industry. To effectively implement a TiMSS plan, a sport organization needs to buy in to

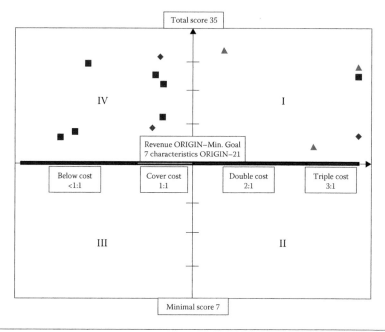

Figure 5.8   Example sales consultant evaluation.

the concept of operating based on analytical, fact-based methodology. This requires significant time for implementation with processes and continual tracking for success. An organization must be ready to measure, learn, and adapt to achieve optimal performance with the TiMSS philosophy approach.

References

Maycotte, H. (2015). Customer lifetime value—The only metric that matters. Retrieved from http://www.forbes.com.

Measuring Your Net Promoter Score[SM]. (2016). Retrieved from http://www. netpromotersystem.com.

Mullin, B., Hardy, S., and Sutton, W. (2014). *Sport Marketing*, 4th edn. Human Kinetics. Champaign, IL.

PwC. (2015). At the gate and beyond: Outlook for the sports market in North America through 2019. PwC, New York.

6

EMPIRICAL RESEARCH METHODS

Season Ticket Holder Management and Fan Engagement

MICHAEL LEWIS, MANISH TRIPATHI, AND MICHAEL BYMAN

Contents

Introduction 89
Valuing and Managing Brand–Consumer Relationships 90
    Customer Lifetime Value and Season Ticket Buyer Behavior 91
    Brand Equity and Fan Engagement 93
Applications of Customer Lifetime Value and Brand Equity 96
    Linking Customer Lifetime Value to Team Performance and
    Fan Behaviors 97
    Fan and Social Media Equity 99
Connecting CRM to Branding 101
Discussion 102
References 104

Introduction

Advancements in business analytics, technology, and customer data warehouses have created opportunities for firms in many sectors to adopt customer-focused approaches to marketing.

Sport businesses are particularly suited to pursuing advanced customer-oriented marketing programs for two reasons. First, given the economic value of season ticket holders, investments in relationship management are economically worthwhile. Second, the current information technology environment makes individual level marketing strategies actionable and measurable. This chapter analyzes how individual and market level data may be used to guide sport business organizations' efforts to increase fan loyalty and engagement.

Concepts from the fields of customer relationship management (CRM) and brand management provide foundational frameworks for the chapter. Specifically, this chapter emphasizes two concepts based on the premise that the role of marketing is to develop and manage a firm's (e.g., team's) customer and brand assets. Customer lifetime value (CLV) is a metric that emphasizes the long-term economic value of a firm's customer assets. CLV is an especially apt metric for season ticket holder management. In the case of major American professional sport leagues, CLVs often grow into six-figure levels. CRM concepts are also relevant because teams have direct relationships with fans and can engage in targeted, individualized marketing efforts. Brand equity is a concept focused on the economic value attributable to specific brands. Brand equity represents the relationship between teams' brands and the fans that drives ongoing buying. Component elements of brand equity such as loyalty and attitude toward the team are the factors that drive fan engagement and passion for teams.

This chapter discusses the concepts of CLV and brand equity in the context of sport business to provide guidance for how these ideas can be implemented. In terms of implementation, it is important to note that using these concepts to understand customers or to improve marketing decisions presents significant analytic challenges. While marketing decisions related to customer and brand management have traditionally been driven by intuition, advances in database technologies and statistical software are now making it possible to make marketing decisions more analytical and quantifiable. However, this shift does require significant investments in data collection and the use of statistical techniques.

Valuing and Managing Brand–Consumer Relationships

The title of this chapter includes the phrase "season ticket holder management and fan engagement." These two items are closely linked, but also differ. Season ticket holders are a specific type of high-value customer, and fan engagement is a psychological construct related to the intensity of interest and loyalty. Season ticket buyer behavior is directly observable, while engagement is an unobservable state that must be inferred. Despite these differences, repeat buying by season ticket holders and the engagement of fans are both driven by loyalty to the team. In this section, we describe two key marketing metrics related to customer loyalty and discuss their relevance to season ticket holder and fan engagement management by sport organizations.

The first metric is CLV (Berger and Nasr, 1998). CLV is relevant to the management of season ticket buyers as it translates the behavioral loyalty of customers to an estimate of long-term profitability. CLV is estimated using observable data and appropriate statistical tools. CLV has multiple applications and can be used as a segmentation variable (Winer, 2001) or as a decision support objective (Lewis, 2005b).

The second metric, or rather set of metrics, is derived from the concept of brand equity (Keller, 1993). Strong brands have economic value because they are the focal point for customer loyalty (Hoeffler and Keller, 2003). This economic value is termed brand equity. Brand equity is therefore a reflection of the attitudinal loyalty, passion, or engagement fans feel for brands. Brand equity is, however, an intangible asset that is driven by psychological preferences that are not directly observable. In order to measure brand equity, the analyst needs to make inferences based on observable market outcomes that are correlated with fans' underlying preferences.

Customer Lifetime Value and Season Ticket Buyer Behavior

Sport franchises operate in an environment where it is increasingly possible to track multiple elements of customer behavior. For example, season ticket contracts allow tracking of retention, seat quality, price paid, parking preferences, and other factors. Bar-coded tickets also allow tracking of ticket usage, reselling, and in-stadium purchases. These detailed customer retention and revenue data make it possible for sport franchises to use customer-focused metrics such as CLV to guide customer level marketing efforts.

The idea behind CLV is that individual customers can be viewed in terms of the revenue or profit they will contribute to the firm over some future period. For example, a customer that purchases a full season ticket package (e.g., 81 home games) of two $100 tickets would provide a baseball team with \$16,200 in revenue per season. If that customer were projected to be retained for 10 years, his or her CLV would be \$162,000.* The key to using CLV as a customer management tool is to link CLV projections to a rich statistical model of how consumers respond to team performance and marketing interventions.

CLV may be expressed in equation form (Berger and Nasr, 1998; Lewis, 2006) as

$$CLV = \sum_{t=0}^{T} \Pr(Retention_t) \times (Revenue_t - Cost_t) \qquad (6.1)$$

where

$\Pr(Retention_t)$ is the probability that the customer is retained in period t

$Revenue_t$ is the revenue produced by the customer in period t

$Cost_t$ is the cost to serve in period t

T is the number of periods used for the CLV calculation

The equation highlights the role of retention since the long-term value of a customer is a function of annual revenues and the length of the customer relationship. A critical issue in CLV analysis is the creation of a statistical model of retention that allows for the quantification of the relationship between team actions and fan decisions. The second CLV equation below makes explicit that retention, revenue, and costs may be a function of team's actions or marketing decisions at time t, A_t:

$$CLV = \sum_{t=0}^{T} \Pr(Retention_t(A_t)) \times (Revenue_t(A_t) - Cost_t(A_t)) \qquad (6.2)$$

One interesting aspect of applying CLV analysis to sport franchises is that it is important to consider factors that may not normally be considered to be under the control or influence of the marketing department. In particular, a critical issue is how to treat team quality. From a consumer behavior perspective, winning is likely the main driver

---

* This simple example assumes that the marginal cost to serve the customer is zero. The example could also be extended to include factors such as inflation and the time value of money.

of fan interest. Given the positive correlations between payroll and winning, and winning and attendance, investments in team quality therefore represent a direct means for driving attendance and retention (Schmidt and Berri, 2001; Lewis, 2008).

Expressing the equation for CLV as a function of marketing makes explicit that the role of marketing is to increase the value of customer assets. A frequent mistake in the field of CRM is to simply treat CLV as a fixed quantity that may be used to segment customers into groupings that vary based on expected CLV (Winer, 2001). This is problematic because it implicitly assumes that CLV is independent of marketing decisions (Lewis, 2005a). In the sport business context, this is a particularly bad assumption as investments in team quality are obviously linked to season ticket holder retention and willingness to pay.

Using CLV as a marketing metric involves challenges yet creates opportunities for teams. Challenges occur because calculations of CLV typically require an extensive data infrastructure and a level of statistical sophistication. For example, it is often useful to use discrete choice models such as binary logits or probits to forecast retention. However, meeting the challenge of creating a statistical model of retention also creates opportunities, since the model may be used to forecast how changes in policies and outcomes might impact the value of the customer base.

Brand Equity and Fan Engagement

Brand equity is a marketing concept centered on the notion that brand names, symbols, and other assets have economic value. A common framework for considering brand equity is Aaker's model (Aaker, 1991). Aaker identifies five components of brand equity: brand loyalty, brand awareness, perceived quality, brand associations, and other proprietary assets. Economic value exists because high-equity brands often result in decreased price sensitivity and increased customer loyalty. The brand equity concept is a natural fit for sports marketing since sports fans have extraordinary levels of loyalty and are often willing to pay substantial prices.

Two measures of fan loyalty or engagement are derived from brand equity concepts. The first, fan equity, is a measure of engagement based on fans' relative willingness to spend after controlling for team performance and market characteristics. The second, social media equity, uses social media data to assess fan support independent of teams' pricing decisions and constraints on observable demand.

The term "engagement" is currently popular in the sport business industry (Yoshida et al., 2014). Increasing fan engagement is a prevalent goal because the traits underlying engagement, like fan interest and passion, are intuitively linked to positive marketing outcomes such as continuing loyalty and willingness to spend. From a practical perspective, there is little reason to view fan engagement separately from brand equity, as the antecedents that drive both constructs and the resulting outcomes are similar.

Measurement of attitudes like engagement or loyalty is difficult, and many organizations rely on survey data. However, survey data on attitudes are often suspect and are especially problematic in sports as this type of data may be polluted by short-term variations in team quality. The academic literature has proposed alternative measures of brand equity that are based on market rather than survey data. For instance, price and revenue premiums have been proposed as measures for brand equity (Ailawadi et al., 2003). A "marketing" premium occurs if a brand is able to outperform the brands of comparable quality on some key measure. In the sport business context, a price premium would be observed if a team were able to charge higher prices than a team of similar quality located in a similar market. The key aspects of these "premium"-based approaches include an ability to monitor the market response metric of interest (e.g., prices and market share) and an ability to identify and control for quality differences. A significant challenge in these "premium"-based approaches to brand equity measurement is the identification of a brand of identical quality. In the case of sports, winning rates provide an observable and objective measure of quality.

This chapter spotlights two "marketing premium" metrics for assessing fan loyalty and engagement. The first metric, fan equity, is similar in spirit to brand equity but is adapted to focus specifically on engagement or loyalty as measured by financial outcomes. The basic approach is to develop a statistical model of team revenues based on team performance and market characteristics. This model can then be used to compare the forecasted revenues with each team's actual revenues. When teams' actual revenues exceed predicted revenues, this functions as evidence of superior fan support.

The fan equity measure has significant benefits. First, since it is calculated using revenues, it is based on spending decisions. In general, measures based on actual purchasing are preferred to survey-based data. The other benefit is that a statistical model is used to control for factors such as market size and short-term variations in team performance. This allows the measure to reflect true preference levels for a team, rather than effects due to a team playing in a large market, or because a team is currently a winner.

A summary overview of the fan equity model is provided below. This equation provides that team i's revenue in season t is a function of the team's performance, the economic potential or characteristics of the team's home market, and the team's fan equity:

$$Revenue(team\ i, season\ t)$$

$$= f(team\ performance, market\ potential, fan\ equity) \quad (6.3)$$

This equation is implemented through a statistical model. For example, this equation would be translated into the following equation to use linear regression:

$$Rev(i, t) = \beta_0 + \beta_1 Win\%(i, t) + \beta_2 Playoff(i, t) + \beta_3 Population + \varepsilon_{i,t}$$

$$(6.4)$$

This provides that a team's revenue is a linear function of its winning percentage in the current season, whether or not the team made the playoffs and irrespective of market population. This is, obviously, a simple expression for revenue. The winning percentage and playoff variables are included to capture team quality and the population variable is intended to control for market potential. The $\varepsilon_{i,t}$ term at the end of the equation is an error term. The coefficients of this equation could be estimated using linear regression and multiple years of data for each team in a given league. This means that the model yields the average value of winning, population, median income, or whatever is included in the model. The guiding theory is that team revenue (or other market outcome) is based on the loyalty of fans, the size of the team's market, the quality of the product, and the entertainment value of the team. The insight or theory that drives the analysis is that it is possible to build a model that can be used to predict the revenue that is due to observable factors like quality and market potential.

The following equation defines fan equity as the difference between the observed and predicted revenues for a team in a given season:

$$Fan\ Equity(i,t) = Revenue(i,t) - Predicted\ Revenue(i,t) \qquad (6.5)$$

The key idea is that revenues that exceed what would be expected due to product quality or market factors are due to the team's brand strength. This occurs because teams with stronger brands are likely to be more resilient to losing seasons and because fans are more willing to pay premium prices. The measure of fan equity is a relative measure, as it is based on performance relative to league norms.

The fan equity metric does possess important limitations. For example, the model includes an implicit assumption that teams price to maximize revenue. The existence of capacity constraints, such as stadium size, is also problematic. While revenue premium measures like fan equity are especially useful metrics, there is also value in other metrics.

Social media is an especially attractive source of data for supplementing the revenue premium type of analysis. Social media metrics such as number of followers or measures of social engagement or sentiment are not constrained by stadium size or local market size. Also, since it is costless to follow a team, teams' pricing decisions do not impact fan activity. Social media equity measurement is similar to the fan equity measurement. The only material difference is that social media following is used as the focal dependent variable, rather than a measure of revenues. The basic approach of modeling social following as a function of team performance and market characteristics and then evaluating over or under performance is the same as fan equity.

Applications of Customer Lifetime Value and Brand Equity

The concepts described thus far should have a logical appeal for sport organizations. There is, however, little published work that reports on the use of CLV or brand equity applications in professional sport (Gladden and Funk, 2002). This chapter section describes two applications of these models. The first application focuses on the modeling of season ticket customers of a Major League Baseball (MLB) team. The second application examines measures of brand equity for National Football League (NFL) teams.

Linking Customer Lifetime Value to Team Performance and Fan Behaviors

In a recent paper, Lewis et al. (2015) present an analysis of season ticket holder lifetime value using data from an MLB team. This paper by Lewis and colleagues focuses on modeling season ticket holder retention as a function of factors such as team payroll, customer level attendance rates, and customer level ticket resales via StubHub. The paper includes a complex econometric model that is designed to account for customer's expectations of prices in the secondary market.

The foundation for the research is a statistical model of retention decisions (buy vs. no buy) based on a variety of consumer behaviors and team performance. This allows the model to be used to relate CLV to factors such as winning rates or individual attendance rates. In practice, the model of Lewis et al. (2015) uses simulation techniques to calculate CLV (Lewis, 2005b). For purposes of illustration, Lewis and colleagues report two simulation studies that evaluate the relationship between CLV and factors of interest. The first simulation examines how CLV is related to a season ticket holder's propensity to resell tickets in the secondary market. The second study examines the relationship between winning percentage and CLV.

Figure 6.1 shows the relationship between reselling rates and CLV for an average quality tier of tickets. This figure shows a positive relationship between reselling rates and CLV. For example, customers that resell only about 1% of tickets have an estimated CLV of about $25,000. In contrast, customers that are more active and sell 7% of tickets are worth about $28,000.

This result occurs because customers who are more active resellers have higher retention rates. One conjecture is that these customers have higher retention rates because they are able to recoup costs

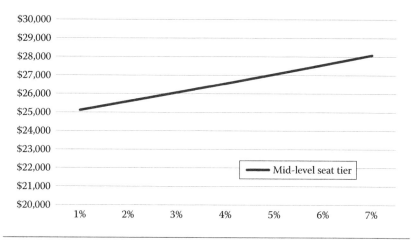

Figure 6.1   Customer lifetime value vs. reselling rates for mid-level seat customers.

through selling unneeded tickets. From a managerial standpoint, this type of finding has at least two implications. First, the team may wish to pay extra attention to customers that resell more frequently as these customers tend to be more valuable. Second, the team might investigate techniques for making reselling more convenient. By facilitating reselling, the team may provide value by allowing fans to unbundle ticket packages.

Figure 6.2 shows the relationship between team performance and CLV. This simulation provides insight on customers who purchase premium and mid-level tickets. For the premium customers,

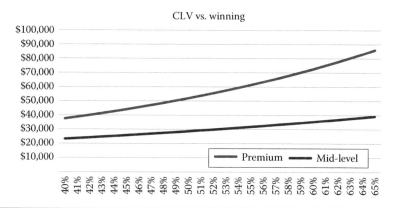

Figure 6.2   Team performance and customer lifetime value.

the predicted CLV increases from about $38,000 for a winning rate of 40%* to $52,000 if the team wins 50% of the games. If the team wins 60% of its games, the average CLV increases to over $70,000. For the mid-level ticket buyers, the impact of wining on CLV is still substantial but less dramatic. The average CLV grows from $23,000 to $35,000 as winning rates increase from 40% to 60%. This application provides an important link between season ticket holder management and engagement as the example illustrates how the greater engagement driven by winning results in greater loyalty and revenue.

Fan and Social Media Equity

This section applies brand equity concepts previously discussed in the chapter by utilizing publicly available data on NFL teams. Two measures of fan engagement for NFL franchises are estimated for the 2014 season. Fan equity is estimated using a revenue premium model of brand equity. This application also estimates a measure of social media equity using data on Facebook "likes" and Twitter "followers."

For both analyses, a statistical model of the focal variable, home box office revenue, or social media following was created, and then teams were evaluated relative to this baseline model of results. These statistical models predict each quantity as a function of team winning rates and market characteristics. Fan equity is then estimated by comparing the differences between actual revenue and the predicted revenue from the statistical model. Social media equity is based on a comparison between a model that predicts social community size and actual social community size.

Figure 6.3 shows fan equity and social media equity results for the NFL for the period from 2012 to 2014.[†] Since fan equity is a dollar metric and social media equity is based on followers, the figure reports indexes for each metric. The index is calculated by dividing each team's score by the maximum score on each measure. This results in a maximum index of 100%.

---

* The simulation assumes that the team wins the stated percentage of games each year. The simulation could also be adapted to include variability in winning rates.

† The years from 2012 to 2014 are used to rank teams. The statistical models are developed using 15 years of data.

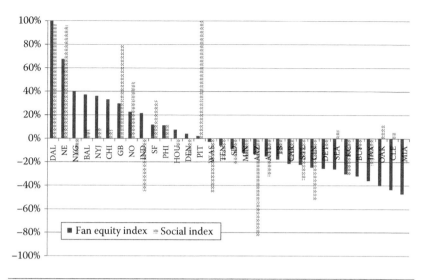

Figure 6.3   2014 NFL fan equity and social media equity comparison.

In terms of the fan equity measure, the Cowboys are the leader followed by the Patriots and the Giants. The teams that lag in terms of fan equity are the Raiders, Browns, and Dolphins. These results have face validity, as the teams at the top of the list are high-profile teams with rich winning traditions. At the bottom of the list, we find teams that have not had significant recent success.

There are, however, several noticeable omissions from the top fan equity teams. In particular, the Pittsburgh Steelers rank in the middle despite having a large and passionate national fan base. A potential issue with the fan equity measure is that team's pricing policies (e.g., there is an implicit assumption that the policies are profit maximizing) and stadium capacity constraints may limit an analyst's ability to evaluate overall levels of engagement.

A potential solution to this dilemma is to use a dependent measure that is not constrained by a team's pricing decisions and stadium capacities such as social media community size. Following a team on Facebook or Twitter does not require a financial sacrifice, and stadium capacities and travel distances allow for a national level measure of a team's brands. The social media equity analysis is conducted using a similar methodology as fan equity. A statistical model is developed to understand the average relationship between social media community size and measures of team performance and market potential. Actual social following levels are then compared to the levels predicted by the model. When the analysis is conducted using social media followers as the key variable, the Steelers score as the top social media equity team.

The difference in the fan equity and social media equity measures reveals important methodological issues and also highlights marketing opportunities. Methodologically, the two measures have different strengths and weaknesses. The financially oriented measure has the benefit of being based on purchasing behaviors, but capacity and pricing constraints limit the researcher's ability to evaluate true engagement. Social media eliminates these constraints but the free nature of following causes the social media metric to be less directly linked to market power and brand strength.

In terms of opportunities, a comparison between the two metrics has the ability to inform marketing policies. At a very basic level, a high social media equity score relative to a fan equity score suggests that the team is pricing too low. Conversely, a fan equity score that exceeds the team's social score might be taken as evidence that the team is pricing too high or "harvesting" local brand equity.

Another salient difference between the measures is that the fan equity metric is predominantly locally oriented while social equity is more nationally oriented. This difference may have important implications for sponsorship decisions. Teams with significant social media followings after controlling for local market potential may be more powerful national brands. This type of national rather than local fan engagement may be useful for opportunities such as stadium naming rights deals.

Connecting CRM to Branding

CLV and brand equity are deeply intertwined concepts. While the former treats the customer as the underlying asset and the latter focuses on the brand, the source of revenues and profits is ultimately the same. Perhaps the most useful perspective is to consider the brand as an element of customer management. Specifically, the brand is the consumer's relationship partner. An important question is how relationship strength is developed over time and how relationship strength impacts long-term behaviors.

Sports are somewhat different from other categories, in that product quality (i.e., winning rates) and therefore brand strength may vary substantially over time. When the fan equity methodology has been applied across major professional and collegiate sports, a consistent finding is that teams with the greatest historical success tend to have the highest equity. This is an important finding when considering the relationship between measures related to consumer attitudes toward teams such as brand engagement and measures based on observable behaviors such as CLV. Team performance likely impacts CLV in two ways. First, there is a direct impact through incremental team quality. Second, there may be a dynamic or long-term impact that occurs through increased engagement or brand loyalty.

CRM and mobile technologies have the potential to create opportunities for marketing to simultaneously improve retention and engagement. For example, technologies such as Experience App have been developed to allow fans greater flexibility and enjoyment via upgrades, unique experiences, and personalized offers. Social media also creates opportunities for teams and fans to communicate more directly and resolve issues. A challenge for teams is how to integrate these new data sources in existing CRM data warehouses and decision support tools.

Technology may, however, create opportunities that have contradictory effects on short- vs. long-term marketing goals. For example, across multiple leagues and at the collegiate level, many teams are now trying to improve event level revenues through dynamic pricing techniques. These techniques are often similar to the revenue management tools used in other industries with perishable inventory, such as airlines and hotels. While basing pricing on market demand levels has the ability to increase revenues, the implications for customer relationships and brand equity are less certain. In one high-profile example, the University of Michigan discontinued the use of single game dynamic pricing. The expressed reason for this change was negative feedback from fans (Baumgardner, 2015).

Discussion

The focus of this chapter is on key metrics and empirical strategies for increasing the value of teams' fan bases. The first metric, CLV, is explicitly focused on the value of individual customers. The key to successfully leveraging this concept is to develop statistical models that connect team actions and outcomes and fan behavior. Understanding these links turns the CLV model into a decision support system. Specifically, including data on explicit consumer traits, marketing activities, and team performance in statistical models of consumer behavior allows organizations to quantify how managerial actions impact long-term customer value. When these actions are quantified, the CLV model essentially becomes a tool for decision support.

The second metric, fan equity, is an intangible quantity that is related to the strength of fans' relationships with teams. Loyalty, engagement, or even "brand love" (Roberts, 2004) is a popular topic across categories. Marketers have come to realize that intense loyalty and consumer passion lead to greatly improved financial outcomes (Reichheld and Teal, 2001). Traditionally, measurement of brand equity and associated elements such as customer loyalty are complicated by the intangible nature of the metrics. Reliance on surveys is problematic for multiple reasons, but surveys are especially problematic in the sports context. For instance, there may be a sense of community pressure that leads consumers to identify as fans of a local team even if these consumers do not spend money on the team. Perhaps a more significant problem is that short-term variations in winning rates may dramatically change survey results.

Sport business, however, is a category that possesses characteristics that facilitate the measurement of brand equity. The public nature of team performance, attendance, prices, local market characteristics, and metrics such as television ratings or social media footprint provide an opportunity to quantify brand effects. In addition, the existence of historical data means that it also becomes possible to understand how team decisions and performance over time create brand equity.

While the focus of the chapter has been on concepts and illustrative applications, implementation issues should also be considered. The two aforementioned examples each require specialized data and statistical techniques. In the case of the CLV application, data requirements include customer purchase histories, secondary market activity, and supporting data such as team results and payrolls. In the fan and social equity study, data are collected from a variety of secondary sources and include social media followings, average ticket prices, attendance, metropolitan area characteristics, and other factors.

From an analytical perspective, CLV analysis may be accomplished via simple or complex methods. However, statistical models of consumer decisions and market outcomes are needed since multiple factors drive behavior. The models may range from linear regression techniques that can be accomplished in standard spreadsheet programs to binary choice models like logistic regression that require specialized statistical software. These types of models can provide great value in terms of understanding the drivers of consumer behavior and can be used to evaluate simple marginal effects. The real complexity in terms of analytical tools occurs when models are used for long-term planning purposes or to maximize CLV. In this case it becomes necessary to use dynamic optimization tools (Khan et al., 2009).

References

Aaker, D. A. (1991). *Managing Brand Equity: Capitalizing on the Value of a Brand Name*. Simon & Schuster, New York.

Ailawadi, K. L., Lehmann, D. R., and Neslin, S. A. (2003). Revenue premium as an outcome measure of brand equity. *Journal of Marketing*, *67*(4), 1–17.

Baumgardner, N. (2015). Michigan football ditches dynamic ticket pricing, announces'15 single-game rates. http://www.mlive.com/.

Berger, P. D. and Nasr, N. I. (1998). Customer lifetime value: Marketing models and applications. *Journal of Interactive Marketing*, *12*(1), 17–30.

Gladden, J. M. and Funk, D. C. (2002). Developing an understanding of brand associations in team sport: Empirical evidence from consumers of professional sport. *Journal of Sport Management*, *16*(1), 54–81.

Hoeffler, S. and Keller, K. L. (2003). The marketing advantages of strong brands. *The Journal of Brand Management*, *10*(6), 421–445.

Keller, K. L. (1993). Conceptualizing, measuring, and managing customer-based brand equity. *Journal of Marketing*, *57*(1), 1–22.

Khan, R., Lewis, M., and Singh, V. (2009). Dynamic customer management and the value of one-to-one marketing. *Marketing Science*, *28*(6), 1063–1079.

Lewis, M. (2005a). Research note: A dynamic programming approach to customer relationship pricing. *Management Science*, *51*(6), 986–994.

Lewis, M. (2005b). Incorporating strategic consumer behavior into customer valuation. *Journal of Marketing*, *69*(4), 230–238.

Lewis, M. (2006). Customer acquisition promotions and customer asset value. *Journal of Marketing Research*, *43*(2), 195–203.

Lewis, M. (2008). Individual team incentives and managing competitive balance in sports leagues: An empirical analysis of Major League Baseball. *Journal of Marketing Research*, *45*(5), 535–549.

Lewis, M., Wang, Y., and Wu, C. (2015). Season ticket value and the secondary market. Working paper.

Reichheld, F. F. and Teal, T. (2001). *The Loyalty Effect: The Hidden Force Behind Growth, Profits, and Lasting Value*. Harvard Business Press, Cambridge, MA.

Roberts, K. (2004). *The Future Beyond Brands: Lovemarks*. Budapest, Hungary: Magyar Könyvklub.

Schmidt, M. B. and Berri, D. J. (2001). Competitive balance and attendance the case of major league baseball. *Journal of Sports Economics*, *2*(2), 145–167.

Winer, R. (2001). A framework for customer relationship management. *California Management Review*, *43*(4), 89–105.

Yoshida, M., Gordon, B., Nakazawa, M., and Biscaia, R. (2014). Conceptualization and measurement of fan engagement: Empirical evidence from a professional sport context. *Journal of Sport Management*, *28*(4), 399–417.

7

DEVELOPING AND MEASURING THE EFFECTIVENESS OF DATA-DRIVEN DIRECT MARKETING INITIATIVES

JOHN BREEDLOVE

Contents

Overview of the Role of Analytics in a Sport Business
Organization 107
    Efficient and Effective Analytics 108
        Efficiency Example: Sales Representative Introduction
        E-Mail 109
        Effectiveness Example: Postgame Guest and Member
        Relations Survey 109
    Keeping Analytics Simple 111
    Aggregation of Data 112
    Using Public Data 112
        Case Study: Raising Ticket Prices 112
        Case Study: When to Spend on Digital Advertising 113
        Case Study: Using Maps 115
Direct Marketing vs. Mass Marketing 119
    Case Study: E-Mail Subject Line Direct Marketing Test 123
    Case Study: Sales Creative Direct Marketing Test 125

Overview of the Role of Analytics in a Sport Business Organization

Most jobs in the workplace require a fair amount of multitasking. Rare is the job where you will only focus on one particular task every day. The analytics role within the organization is no exception.

Analytical positions will generally be responsible for much, if not all, of the following:

- Maintaining the customer database, e-mail database, and/or data warehouse
- Keeping the flow of data between the systems working efficiently
- E-mail marketing efforts (creation, testing, and tracking of e-mails)
- Research, both proprietary (in-house surveys and analysis) and syndicated (Scarborough and Nielsen)
- Digital and social analytics (website metrics and social media metrics)
- Advertising analytics (digital retargeting, search engine marketing, mass media tracking)
- Sales reporting and analysis (campaign tracking and sales representative key performance indicators)
- Season ticket holder renewal tracking and indicators
- Any additional data analyses or system evaluations

As a result of this variety of responsibilities, the analytics department will typically work with the majority of other departments within an organization including sales, marketing, customer service, sponsorship marketing and activation, community relations, ticket operations, business operations, finance, and legal.

Efficient and Effective Analytics

Progress isn't made by early risers. It's made by lazy men trying to find easier ways to do something.

Robert Heinlein

Efficiency is doing things right; effectiveness is doing the right things.

Peter Drucker

With so many tasks to be done, efficiency and effectiveness are the primary principles for an analytics department. As long as these principles are kept in mind when working on every project, then the end result will always be one that helps move the business forward either by freeing up time to work on more tasks (i.e., efficiency) or by improving the end result compared to what was done before (i.e., effectiveness).

Efficiency Example: Sales Representative Introduction E-Mail   A simple example of improving efficiency is the automation of sales representative introduction e-mails. Historically, when a sales rep would make a call and leave a voicemail message, the sales representative would then type a follow-up e-mail with relevant information about tickets. The problem with this approach is that each sales rep used different formats and included different contents in these e-mails, with some of the sales reps using outdated images or creative and others including grammatical errors in the follow-up notes. Also, the time spent sending e-mails was the time that the sales reps were not making the next phone call to prospective season ticket holders. In order to make the process more efficient, sport organizations could add a check box in the team's customer relationship management (CRM) system where all the sales rep needed to do was check the box when he or she logged the call in the system; the CRM system would then automatically send out an e-mail to the prospective season ticket holder in which the note appeared to come directly from the sales rep (see Figure 7.1). Aside from saving time, this new e-mail looked better and also used the correct marketing copy and imagery.

Effectiveness Example: Postgame Guest and Member Relations Survey   A standard means of improving CRM operations is to send out postgame surveys to attendees measuring satisfaction with the various aspects of the game experience (e.g., parking, entry, concessions, and ushers). Sport teams are able to take this approach one step further by allowing Guest and Member Relations staff to individualize the analysis based on the game experience of each ticket holder. For example, on the morning after a game, each Member Relations Associate would be able to run a CRM report with respect to specific season ticket holders that took the postgame survey, identify which fans had a poor experience, and then reach out to those fans in an effort to resolve the situation. Despite each sales rep being responsible for thousands of accounts, the report enables each sales rep to reach out to the accounts

My name is `Intro_Email___Sales_Rep_Name1`, and I wanted to introduce myself as your personal connection with the Tampa Bay Buccaneers. Now is the time to secure your seats for the 2016 Buccaneers Season! Get the full benefits of being a Buccaneers Season Pass Member and experience the thrill of gameday!

VIEW AVAILABLE SEASON PASS LOCATIONS

Help us usher in a new era of Buccaneers football with Head Coach Dirk Koetter and Pro Bowl quarterback Jameis Winston. We're also excited for the upcoming renovations coming to Raymond James Stadium. The first phase is already underway and will include over 28,000 square feet of all-new HD video space (the third most in the entire NFL!) as well as an immersive, 360-degree surround sound system.

Please feel free to contact me at `Intro_Email___Sales_Rep_Email1` or
`Intro_Email___Sales_Rep_Phone1` to discuss all of our exciting options to experience the Buccaneers gameday experience.

I look forward to hearing from you soon.

Sincerely,

`Intro_Email___Sales_Rep_Name1`
`Intro_Email___Sales_Rep_Title1`
Tampa Bay Buccaneers

Figure 7.1   Sales representative season ticket e-mail through customer relationship management.

Figure 7.2 Postgame guest and member relations survey.

the rep will be able to impact the most and to do so within 24 hours of the game (see Figure 7.2).

Keeping Analytics Simple

An analytics department will often be more efficient if it keeps the analysis relatively simple. Given the choice between a model that takes weeks to develop and can explain 85%–95% of a particular relationship versus a heuristic (rule of thumb) that takes under a day to develop and can explain 75%–85% of a particular relationship, I would take the heuristic every day. Going back to economic principles, there is an opportunity cost to spending those extra weeks to marginally improve the end result. Rather than improving that one method by a fractional amount, that time could have been spent generating solutions to a multitude of other problems. This chapter provides several examples of how relatively simple analysis can still yield meaningful returns.

Aggregation of Data

Sometimes all you need to do is aggregate the data that you have and use that to make more informed decisions. For example, suppose the following conditions are considered:

- 80% of season ticket buyers live within 75 miles of the stadium.
- 80% of season ticket buyers are male.
- 72% of individual ticket buyers are between 25 and 54 years of age.
- 60% of new season ticket buyers renew; 90% of season ticket buyers who are entering their fourth season or greater renew.
- 75% of food and beverage revenue comes from the "100 (lower) level" of the stadium.

Even with just the pieces of information above, think about all the decisions that can be made more effectively and efficiently. When asked where to spend your mass media budget, would you be able to give some direction on location and targets? When determining which customers to focus your sales staff on during renewals, would you be able to? What about how to distribute your game day concession staff?

Using Public Data

While you will often spend your time analyzing proprietary data that only your organization has access to, one source of data that is often overlooked is public data. The following are a couple of examples in which publicly available data can be used to make better analytics-driven business decisions.

Case Study: Raising Ticket Prices   At the end of the 2012 season, the Tampa Bay Buccaneers were considering raising ticket prices. It had been 4 years since the last price increase, which is a fairly lengthy time in the world of sports, and a ticket to a Buccaneers game was one of the lowest priced tickets in the National Football League (NFL). With the recession still affecting much of the country, especially Florida, the team wanted to make sure that it properly analyzed what the market could bear. For a high-level assessment of the local market, the Buccaneers analyzed the U.S. Census data. By analyzing various metrics of available discretionary spending for the 30 NFL markets (i.e., mean income, median income, unemployment, median home value, and change in median home value from 2007), the team was able to compare these metrics for the Tampa market with all other NFL markets. For example, this analysis found that the Tampa market was lowest in key categories such as mean and median household income and was also in the bottom 10% of all NFL teams in categories such as median home value and change in home value (see, for instance, Figure 7.3). As a result of this analysis, the team decided against raising prices for the following season. Ticket prices to Buccaneers games remained near the lowest in the league. The analysis to aid in that decision was simple and quick but very effective.

Case Study: When to Spend on Digital Advertising "Retargeting" is a strategy that occurs when an individual visits a website, and then after leaving the site, they begin to see the company's advertising throughout the Internet on other sites they visit. The benefit of retargeting is that you do not have to purchase advertisement space on specific sites. Instead, ads go out on an ad network that covers the majority of the Internet. A sport organization may have one segment of fans that prefer to visit CNN and another segment that only visit Fox News. With retargeting, both segments of fans will see company messaging because the determining factor is only that the fans have previously visited a specific website.

One of the major questions for any type of advertising is how to allocate spend. There is a finite budget that can be spent, and you want to make sure that you are maximizing the use of it. One publicly available tool that you can use to help make these decisions is Google Trends. The Google Trends tool shows you a graph over time of the relative search volume for whatever words or phrases you are interested in tracking and analyzing. The analytics tool also allows you to view those results by a specific geography. Figure 7.4 is the generated graph for searches for "Tampa Bay Buccaneers" originating from the state of Florida for the time period from January 2012 to January 2014.

As you would expect, interest in the Buccaneers does not remain steady throughout the year. You can see that there is a ramp up when

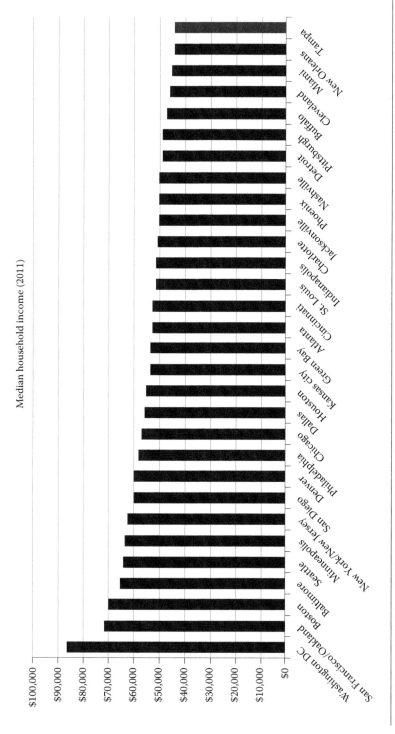

Figure 7.3 Median U.S. household income (2011). (From U.S. Census Bureau, American Community Survey 2011, Washington, DC.)

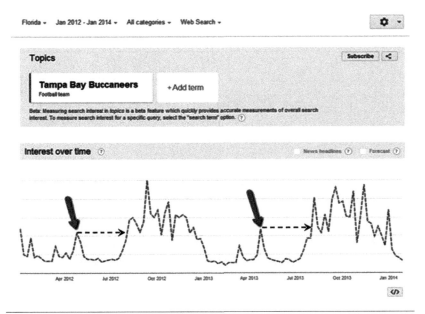

Figure 7.4 Tampa Bay Buccaneers Google Trends.

the season begins in August and then a decline in interest once the season is finished. The most interesting aspect of the graph is the peak marked with an arrow that occurs in late April each year. This peak coincides with the NFL Draft, and you can see that the level of interest generated around the draft is not matched again until August. The smaller peak prior to the NFL Draft represents the schedule release, which occurs a couple of weeks prior to the NFL Draft. Taking all of this information into consideration for the distribution of digital spend, the Buccaneers decided to reduce money that was spent during the off-season, using some of that money to increase spend around schedule release and the NFL Draft while primarily focusing overall spend on the beginning of the season. By tripling the digital spend in August and September, the team was able to generate a 22× return on investment during those 2 months. Again, the analysis itself was simple, quick, and effective.

Case Study: Using Maps   Any type of geographic data is a natural fit for a map, and it is a fairly common exercise to plot ticket buyers on maps of the local region so that a sport team obtains a better idea of where ticket buyers are concentrated. Taking this analysis an additional step

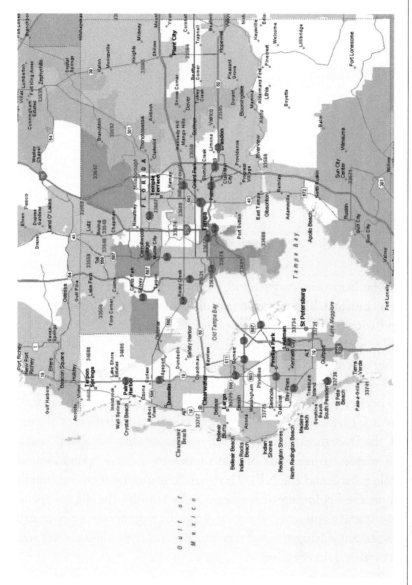

Figure 7.5 Tampa geographic area marked with ticket buyers.

and plotting another layer of information onto the map can yield further insights that a team can use for a variety of purposes. For example, when choosing which billboards to display ads on, the Buccaneers plotted the location of the local billboards on top of where ticket buyers were concentrated (see Figure 7.5).

It is now much easier to see which billboards are better options, working under the assumption that high concentration areas contain additional nonbuyers who the team should be targeting.

The analytics team could then produce a map of information similar to the map in Figure 7.6 for use by the corporate partnerships and sales departments.

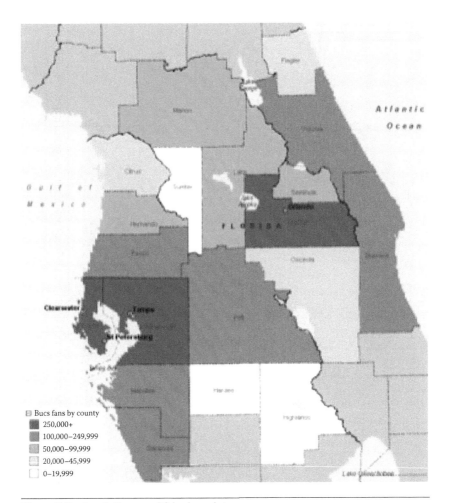

Figure 7.6   Fans in Tampa and Orlando markets.

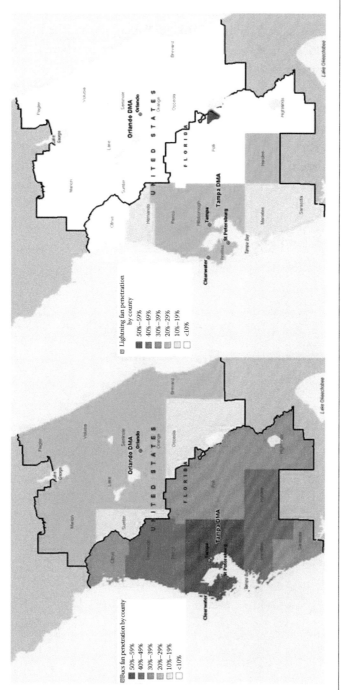

Figure 7.7   Plot of Tampa Bay Buccaneers ticket buyers in Tampa and Orlando designated market areas (DMAs).

The analytics team can help colleagues in other departments illustrate how far the team's reach extends by including a comparison against other teams that might be competing for the same sponsorship and ticket dollars (see Figure 7.7).

The Buccaneers could also choose to overlay important sponsor locations to the map of ticket buyers. Figure 7.8 is a plot of new Lennar, Florida communities against Buccaneers ticket buyers, which the team could use to show that ticket buyers live near the new home communities—and are therefore potential ticket buyers within those communities (see Figure 7.8).

Direct Marketing vs. Mass Marketing

There are two major categories of marketing: mass marketing and direct marketing. Mass marketing tries to reach the largest number of people possible, with the goal of keeping the brand and associated products and services top of mind so that when a consumer goes to make a purchase they remember that brand and hopefully decide to choose it over other options. Mass marketing is definitely effective, but it requires a substantial investment in terms of both money and time. Mass marketing requires an organization to saturate the various advertising channels (television, radio, print, and Internet) with a marketing message and to then do so over an extended period of time. For large brands (e.g., Apple, Nike, and Coca-Cola), this is not a problem. But if a company's advertising budget is limited, the organization can have difficulty achieving the necessary level of saturation and the marketing message will get lost amongst the sea of other advertisers.

Direct marketing (also known as direct response marketing) is a more targeted form of marketing where a company aims to advertise to a specific segment of consumers with the purpose of eliciting an immediate response. Typically that response is a purchase, although the response could also be filling out a form for more information or registering for an account on a sport team's website. Methods of direct marketing include direct mail, e-mails, and targeted Internet advertisements. While mass marketing advertisements are typically focused around reiterating brand characteristics (think about ads for Coca-Cola) or a one-size-fits-all offer (e.g., $1000 cash back on all

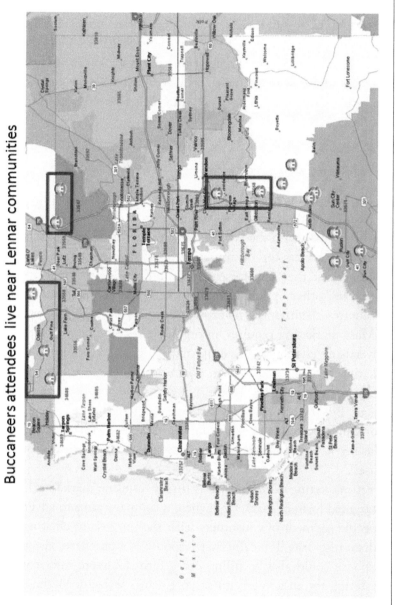

Figure 7.8   Tampa Bay Buccaneers sponsor locations in Tampa communities.

Toyota sedans purchased this month), direct marketing ads typically have the following main characteristics:

- *Direct marketing ads are targeted to a specific segment with a specific offer*: Rather than being broadcast to everyone, direct marketing attempts to tie a particular offer with a particular target segment that is more likely to respond to that offer. For example, targeting past individual buyers with a postcard mailed to them advertising season tickets.
- *Direct marketing ads have a "call to action"*: Direct marketing ads always encourage that the recipient take action, or respond, in some fashion (hence the term direct response marketing). While mass marketing ads may also encourage a response, direct marketing ads should always have a "call to action."
- *Direct marketing ads are trackable*: As a result of having a call to action, there is a definitive way that the action can be tied back to the ad via a specific phone number, a special offer code, or a direct click-through.
- *Results can be measured*: A corollary to being trackable, once you can track the results of something, you can then also measure performance. It can be difficult to track results of mass media (e.g., did the Coca-Cola ad about happiness lead to you buying a Coke?). Conversely, it should be easier to track a direct marketing ad (e.g., you clicked through in the e-mail you received about tickets being on sale and subsequently purchased a ticket).

The three parts of a direct marketing ad are as follows:

1. *The list*: Who the ad is targeting
2. *The offer*: What the company is offering to prospective purchasers
3. *The creative*: The image(s) and copy within the ad

With a direct marketing campaign, an organization attempts to target the right people (the list) with the right offer (one that prospects are likely to be interested in) in the right way (using creative that resonates with prospects). When it comes to driving results, the general rule of thumb is that the list and the offer will account for 80% of the effectiveness, while the creative only accounts for 20%.

Some industry leaders insist that creative only accounts for 10% of campaign effectiveness. This makes sense when you think about it: imagine a piece of amazing creative—it could be a hand-addressed letter coming from the star player on a team, where when you open the envelope a holograph of that player appears out of thin air and delivers a passionate pitch to you on why the team needs you to buy season tickets. Now imagine sending that letter to a list of people who are not ambivalent to sports—but actually despise attending sport events—with the offer being a season ticket package that costs $10,000. It cannot be hard to imagine that the response on that piece of advertising would be 0%, no matter how amazing the creative. Take the reverse of that situation: a simple postcard sent to a list of die-hard fans who have purchased individual tickets and team merchandise and are on a waiting list for season tickets. Offer them a season ticket package costing $200 plus the opportunity for a personal meet and greet with the star player and an autographed item. Response rates would be great, even though not much effort was spent on the creative.

The methods typically used for direct marketing (direct mail, e-mail, and Internet advertising) all allow for relatively easy changes to the important aspects of the advertising (the list, the offer, and the creative). Combined with the ability to track and measure results, another key concept tied to direct marketing is "test and learn." Just like every other analytical endeavor, no matter how well a direct marketing piece performs, you will always want to think of ways that the initiative can be more effective. One of the best strategies when starting off with direct marketing is to employ a basic A/B split test. To run a split test, you first develop a single version of your direct marketing ad, send it out, and then use that to establish a baseline against which you will test. The baseline piece is called the control. You then develop an alternative piece changing only one variable, which is the test. In an e-mail, you may change the subject line, the list, or a portion of the creative itself. However, you do not want to change multiple portions of the piece because then you will not know which change is responsible for the variation in result. Multivariate testing allows analysts to make multiple changes and still determine what portions affected the result.

When it comes to analyzing your test, you will want to measure conversions. A conversion represents the recipient or viewer of your advertisement taking the desired action you want them to take. This action could be a purchase, a click, an open, signing up for a newsletter, downloading a case study, or making a phone call to a team's sales center. Once you have tracked the conversions for a suitable length of time, you need to determine which split performed better. Sometimes the difference in results is obvious (e.g., suppose the A version had a conversion rate of 10% and the B version had a conversion rate of 20%) but other times the difference may not be as readily apparent. You need to have more than just a difference in the comparison metrics—a statistical difference is key. Luckily, there is a fairly simple test to determine if the results are statistically different. This test involves analyzing the margin of error (i.e., confidence interval). The following four data points are essential to calculate the margin of error:

1. *The population*: The total number of people who could conceivably receive or be shown the advertisement (e.g., could be the size of a CRM database or the size of the team's target market)
2. *The sample size*: How many people the advertisement was sent to
3. *The confidence level*: How confident a team can be that the sample accurately reflects the actual behavior of the population
4. *The conversion percentage*: The percentage of the sample that took the action that the team wanted them to take

Case Study: E-Mail Subject Line Direct Marketing Test

The Tampa Bay Buccaneers had a merchandise offer for the month of June that included free shipping on any orders totaling $75 or more. The team decided that it would test subject lines in e-mails, with one making reference to Father's Day and then another without the reference in order to see if the holiday mention would spur any additional e-mail "opens." The conversion in this test was simply an "open" of the e-mail. The creative remained the same for both versions of the advertisement (see Figure 7.9).

Figure 7.9   Tampa Bay e-mail subject line direct marketing test.

Table 7.1   Results from E-Mail Subject Line Direct Marketing Test

SPLIT	SUBJECT	E-MAILS SENT	E-MAILS OPENED	CONVERSION (OPEN) RATE (%)
A	*Free* shipping on Buccaneers merchandise orders of $75 or more	30,000	6000	20.0
B	Get your Father's Day presents now: *free* shipping on orders of $75+	30,000	5775	19.3

The results of this e-mail subject line direct marketing test are presented in Table 7.1.

At first glance, it looks like the A split was the more effective advertising strategy. However, we should confirm by checking the margin of error. Assuming that the potential total population that we could have sent the e-mail to was 500,000, then the margin of error

Table 7.2 Range of Results in E-Mail Subject Line Direct Marketing Test

SPLIT	LOW END	MIDDLE	HIGH END
A	*19.56*	20	20.4
B	18.87	19.3	*19.73*

for split A was 0.44 and the margin of error for split B was 0.43. To compare the two splits, you then compare the range of the result ± the margin of error. If the ranges overlap, then statistically you cannot be confident that they are truly different results (see the ranges indicated in italics in Table 7.2).

Since the low end of A overlaps with the high end of B, the result of this split test was that including the Father's Day message did not statistically alter the open rate, even though the raw numbers made it appear that it did. You will notice that the margin of error was basically the same for split A and B in the previous example; this will typically be the case when the observed percentages are close to each other. Something to keep in mind with margin of error is that when given the same sample and population size, it will generally be largest in the middle at the 50% mark and smallest at the extremes (either very low such as 1% or very high such as 99%).

Case Study: Sales Creative Direct Marketing Test

The Buccaneers implemented another Father's Day themed direct marketing test (don't worry, the Buccaneers have Mother's Day promotions as well). This time the promotion related to the ticket sales side and involved changing the creative rather than the e-mail subject line. Direct marketing e-mails can get rather copy intensive at times, and the Buccaneers wanted to test whether a simpler layout with fewer words and a more prominent call to action would deliver better results. The control was a standard e-mail layout that contained quite a bit of text (see Figure 7.10). The test e-mail had a much "cleaner" look (see Figure 7.11).

Note that in both e-mails, the Buccaneers used HTML text rather than designing the whole e-mail as an image. Have you ever received an image-only e-mail with your images function turned off? If you design your e-mails with HTML text embedded, the text will still

GET DAD WHAT HE REALLY WANTS!

Dear John,

Invite Dad to witness history and celebrate one of his Tampa Bay Buccaneers heroes with all-new 5-Game Plans!

Each 5-Game Plan includes a ticket to the Ring of Honor Game and Ceremony of your selected Legend, tickets to the four other included Bucs games, a 10% savings off individual ticket prices and the same seat at all five games!

Plans start at just $150! Choose your plan below to give Dad what he really wants this Father's Day!

CLICK HERE TO BUY A 5-GAME PLAN

Want to get him into every can't-miss matchup this year? Tampa Bay Buccaneer Season Pass Memberships are still available. Get your seat at every single 2015 Bucs home game on top of plenty of great savings, benefits and Member-exclusive events year-round.

Buccaneers Season Pass Membership benefits include a dedicated account rep, savings up to 21% over individual prices, exclusive Buccaneers events, discounts on concessions and merchandise and much more!

CLICK HERE TO BUY A SEASON PASS MEMBERSHIP

Finally, make sure you're all decked out in the latest red and pewter apparel from the Buccaneers Team Store! Choose from all-new Nike inventory, jerseys of all your favorite players, hats, collectibles, décor and much more. Bucs Season Pass Members also enjoy 15% off all shop.buccaneers.com merchandise!

To learn more about Season Passes, the all-new Hall of Fame Club and all of our ticket options or to book your appointment for The New Raymond James Stadium Experience PreView Center, call **866-582-BUCS (2827)**, visit our website, request more information, or chat with a live rep.

—————— 2015 TAMPA BAY BUCCANEERS HOME OPPONENTS ——————

| MON 8/24 8:00PM | SAT 8/29 7:00PM | SUN 9/13 4:25 PM | SUN 10/4 1:00 PM | SUN 10/11 1:00 PM | SUN 11/8 4:05 PM | SUN 11/15 1:00 PM | SUN 12/6 1:00 PM | SUN 12/13 1:00 PM | SUN 12/27 1:00 PM |

Figure 7.10   Father's Day sales creative test—control e-mail.

Figure 7.11   Father's Day sales creative test—test e-mail.

Table 7.3   Results of Father's Day Sales Creative Direct Marketing Test

SPLIT	SUBJECT	E-MAILS SENT	PURCHASES	CONVERSION RATE (%)
A (control)	Give the gift of football for Father's Day	47,000	197	0.42
B (test)	Give the gift of football for Father's Day	47,000	378	0.80

be displayed even if the images are not, thus enabling the recipient to still see the communication. Table 7.3 spotlights the results of this sales creative direct marketing test.

Sometimes you do not need to check the margin of error when one version just blows the other one out of the water (in case you were wondering, the margin of error was 0.09%). Clearly the phrase "less is more" applied in this instance. While in both of these examples we have only utilized two versions, you can actually create as many versions of a test as you want and the same methodology applies. So you can do A/B/C testing or A/B/C/D testing—the only key is to make sure that you are changing the same variable amongst all your versions and then you are testing all the ranges for statistical significance. Of course, with more versions you have a greater chance of finding that A and B are not statistically different but that A and B are significantly better than C or D. Also, while these examples have been e-mail examples, split testing works in any instance where you randomly split a list of people and have them receive different messages. That means you could split test direct mail, website visitors (programs exist that can randomly show completely different creative for the same web page so that you can test any number of calls to action), or even the phone campaign that a sales rep is working through.

Another strategy you can employ with split tests is that rather than a 50/50 split test you can use a test and winner strategy. With this strategy, you deploy only a portion of the list for testing and then after some set amount of time (could be hours or days) you send the winning creative to the remainder of the list. For example, you might send A to 10% of the list and B to another 10%, then hold back the remaining 80%, and send them whichever version performs better. This helps you get a more immediate benefit from the winning version, since the majority of your list or segment will receive the preferred version of prior recipients.

A/B tests are convenient analytics tools because these tests are relatively straightforward and easy to understand. However, if you are interested in changing multiple variables, it can take time to run through them all with A/B tests. You also run the risk of missing out on interactions between variables. For instance, if the B subject line and the B creative both win in sample tests, you would think that the combination of the two would also be optimal. It may turn out though that the actual optimal solution is the A subject line coupled with the B creative. In order to test multiple variables and measure every aspect of the test, you would need the product of the number of versions for the first variable and the number of versions for the second variable. Suppose you wanted to test both subject line and creative, and you had two versions of each. That would require four total combinations. If you had three versions of each, it would require nine combinations.

You can see how this could get complex quickly because adding more variables means you need to multiply once more—testing 3 offers, 3 subject lines, and 3 creative messages would result in 27 overall versions. Testing every possible permutation is called the "full factorial method." There are methods that will permit you to do multivariate testing with only a portion of the possible combinations, but still use statistical analysis to show the effect of each variable—these are called "partial factorial methods." For either of these methods, it is recommended that you use a program that will help evaluate the responses for you, as the statistics involved are more complex than A/B tests.

A primary goal of this chapter was to provide an overview of various direct marketing business strategies. Data-driven decision-making is key to the overall success of these marketing initiatives.

8

FAN ENGAGEMENT, SOCIAL MEDIA, AND DIGITAL MARKETING ANALYTICS AT DUKE UNIVERSITY

RYAN CRAIG

Contents

Case Study: #DukeMBBStats Data Visualization Platform 132
Fan Profiles 137
Summary 143

Relationships and awareness—successful marketing relies on the optimization of both. Even the most remarkable product, discount, or opportunity is destined to fail if nobody is acquainted with its existence. Likewise, even the most intriguing marketing campaigns are fated to go ignored if the messenger does not develop equity with the consumer. It is important to realize, though, that "success" is not solely reliant on the variables that exist on the consumer's side of the marketing equation. Marketers must gather the appropriate information and ascertain the ideal target market before even beginning the marketing campaign. A misaligned campaign wastes both financial and physical resources and will set growth back indefinitely.

This chapter discusses marketing practices, concepts, and applications rooted in "analytics"—a catchall term that increasingly borders on cliché—but a space that offers tremendous benefit when applied in strategic fashion. Analytics have historically been associated with inward-facing platforms, such as those that allow an organization to understand more about itself or its patrons; for coaches to understand more about their players, teams, or prospects; or for athletes to understand more about themselves. Duke University is utilizing analytics for many of those same reasons, from player development to segmented marketing, and in that sense, is less of an innovator than an adopter—albeit a fairly early one in the college athletics space. One area in which Duke is on the leading edge of analytics within college athletics relates to its fan-facing, crowdsourced data visualization platform known as #DukeMBBStats.

Case Study: #DukeMBBStats Data Visualization Platform

Duke University began working on this project well before it was even aware it was doing so. In the early 2000s, Curtis Snyder, an avid Duke basketball enthusiast and veteran of college sports administration, took on a pet project to be completed on his own time: digitize and organize every Duke basketball stat on record into a multilayered, searchable database. From computer files to drawers of folders to microfilm, Snyder tracked down box scores from as early as the 1905–1906 basketball season and added those statistics to the collection. Several modifications and roughly 10 years later, Duke University has arrived at a truly unique intersection of historical data and modern fandom.

Previously, the database had functioned as a resource for the media and school officials as well as a destination for the dedicated core fans who sought story lines in stats long before this became a mainstream mindset. As Duke University Athletics leaders planned out the latest version, the goal for the application changed. Athletics leaders saw an opportunity for the platform to appeal to a wider audience, more specifically, the ever-expanding collection of fans—diehard and casual alike—that see and feel the game through numbers, comparisons, streaks, and records.

In addition, the project would adopt a "For Duke, by Duke" mantra. Instead of a singular entity providing the vision and executing the build, Duke students, professors, and alumni would become the bedrock of a product destined to enhance the experience of the wider Duke community, including its loyal fan base both domestically and around the globe. In response to the growing amount of data available, player tracking analytics would be included, as would algorithms that could scrape the updated number sets and automatically generate insights and unearth trends within seconds that would take months to brainstorm and research otherwise. Campus outlets would be given access to the data for use in projects that consistently require unique and interesting data sets, and from those work streams, additional interactive visualizations will be built and added to the platform. In totality, the goal to create was a dynamic, developing statistical and visual repository.

A traditional, static box score helps you answer a question. For instance, how many points did Brandon Ingram have in the team's last game against North Carolina? It is a simple enough query. But how does that point total compare to what other freshman did against Duke's archrival? How many times had that mark been achieved before? Based on historical comparisons, does that performance portend good things for his and the team's future?

#DukeMBBStats begs you to ask more questions. Think YouTube, minus the ads and multibillion-dollar valuation. While #DukeMBBStats does not (yet) include an algorithm that suggests other stats you may enjoy as YouTube does with recommended videos, it does induce the same inquisitive mindset. While you may visit the page with only one idea, request, or bar room debate in mind, the sheer volume of information, coupled with logical organization and easy navigation, will invite you to explore many more. The platform will allow people to look up program records, individual statistics, team accomplishments, and opponent data. Does it feel like the team is rebounding better than in years past? Does the rotation seem shorter and do the starters' minutes seem untenable? In a few clicks, you will be able to see how the team's profile stacks up against years that have resulted in a conference or national championship. You will also be able to share the results you find with built-in social media functionality that makes use of the hashtag that was intentionally used in the name of the platform itself. After all, what good is your newfound knowledge without a community of people to share it with?

#DukeMBBStats serves two purposes—one internal to Duke and one felt beyond the walls of the campus in Durham, NC. Internally, a project like this helps bridge the gap that often exists between the academic entities within higher education and the institution's athletics arm. Outside of Duke, the core function is to bring the fans unique, compelling, interactive, and ever-evolving content and supply fans with a reason to consistently engage with GoDuke.com, the digital hub of Duke Athletics and an ecosystem that allows the department to involve fans in a variety of cross-marketing and revenue-generating initiatives.

Of all of the adjectives used to describe #DukeMBBStats, let's take a minute to further examine one of them: "unique." In the case of this particular project, its "unique" label does not simply pertain to the content itself, but in the concept or genre. "Unique" is a hackneyed term whose meaning has been devalued by people that are actually discussing something that is one of a few, but at its core, something that is truly unique represents one of one.

What if you were the first to execute a raffle, the first to offer a "buy-one-get-one" deal? Someone had to be first and at that time, that offer was rightly labeled "unique." That is what Duke Athletics has accomplished with this project. The first flat-screen television made waves for the way it changed the manner in which society consumed its living room entertainment. But those waves were the kind a pebble makes in a pond compared to the oceanic rip current that was felt through civilization when the first television of any kind hit the market. Sure the flatter screen enhanced the experience, but the first television revolutionized entertainment as it was known at the time. Duke Athletics hopes that #DukeMBBStats provides a similar disruption with regard to the way college sports programs engage with fans and schools through stats.

Marketers need to timely adjust to the changing mentality and intelligence of fans. Supporters are smarter than ever and the relationship is no longer a one-way interaction whereby the school or franchise simply directs its patrons with respect to where to go and what to do. Consumers have more options and require a deeper connection in order to take action, spend money, or give of their time. It is incumbent on Duke Athletics as a department, therefore, to adjust to where and how people are living their lives. Content on any website needs to be mobile optimized for an increasingly on-the-go audience. Social media platforms emerge, fall off, and evolve, forcing institutions to cater messaging to the various spaces depending on the type of content and the target demographics.

In reality, fans are looking for one thing: effort. They want to know if a sport property has taken the time to provide them with something of value, understand them as people, and appreciate how and where they want to receive marketing messages. We all know what a lack of effort feels like. Have you ever received an e-mail or letter with the wrong name in the salutation? What about the envelope meant for "the current owner" of your home, condo, or apartment? How likely are you to open, much less read and lend thought to, that correspondence? Likewise, if every communication came with a request, a deadline, or an overt purchase solicitation, it would be easy to see how those on the receiving end would tire of the endless money grabs.

You want your brand to be one predicated on relationships, trust, and personalization. Bring people into your program/team and treat them as a part of what makes it great, because that is what fans are. Without fans, there are no teams. Too often, enthusiasts are treated like charity dinner guests—sure, they are welcome to sit at the table, but only at a cost. Yes, you need to sell tickets, merchandise, and concessions to pay for the salaries and facilities that allow the department to run successfully, but that does not mean there should not be methods for people to fully and genuinely interact with the program in ways that are complimentary.

The fans of Duke are perhaps more ingrained in the identity of the school and its athletic program than most. After all, Duke is known for its "Cameron Crazies"—technically speaking, the passionate student section that populates the entire lower bowl of Cameron Indoor Stadium on the side opposite the team benches. But the personality of the "Crazies" has moved well beyond that 100 foot stretch of bleachers. It permeates the rest of the building on game days and the homes and watering holes of the millions that watch games from wherever they are in the United States or abroad. That type of passion, commitment, and support—the type that leads the student contingent to eschew the dorm room that is costing them tens of thousands of dollars per year for a fabric tent on a plot of land known only as Krzyzewskiville—needs to be matched by a commitment on the University's behalf. The fans have shown their interest, and now they should be rewarded.

If properly built, those relationships can help you reach marketing nirvana, the ideal scenario where your brand thrives in an environment exclusive of your team's record. As of the writing of this chapter, the Chicago Cubs have not won the World Series in more than a century, but the seats are often packed in Wrigley Field because the games are a destination. The history and aura of the club and ball-park outweigh the subpar results that have been achieved between the ballpark field lines. Fans of the Cubs identify themselves not as winners or losers, but as Cubs fans. Sure, everyone loves to support a champion, but any team can sell tickets, jerseys, and hope during a winning streak or in the middle of the glory years. It is when losses start to outnumber wins that people truly decide whether they identify themselves as fans of your team or as passengers along for the ride while the getting is good. Relationships help convert the latter into the former.

Duke University is nearing a crossroads of sorts. The basketball program has been fortunate to call Mike Krzyzewski its head basketball coach for more than 35 years, with over 1000 wins and 5 national championships to date. But sooner than later, although some might hate to admit, Coach K. will no longer be roaming the sidelines in his suit and tie. Sure, he will be a part of the program forever, but when arguably the game's greatest coach steps aside, a regression to the mean is (if not a certainty) a possibility that needs to be acknowledged. Now more than ever, Duke Athletics needs people to understand and appreciate that Duke basketball, and inherently Duke Athletics, is about much more than wins or losses. It is a family that extends beyond the campus and into the minds, hearts, homes, computers, and smartphones of all of the fans that identify themselves with one of the most prestigious universities in the world. At that point, it is less about being a fan of winning and more about aligning yourself with the University and its student-athletes.

With that, let's revisit the ecosystem mentioned earlier in this chapter, which includes GoDuke.com and its social media presence, and the concept of "awareness" that was discussed at the beginning of the chapter. With a newly minted fan engagement platform that should hopefully help instill trust in fans, enhance the program brand, bolster relationships with those across campus and across the world, and make GoDuke.com a destination for the millions that call themselves Duke backers, Duke Athletics now has an audience that is both frequently present and willing to listen. From there, the opportunities to cross-market and promote the stories of other athletics teams and athletes and generate revenue through avenues like video subscriptions, e-commerce, sponsorship, and philanthropy are nearly limitless.

In order to capitalize on those opportunities, you need people in your environment long enough and often enough for them to see the banner advertisement that may rotate through the server or notice the e-mail sign-up link that will allow you to communicate more directly to them when they are not visiting the website. A discount on video subscriptions is only as good as the number of customers that see it. Think of it as the digital version of the "tree falling in the woods."

Your visitors are not the only ones to consider when bringing people to and keeping people in your ecosystem. As more advertisers move away from their fixation on "quantity metrics" like page views, key performance indicators (KPIs) like reach and time spent on page have become more central to the story sales teams are telling. A platform like #DukeMBBStats, and others like this platform, registers high marks in both KPI and page view realms. The amplifying powers of the baked-in social media components can disseminate the content among users and their network of friends, family, and colleagues far faster than anyone could utilizing traditional communication channels. Also, the "unique" content entices a lengthier stay on the webpage. The days of performance-related stats and analytics being used solely for player development and coaching are over. Fans want to be involved as well, and platforms like #DukeMBBStats bring that desire to life.

Fan Profiles

This chapter previously discussed the importance of effort and the current expectation from fans that fans be understood and appreciated. While #DukeMBBStats represents a real-life example of how that is accomplished through men's basketball, in order to scale that to the entire department, Duke is investing a great deal of time and energy into the next major emerging division in college athletics: data and analytics.

Professional sport teams, Fortune 500 companies, and behemoths like the government have been in the "big data" game for years, but for the first time, we are seeing college athletics put its hat in the ring. As pressure mounts to generate more and more revenue to help pay the increasing costs of scholarships, facilities, and recruiting, even the most monetarily successful departments are forced to mine for additional sources of revenue.

For some athletics departments, that means expanding stadiums and adding premium seating. For others, it means raising ticket prices or establishing capital campaigns. And for others still, it means developing and enriching the fan base and, as a result, the number of prospective customers. While the first several options are certainly plausible and perhaps even necessary, this chapter will now take a deeper dive into that last area—cultivating the fan base.

There are two ways to increase the potential purchase power of fans: add more of them or learn more about the ones you already have. I would argue the best strategy involves a hybrid of the two. First you learn about whom your fans are, and then you go about supplementing your contact lists with people fitting that profile. Sure, from simply a "reach" perspective, anyone can be a fan. But through some digging, you can find people that are more likely to purchase tickets, come to a game, and buy merchandise. With staffing the ubiquitous issue that it seems to be in college athletics departments, making the most efficient use of your time is paramount. When you are in essence preselecting fans that are more likely to purchase, and concentrating your marketing efforts on them, you are allowing staff to work with a stacked deck. Fan profiles—a panoramic view of your customers and any of the touch points they have with your franchise or program— allow you to start shuffling through the cards.

The idea here is to have a gauge on the full breadth of someone's interaction with you and your team. You want to know what they have purchased, how much of it they have purchased, where and how they purchased it, and how many times they have done so. Knowing someone is a season ticket holder is important. But knowing that they have been a season ticket holder for 8 straight years, that they bought the tickets online the day they were available for the past five of those seasons, and that they have increased the number of tickets each of the last 2 years is even better.

Additional information, without exception, helps formulate your strategy. Have they changed locations within the stadium? How many sports are they buying tickets for? Have they purchased any merchandise or VIP packages in their time as a fan? How far are they driving, or flying, to attend the games? There are dozens of questions you can ask about the same person and that can happen only when you examine the ticket purchase.

For a season ticket holder at Duke, analytics and sales leaders might also ask about whether they have purchased an auction item related to the team, donated money to become an "Iron Duke," downloaded the team's schedule to their computer or mobile device, purchased a subscription to the Blue Devil Network Plus platform, purchased a ticket miniplan, signed up for an e-mail newsletter, or partaken in any of a plethora of other existing associations with the athletics department. All of those questions are designed to do one thing: give athletics leaders the best idea possible of who fans are and how fans behave.

Remember the piece about the mislabeled e-mail and how unlikely you were to click through and read what it had to say? What about the opposite end of that spectrum? What if you were able to segment the population you were sending that e-mail to as a way of letting the consumer know "we are not going to bother you with something you are not interested in?" What if you could let the fan know that you have done your homework? Imagine how much more likely you would be to not only open the correspondence but also to read the marketing material. This is where fan profiles become the basis for your specialized, segmented marketing efforts.

With a thorough understanding of your fan base, you can begin to narrow the scope of your marketing campaigns. Gone are the days of the 90,000 person e-mail blast—the message is too generic and the audience too large. Almost by default you are going to include thousands of individuals that are at best disinterested or at worst annoyed by seeing that tactic employed at the expense of space in their inbox. By coagulating your fan profiles into a data warehouse that allows you to run reports and consolidate like-minded or behaviorally similar consumers into a variety of categories, you can more precisely cater the pitch to a fan base that increasingly craves and demands that specificity. Instead of alerting everyone that has ever given a dollar to Duke in any form or fashion that a football jersey is being auctioned off on GoDuke.com, why not limit that e-mail to people that have shown an affinity toward football?

Could you be leaving sales on the table? Yes, you likely are. But I would argue the cumulative effect of the "blanks" you would be firing would be far more detrimental to the department or franchise than the loss of those dollars. You never want e-mails or phone calls coming from your organization to become white noise. If they do, you are going to cultivate a group of fans that tune out, instead of listen, by default. As a consequence, you are going to spend an inordinate amount of time on the phone with those customers, either handling complaints related to the parking pass they did not renew because it was in one of those e-mails they now always ignore or answering questions that would have been resolved on the landing page you disseminated that went overlooked since the reader was on autopilot and not actually taking in the information.

Try and limit contact to the most critical messages (e.g., season ticket renewal, changes in procedure, and pricing changes) or times when you feel like a conversion is most likely. The credibility and relationships you will build up will far outweigh the dollars "left on the table."

That credibility can manifest itself in a number of ways, including more thoughtful customer feedback. That, in turn, can help you establish value on subjects related to the game day experience or the program/team as a whole. Instead of merely receiving comments in the form of criticism, which is often when people feel moved to write or call in, customers can instead be asked to take part in a focus group, participate in a conjoint analysis, and fill out a survey or do a phone interview with a customer service representative. The best way to know what a fan prioritizes among ticket price, food, and parking is to ask, but fans will not answer if they do not have a relationship with the organization. This segmentation should also lead to more conversion success. Specification and conversion have a fairly linear relationship to each other. In taking a holistic look at the profile of a fan, you can begin to understand their habits and upsell them into areas they are likely to see a fit.

If someone, for instance, is an Iron Duke, a season ticket holder for lacrosse and has downloaded the lacrosse schedule into their mobile device, then this person has in essence raised their hand from the crowd and shouted, "I'm a lacrosse fan!" In that case, they are more likely to feel moved by a campaign advertising an autographed lacrosse helmet on the auction platform or a chance to watch replays of games they missed (or ones they wanted to see again) on their mobile device through Blue Devil Network Plus.

Someone that has not attended a game or shown interest in the program would see the same marketing e-mail as white noise. They might be more interested in soccer, field hockey, basketball, or one of Duke's other 26 sports, so a campaign for them should look much different.

In building the profiles, you are in essence allowing the fans to identify themselves. Instead of having to ask them which sports they like, or which areas of the department they desire to hear more about, you can make inferences by simply organizing the information they have volunteered throughout the years. In this way, the connection is both less intrusive and more constructive.

So far this chapter has discussed the potential uses for big data and analytics when it comes to customer information that is already available to you. But what about adding to your potential client base? A more complete understanding of your fans can also steer the process of data augmentation. Third-party vendors can assist with cleansing, deduplicating, and visualizing data. Oftentimes, these vendors also allow you to enrich the profiles by adding data to the blank spaces you come across during the build. This information can be acquired in several ways: it can be provided by your analytics vendor, purchased on your behalf by your analytics vendor, or purchased on your own through a separate external source.

Since you will likely be paying by volume, zeroing in on what and who you want is vital. A thorough grasp of the information you already have will help lend clarity to both of those segments. Ultimately, you want to try and build out groups for each of the areas you would like to target. For Duke, that could mean any one of a number of clusters: potential Iron Dukes, probable football season ticket holders, or prospective auction bidders. In time, you will come to understand, for instance, what the typical Duke football season ticket holder looks like. From there, you apply that same set of demographic information to the general population and retrieve thousands of accounts that fit that description. Narrowing your scope and marketing to a group that is more likely to engage shows the fans, even subconsciously, that you have put in the effort.

The additional accounts born of that augmentation process become your next set of leads for the development office, ticket sales team, and marketing department. It is the equivalent of replacing a blind date with one that you have had a chance to see and learn more about. You still are not sure there will be a connection, but you have a whole lot more information going into the first meeting than you would have had otherwise. You can cater your message to them more personally and both the customer service representative and the consumer can feel like they are talking more with a casual acquaintance than a complete stranger.

Sometimes, it is easier and more fruitful to simply keep the people you have instead of trying to recruit others. People are inherently less likely to give up something they already own than purchase something they have lived without until that point. In behavioral science, this concept is known as "loss aversion." In that way, reducing churn, whether it is related to ticket sales, donations, subscriptions, or any other rollover revenue streams, can be as valuable an exercise, if not more so, than going through the process of generating new customers. Obviously, you would want the two streams to be working in parallel with each other, but it is important to make sure the focus does not shift too much into generating new revenue and not enough into keeping what is already there.

Just like you can narrow down your marketing campaign to fans that fit a certain profile and you can seek to augment your contacts with similar individuals, you can also use your analytics to hone in on the inverse. While certain characteristics and buying habits would lead you to believe someone is more likely to purchase, renew, or engage, other traits can paint the picture of someone that is likely to churn, cancel, or leave. You should be putting as much time into the latter as the former.

As frustrating as it may sound, in many cases, new money often only serves to balance out money lost through churn. You can drive $1 million of new revenue, but if you lost $1 million worth of season tickets from people that did not renew, what have you really gained? Sure, you have not lost ground, but you also have not grown your business at all. The most efficient organizations work on both ends of the spectrum simultaneously.

Once you have a better idea of who that group of people might be, you can "randomly select" them for seat upgrades, VIP events, or other exclusive experiential perks to help transform them from someone riding the fence about their renewal into a long-term stakeholder.

Summary

The applications of data and analytics to college sports are a lot like your experience with this book. You have chosen to read this book. If you were not interested in the general topic of data and analytics, you would not have picked it up. But how did you come across it?

If someone had shoved a book in front of you about a subject you had no interest in, you would likely never get past the cover and have an impolite thought about the person who forced you to look at it in the first place. But that is just one barrier to entry.

Even if you did choose it yourself, there would have to be something to keep you rifling through the pages. Just because you like a genre or topic does not mean you will like every illustration of it. Every action movie aficionado has rolled his or her eyes at an unrealistic car chase. All sports fans occasionally turn away from a game because the scoring margin or pace is unappealing.

It is all about finding an interested audience and keeping their attention—in the end that is how you build trust. If you like an actor and have seen them in several movies, you are more likely to give another movie they are starring in a shot, even if you are not sure what it is about. That is because they have built credibility with you and you are willing to invest in something based on that connection. If you have enjoyed this book and this specific chapter, the next time you see the author on a panel at a conference or witness their name in a byline, you will be more likely to check in on what he or she has to say.

None of that has a chance at happening, though, if someone or something had not tipped you off to this book's existence. There was a moment in time when you had to make the decision to obtain a copy, but that moment could not have happened if you did not even know there was something out there to obtain.

From books to tickets to social media, your chances of having a long-lasting and consistently positive interaction with your constituents dramatically increase if you put in the effort to cultivate a relationship, offer something unique, and make the world aware it is there.

Hopefully, this chapter has served to check all three of those boxes.

9

LEVERAGING DIGITAL MARKETING TO ENGAGE CONSUMERS AND DRIVE REVENUE

MICHAL LORENC AND ALEXANDRA GONZALEZ

Contents

Digital Marketing and the Sport Business Industry 145
Ticket Sales 146
Video 148
Fan Acquisition 150
Digital Marketing Analytics 153
References 156

Sport consumers have unprecedented access to their favorite teams: continuous coverage, social media feeds, and play highlights that can be repeatedly shared on YouTube. This amplified consumer access to highlights and data also allows teams to leverage more technology than ever before to connect with spectators, building a loyal fan base that sport organizations can market and sell to.

Digital Marketing and the Sport Business Industry

Digital has democratized team–fan connections. Sport organizations at all levels, from corporate brands to professional sport teams, can utilize digital to connect with fans, promote live events, and sell tickets. Google Search facilitates teams' connections with potential customers who might be seeking tickets to next week's game. Online video, specifically on YouTube, gives teams the opportunity to easily share exclusive, interactive content with fans. Digital advertising and retargeting, the ability to show advertisements to past site visitors, creates a space for teams to speak directly to their target demographic, even if prospective ticket holders have never been to a game. These digital formats provide teams with the ability to create flexible, responsive marketing campaigns to increase their fan base and visibility. Most important, these formats can be evaluated with digital analytics platforms, allowing teams to continuously improve their marketing strategies and optimize generated revenue.

Ticket Sales

In the 2013–2014 National Basketball Association (NBA) season, the Washington Wizards made the playoffs for the first time in 5 years, bringing the team unexpected success and visibility. Prior to this successful season on the basketball court, the Wizards relied mostly on traditional media like print and radio; the unprecedented attention that evolved from the team's success encouraged the team to expand its marketing efforts to digital. Hoping to draw new fans and further improve ticket sales, Wizards' owner Monumental Sports and Entertainment spent 25% of the team's overall marketing budget on Google AdWords.

According to Josh Brickman, senior director of strategy and research at Monumental, "a simple Google AdWords ad drove more conversions than any other campaign" the Wizards used. The strategy was simple: use digital ads to serve information fans want, like game schedules, and use data to put more dollars behind campaigns that drive high engagement and sales. With this cost-efficient strategy focused on campaign engagement, the Wizards drove a 293% return on ad spend for the entire NBA season. Team revenue increased as well. The average total transaction through AdWords was 16% higher than online transactions from other mediums.

It is no surprise that the Wizards' digital marketing efforts yielded record-high resultant ticket sales. Data collected by Google indicate that 87% of consumers make a purchase after an online search for sports tickets and 82% of all consumers research online before buying a sports ticket (Guilfoyle and Google, Inc., 2014). The majority of sport ticket sales occur via the Internet. For example, in 2013, 68% of sport event tickets were purchased online (Guilfoyle and Google, Inc., 2014). Live event ticket sales account for a sizable portion of

North American sport team revenue. In 2014, gate receipts accounted for approximately 29% of total revenues; ticket-related revenue exceeded revenue generated from other key revenue categories such as media rights, merchandising, and sponsorships (PwC, 2015). As this key revenue source moves online, teams and leagues need a digital strategy to support this revenue category.

Table 9.1 provides an overview of online sources used by ticket purchasers during the ticket research and decision-making process.

Table 9.2 spotlights consumer mobile device activity during the information-gathering process with respect to purchasing tickets to a sport event.

The Wizards relied on a return on investment (ROI) driven strategy, made possible by the depth of AdWords data readily available. Campaign managers analyzed conversion metrics such as which

Table 9.1 Online Sources Used to Gather Information on the Internet

	AT THE VERY BEGINNING OF TICKET RESEARCH (%)	IN THE MIDDLE OF TICKET RESEARCH (%)	AT THE VERY END OF TICKET RESEARCH (%)	THROUGHOUT DECISION-MAKING PROCESS (%)
Search engines	47	19	5	33
Team/league websites	30	22	8	42
Venue websites	26	22	12	42
General ticket websites	25	14	24	43
Social networks	22	33	7	40

Source: Guilfoyle, E. and Google, Inc., Live events: 2014 IPSOS ticketing study, 2014.

Table 9.2 Device Activity while Gathering Ticket Information

Looked for event ticket availability	26%
Compared prices	25%
Looked for promotions or coupons	17%
Read reviews	13%
Located a ticket seller to purchase tickets from	9%
Contacted a ticket seller	9%
Watched an online video about a particular live event	7%
Other	3%
Did not use mobile device	45%

Source: Guilfoyle, E. and Google, Inc., Live events: 2014 IPSOS ticketing study, 2014.

devices, locations, and queries drove the most ticket sales. Wizards team representatives analyzed performance metrics, such as which ads drove the most clicks or highest click engagement, along with competitive metrics, such as how often a Wizards ad showed for a valuable query. These metrics allowed the team to put more budget behind campaigns that were driving profitable sales, achieving almost a 400% return on ad spend in the last 2 months of the 2013–2014 NBA season (Google, Inc., 2014a). Using the same analytics metrics, the Wizards pulled back from campaigns that drove lower engagement or less volume, saving valuable dollars that could be spent on sales-generating campaigns.

In addition to maintaining a positive ROI, the Wizards wanted to focus on targeting new ticket holders. The team accomplished this objective by reaching users in the moment of consideration, when a fan is deciding which ticket to buy. Most sport event ticket purchasers do not have a specific game in mind when they begin shopping and, on average, ticket purchasers consider two events before buying a ticket (Guilfoyle and Google, Inc., 2014). To capture users in this research phase, the Wizards included multiple matchups in their Search ad extensions, tailored to a user's interests. This allowed users to compare ticketing options right on the Search results page; if a fan was interested in tickets for a specific game, he or she could click on the relevant extension and buy tickets immediately. This strategy helped drive sales from new ticket holders by giving consumers more flexibility between games. In the 2013–2014 NBA season, 72% of Wizards ticket sales came from new customers (Google, Inc., 2014a).

Video

Sport teams have found digital success because of the countless ways fans can engage with a team's content. This revolution is most noticeable in the world of video, where fans can live-stream games, catch up on the latest news, watch interviews with their favorite players or coaches, and find clips of any highlight. In 2014, fans spent 2.4 billion hours globally watching sports video; this number is projected to reach 6.6 billion hours by 2018, and more of this watch time is happening online (Statista, 2015). In 2014, 89% of fans live-streamed sport events on a computer, while 39% streamed on a phone (Statista, 2014). When it comes to short clips or highlights, digital use is even stronger: 78% of fans watch short clips on a laptop, 58% view on a mobile device, and 33% consume on a tablet (Statista, 2014).

The evolving interest of consumers in online video presents a unique challenge for sport teams: how can teams harness the power of video to engage fans, build loyalty, and ultimately drive revenue? By leveraging the immersive format of video and focusing on a data-centric approach, the Orlando Magic launched a successful AdWords campaign to bring tourists to games. As the team entered the 2013–2014 NBA season, Magic executives wanted to leverage the organization's unique consumer marketplace. In addition to competing with other sport events, the team competes with hundreds of other entertainment options and tourist attractions in Orlando, such as Disney World and Universal Studios. Anthony Perez, the Magic's executive vice president of strategy, decided to utilize tourism to the team's advantage. Perez coordinated a collaborative partnership with the digital agency Net Conversion for the Magic's first AdWords campaign, hoping to draw more international tourists by positioning Magic games as an "authentic NBA experience" (Google, Inc., 2014b). Video comprised a crucial part of this ticket sales strategy, as it represented the most effective and efficient method to immerse tourists in a live Magic game environment.

Frank Vertolli, Net Conversion cofounder, explained that campaign videos focused on showing tourists the full experience that comes with a Magic ticket—not just basketball, but dining, shopping, and other forms of entertainment. The videos were meant to "engage very specific users who, without a stimulus, might not see the Magic and visit the arena on a night out" (Google, Inc., 2014b). Video content was customized to the appropriate market. For example, local videos pushed season-long game packages, while videos shown in Brazil advertised individual tickets and used Portuguese. This customized approach allowed the Magic to visually put fans in the most engaging, realistic environment possible. These highly targeted ads achieved a return on ad spend of 5.0 and increased attendance from Brazilian tourists 35% year-over-year. International traffic also rose on the Magic's website; year-over-year, traffic from Brazil increased

21%, traffic from Canada increased 32%, and traffic from the United Kingdom increased 35%. Visits to the team's website increased most noticeably in markets outside of Florida, where visits rose 20% (Google, Inc., 2014b).

With the power of video, the Magic strategically provided international tourists with a vivid, realistic idea of an NBA game experience. With fans worldwide hungering for more interaction with their favorite teams, more clips of their favorite plays, and more interviews with their favorite coaches, video advertising is poised to let teams connect emotionally with fans. Vertolli put it best when he said, "the more that we can target these things, the more that digital advertising becomes a service to the customer" (Google, Inc., 2014b).

Fan Acquisition

The digital revolution created a new opportunity for sport organizations to engage potential consumers and acquire loyal fans. Every online interaction (e.g., a search, a view, or a click) is an opportunity to engage a user and create brand loyalty. A potential customer might search for tickets or game schedules; when they do, a strong search engine optimization (SEO) presence and well-targeted Search ads puts the right team front and center for the consumer. A casual fan might watch highlights on YouTube or browse the latest ESPN article. Relevant video and display content keeps a team top of mind in these moments and helps build fan loyalty. Fan acquisition is made easier with the nimble, flexible nature of digital marketing. Teams no longer have to plan television spots months in advance, hoping their target demographic continues to watch a specific channel. Instead, teams can create digital campaigns easily and respond in real time to user behavior.

The complexity of the contemporary Internet impacts a team's fan acquisition strategy. In past years, building a team website might have been enough. A website could become the hub for the overwhelming amount of information or media associated with a team, guaranteeing traffic from loyal fans and interested readers. When online journalism evolved, sports-related websites became the next "must-be" spot, an easy way to reach more casual fans interested in news at a league level. Now, only 14% of sport event discovery happens on a league or team website (Guilfoyle and Google, Inc., 2014). Much of that traffic emanates from fans who know what they are looking for and who have already established loyalty to a specific team. If loyal fan traffic functions as the majority of website traffic, how can teams find the customers who are on the cusp of fandom, eager to attend a live event?

The answer lies in digital marketing. Over one-third of sport event discovery occurs through social network websites (20%) and venue sites (17%); collectively, these two are the largest online resources utilized by consumers during the event discovery process (Guilfoyle and Google, Inc., 2014). These resources also function as some of the easiest spaces to reach with digital marketing campaigns, which means teams can connect with users during moments of purchase consideration. Facebook, Instagram, and Twitter all offer advertising platforms. The first display ad was sold in 1993; over 20 years later, display advertising remains a crucial part of digital marketing initiatives, and the proliferation of ad networks makes it easy to reach a wide audience (Jandal, 2011). Google's own Display Network includes more than two million publisher sites and reaches 90% of global Internet users.

Table 9.3 lists the primary online resources that consumers utilize when researching and gathering information during the ticket purchase process.

With the flexibility and robust targeting potential of digital marketing, teams can reach social networks and venue sites without huge budgets. Many social network advertising platforms are easy to develop and use—one reason why many small businesses, with

Table 9.3 Sport Event Discovery: Online Resources Utilized by Consumers

Social network websites	20%
Venue websites	17%
Team/league websites	14%
Search engines	13%
General ticket websites	8%

Source: Guilfoyle, E. and Google, Inc., Live events: 2014 IPSOS ticketing study, 2014.

generally fewer resources, use social media as a key foundation of their digital marketing plans. Even with display advertising, teams can create and manage effective campaigns without a large agency or a robust internal marketing department. This bodes well for small organizations, which need effective fan acquisition strategies if these organizations hope to grow. More fans mean more tickets are purchased; more tickets mean more revenue; and more revenue means teams develop the resources for growth and expansion.

AFC Ann Arbor, a new minor-league soccer team, relied on fan acquisition to draw attendance for its inaugural season in 2015. The team was most interested in young families that lived within 40 miles of Ann Arbor, Michigan, as analytics indicated that this target demographic had the time, money, and potential interest necessary for following a new sport team. Facing stiff competition from the University of Michigan sport events, AFC turned to YouTube to launch its digital marketing efforts. By the end of the season, YouTube comprised 75% of overall marketing efforts, and the team's YouTube channel had received 175,000 views.

AFC Ann Arbor used Google TrueView in-stream ads, an ad format that plays immediately before a YouTube video and gives users the option to skip after 5 seconds. This platform provides advertisers with a minimum of five free seconds in front of their audience, and campaign metrics inherently focus on user engagement and interest. Bilal Saeed, co-owner of AFC Ann Arbor, recognized the value of the TrueView format: "You have five seconds for making an impression...Viewers might skip the first few times, but that fourth or fifth time we can definitely capture them. That 5-second model is genius" (Google, Inc., 2015).

At first, AFC Ann Arbor used promotional videos as in-stream ads, hoping to immerse viewers in a realistic game environment and entice them to attend a game. Although promotional videos drew attention, Bilal noticed that fans were more interested in profiles of players, as well as recaps of recent games. As explained by Bilal, "We wanted to roll things out, see what happened, and adjust immediately" (Google, Inc., 2015). This constant optimization led AFC to create videos that met consumer demand and promote the videos through in-stream ads. As the team's content improved, so did its campaign metrics. Fans were more engaged, especially on mobile devices. Video views continued to grow, as AFC developed a remarketing list of 100,000 users who viewed an in-stream ad. AdWords automatically built a second remarketing list of 80,000 users with similar interests and demographics, which the team could leverage to acquire more fans before the start of the team's second season. Online visibility translated to offline success quickly. An average of 1200 fans attended home AFC Ann Arbor games, significantly more than expected. AFC Ann Arbor landed multiple sponsorships, including one before its first game.

Digital Marketing Analytics

Every online interaction is an opportunity to engage fans. These interactions send clear signals about a user's interests, such as whether users are ready to buy a game ticket or just starting to learn about a team. But, those signals alone are not enough to inform a marketing strategy. Teams need to be able to find valuable customer insights and patterns of behavior in these interactions, so that sport organizations can leverage insights to improve operational performance. Without the proper data or analysis, user interactions become meaningless, and teams can easily employ a faulty strategy.

In the digital world, marketing analytics is the cornerstone of success. The increasing complexity of the web results in thousands of data points that need to be sorted, understood, and turned into successful strategies. Robust digital analytics makes these data easy to act on and lends needed context to user behavior that might not otherwise be understood.

Digital analytics can be understood in four categories: audience, acquisition, behavior, and conversions. These categories are used to sort data in Google Analytics, a free tool that provides businesses data on website traffic, allowing companies to make data-driven marketing and business decisions.

Audience data provide a business with information about visitor traffic, specifically about the users who visit a website and interact with website content. A sport team can locate and analyze data on user demographics, interests, locations, and devices. None of these data has personally identifiable information, but it helps to paint a larger picture of a target audience and allows a team to improve the overall user experience. For example, teams can see the routes users take through a team's website. If a significant percentage of users drop off before the final purchase page for tickets, a team can respond to that issue by working to improve the website experience or clarifying the purchasing process. If most of the users are on mobile devices, a team might need a mobile-responsive website or mobile-friendly design. Audience data can extend beyond website traffic; for example, data relating to views of a single video posted by the team on YouTube can provide significant insights as well.

Acquisition data focus on how a user arrived at a website. Users can arrive directly by typing the URL into their web browser, or users can click through from a search engine, social channels, a link on another website, or a digital ad. This section of data helps teams evaluate the effectiveness of a marketing campaign and places campaign traffic in a larger context. For example, if a team is struggling with their SEO presence, the team can use acquisition data to evaluate which paid channel is driving the most ticket sales.

Behavioral data give a team an understanding of user actions on the website; these data focus on site content, site speed, and user behavior. Teams can evaluate a behavioral flow (i.e., how users move through the site, including clicks, page views, and time on each page). This puts a team in the shoes of its customers and, like the audience data, can help a team address any user experience issues. Teams can also see what percentage of visitors are new as compared with returning users, which is an important data point for teams that are trying to acquire new fans. Finally, behavioral data include bounce rate (i.e., the percentage of single-page visits in which a user exited the page without interacting). Bounce rate is a strong indicator of user interest and, in marketing campaigns, a strong indicator of relevance. For example, if a user clicks on a Search ad that reads "Buy Season Tickets Now," that user likely expects to be taken to a purchase page. If that user arrives on the team's home page, they might get discouraged or distracted and leave without purchasing a ticket.

The last category of analytics data is *conversions*. Traditionally, a conversion meant a sale, but the term now has a much wider definition in the world of digital marketing. A conversion can be any valuable action that a user takes as defined by the analytics creator/coder. This means that sport teams can track online ticket sales; teams can also track when users place something in a cart, when users visit a specific page, or when users take a specific action, such as playing a video. Conversion tracking allows a team to identify the actions that matter most and analyze those actions over time. Conversion data show teams completed conversions with accompanying data (e.g., location, device, and day) as well as attribution models that allow teams to evaluate marketing funnels. For example, if a team sold 100 tickets in a week, the team can identify which paid channels led to these purchases and determine a return on ad spend for each of those marketing channels.

While digital analytics can seem overwhelming, it is a needed and valuable component of successful marketing. Analytics provides sport teams necessary data to understand web trends, user behavior, and an evolving consumer audience. These data must be leveraged to test new strategies and adapt existing strategies until a team finds optimal success. Once teams succeed, they can repeat and further refine the digital marketing strategy. For example, if a sport team tracks online ticket sales through Google Analytics, the team can use their analytics data to understand where these purchases are happening geographically. That data can be a list of cities or regions most important to a team's ticket revenue. The team can then use that information to inform radio, television, print, or other advertising.

An example of one practical application of digital marketing analytics relates to the ability of a team to import its own customer relationship management data and strategically target (or exclude) specific target markets on Google and YouTube, as well as on social media sites. This segmentation capability, based on digital marketing data, promises to further fine-tune the effectiveness and impact of digital marketing. For example, a team could target all past season ticket holders (active and lapsed) during renewal season or run a ticketing campaign targeting everyone except season ticket holders. These data-driven business strategies provide sport marketers with opportunities to efficiently engage users with the right message at the right time.

Digital marketing analytics extends beyond testing new marketing strategies. Even when a sport team has successful strategies in place, the team can leverage analytics to further analyze key prospective consumers. For example, YouTube ads allowed AFC Ann Arbor to promote team home games and also provided the team with valuable data on key prospective consumers. AFC Ann Arbor was able to analyze demographic data (e.g., gender, age, and parental status), interests (e.g., whether a user was considered a soccer fan), and behavior (e.g., how many seconds a user spent watching an ad or how often they skipped). These data showed AFC Ann Arbor that the team's targeted primary demographic was spot-on: young families within 40 miles of Ann Arbor were more likely to buy home game tickets.

References

Google, Inc. (2014a). The Washington Wizards add 72% more new fan ticket sales with AdWords.

Google, Inc. (2014b). The NBA's Orlando Magic enjoy home-court advantage with Google AdWords.

Google, Inc. (2015). AFC Ann Arbor perfects its pitch with TrueView in-stream ads.

Guilfoyle, E. and Google, Inc. (2014). Live events: 2014 IPSOS ticketing study.

Jandal, H. (2011). *Display Advertising: The Billboards of the Web*. WSI Research & Management.

PwC. (2015). At the gate and beyond: Outlook for the sports market in North America through 2019.

Statista. (2014). Types of devices used to watch sports content online in United States as of June 2014.

Statista. (2015). Time spent watching e-sports video worldwide in 2012, 2013 and 2018 (in billion hours).

10

COMMUNICATING THE VALUE OF SPORTS SPONSORSHIP

ADAM GROSSMAN AND IRVING REIN

Contents

Introduction 157
What Is Sponsorship? 159
How Have Properties Valued Sponsorship? 160
How Can Sport Organizations Value Assets in the Future?..........162
    Inherent Valuation...162
    Relative Valuation 165
    Comparable Valuation...166
How Do You Communicate Sponsorship?....................................167
Conclusion 170
References 171

Introduction

In a conference focused on numbers, the most important takeaway was how to communicate the *value* of those numbers. The Sports Analytics Innovation Summit brought together sport business industry leaders to discuss how sport organizations can use quantitative data to improve their organization's performance on and off the field. It would be difficult to find a conference with people who loved the intersection of sports and numbers more than this conference in San Francisco. Topics ranging from predicative modeling, analytics, economics, data science, and data programming dominated the conversations during panels. Even with all of these disparate topics, one central theme emerged from this conference. While more data are being produced in the sport business industry than ever before, there are also more people who can "crunch the numbers." The people who will have a sustainable advantage in the sport business industry are the ones who are able to analyze data and communicate their findings to a sport organization's different internal and external audiences.

Nowhere was this central conference theme more important than in sports sponsorship. Corporate advertisers expect sport organizations to provide them with information on the return on their investment (ROI) spend. Yet sport organizations have typically communicated sponsorship information using qualitative reports that no longer meet their partners' expectations. To be successful in attracting and retaining sponsors, sport organizations need to focus on how to understand and efficiently communicate quantitative data.

Big data has already had a big impact on the sport business industry. The book and movie *Moneyball* has popularized how using this data can help teams find undervalued players to create a winning team on the field with lower player salaries. While analytics has continued to impact the team operations side of sport organizations, business operations have been slower to adopt a quantitative approach. One of the main reasons for this is that many people in sport organizations do not possess the ability or language to communicate quantitative concepts. Dynamic ticket pricing is a good example of this issue. The goal of dynamic ticket pricing is to enable sport organizations to sell tickets at prices that reflect the true demand for the product. However, how do you communicate to fans what factors go into a dynamic ticket pricing model? How do fans really know if they are receiving the fair value for their tickets or are getting the best price? These models can be so complicated that sport organizations often are hesitant to detail how they work.

Sports sponsorship is dealing with a similar problem. The sponsorship industry generates over $57.5 billion globally per year, with sports making up a majority of that spend (IEG, 2015). With so much volume and competition, how do sport organizations determine if a sponsorship is generating value? Companies now scrutinize their advertising spend more closely than ever before. New digital, social, mobile, and geotargeting platforms deliver metrics where brands can see who views an ad, how long someone views an ad, and how many people click on an ad. In addition, media, entertainment, and video streaming companies are providing detailed information on how much value companies receive related to a company's advertising spend. Sponsors now expect their experience with sport organizations to receive the same level of transparency that sponsors obtain when advertising through other channels.

The sport business industry needs people who can deliver this experience because many organizations at the professional, collegiate, and high school level lack this expertise. This chapter provides the strategies and tactics to be successful in addressing the most critical sport business industry sponsorship challenges. The next section of this chapter discusses exactly what sports sponsorship entails and how sponsorships have been valued in the past. This chapter then highlights the challenges that have prevented sport organizations from adopting a more quantitative approach to sponsorship valuation and evaluation. This chapter also describes an approach on how to quantify and communicate sports sponsorship values using real-world case studies as examples. This chapter concludes by showing how the industry will evolve and the pressing need for people who can connect numbers with sponsorship.

What Is Sponsorship?

Before quantifying the value of sponsorship, it is imperative to have a clear definition of what sponsorship means. Sports sponsorship is defined through the relationship of sport properties and corporate partners. Sport properties are the rights holders of assets that can be sold to corporate partners. Properties are usually teams, leagues, schools, competitions, or events. Corporate partners are companies or organizations that buy these assets to achieve their sales, advertising, marketing, and brand goals.

Inventory items are typically classified into seven main categories. While the following list is not an exhaustive list, it covers the primary sponsorship inventory items purchased by corporate partners:

- *Venue*: While the most common form of inventory is signage, venues have a number of inventory items, including naming rights deals, call-to-action campaigns on display boards, luxury/hospitality suites, game tickets, and sales booths or tables.
- *Traditional media*: Television, radio, and print (newspapers, magazines, and fliers) comprise traditional media. The most common forms of advertising are a 30 second advertising spot

on television or radio along with print advertisements. Other common activation elements include media billboards, product placements, on-air reads, and coupons.

- *Digital and mobile media*: Digital refers to advertising that occurs on a sport property's website or social media platforms. This normally includes digital billboards, videos, or promoted social media posts. Mobile focuses on sponsorship inventory that can be accessed on mobile devices. This usually involves geographic targeting that enables properties and partners to target users in specific locations.
- *Intellectual property*: The intellectual property of teams, leagues, and individual athletes is a valuable asset for corporate partners. The most common example is using a team's or league's logo that is featured in an advertising campaign. For instance, Anheuser-Busch InBev's (AB-InBev) partnership with the National Football League (NFL) enables the company to place NFL team logos on its Bud Light cans (Grossman, 2015). Having exclusive rights to use intellectual property rights for a certain product or service category (i.e., Anheuser-Busch has exclusive rights to the NFL spirits category) has been an attractive asset for properties and sponsors. Buyers and sellers of sports sponsorship believe that this type of inventory provides significant competitive advantage for the sponsor in the marketplace (Grossman, 2015).
- *Experiential*: Corporate partners often want to activate sponsorships with events, booths, or displays both inside and outside of the venue. This includes special events for customers or employees at a venue on non-game days or player appearances at corporate activities.
- *Jersey*: Jersey sponsorships occur when an organization's brand or logo is placed on the front and/or back of a jersey.

How Have Properties Valued Sponsorship?

Many individual sport organizations are generating millions of dollars from sports sponsorships. In addition, the largest companies in the world work with leading advertising agencies, including Octagon, IMG, OMD, and Tribune Media Group, to source, buy, and manage sponsorships for sport organizations. That means industry leaders that sell and buy sports sponsorships interact to discuss opportunities on a regular basis.

Despite sponsorship representing such a significant portion of an organization's revenue stream and sport organizations working with *Fortune* 500 companies, quantitative sports sponsorship valuation is only beginning to permeate the industry. Most sport organizations currently use "recaps" to communicate the value of sponsorships to their corporate partners. These recaps are usually PowerPoint and PDF documents featuring images of sponsorship activations. These recaps typically include photos of activation elements across the different categories of sports sponsorship so organizations can see how different audiences interact with their brands.

Sponsorship recaps often have limited quantitative data because corporate partners often do not ask for or require this information. For many corporate partners, just seeing their activation elements provides the necessary support to renew their sponsorships. In addition, providing tickets to sporting events for sponsors is a unique way to reward the people who generate the most for the sport organization's bottom line.

The economic downturn in 2008–2010 combined with the growth of big data and new marketplace technologies changed this dynamic. Financial services, automobile, and insurance companies are among the largest sponsors of sport organizations. Companies in these industries are also the companies who were the hardest hit by the economic downturn. As companies such as Bank of America, General Motors, and AIG were all receiving federal aid, more scrutiny than ever before was being placed on these organizations, especially on their marketing and advertising spend.

At the same time, big data and technology continued to change the way that advertising is purchased. In particular, companies could receive detailed information on their customers through new digital channels. Real-time digital analytics enabled companies to know how many customers saw an advertisement, watched a video, or clicked on a promotion. In addition, new marketplaces emerged that enabled buyers and sellers of advertising to see inventory and prices in real time. Google, Microsoft, and Facebook all have advertising exchanges where sport organizations can purchase inventory.

To remain competitive, traditional media companies also started to more frequently provide detailed pricing and consumption data to their advertising customers.

How Can Sport Organizations Value Assets in the Future?

When investment banks, private equity firms, or venture capital firms evaluate companies or assets to purchase, they primarily use three valuation approaches—inherent, relative, and comparable valuations. Inherent valuations analyze the dollars or profits generated by a company or asset to determine its overall value. Relative valuations analyze ratios to determine value. The most common type of relative valuation is a price-to-earnings ratio—the price of a company compared to its earnings. Comparable valuations examine the prices of similar assets to determine value—for example, what the prices of comparable companies are within an industry. Sport organizations can employ a similar approach when determining values for sports sponsorship inventory. This approach can start with an inherent valuation.

Inherent Valuation

For sponsorship inventory, companies analyze the number of impressions generated rather than dollars. Impressions are the number of people who consume a piece of sponsorship inventory. This usually means how many people can see sponsorship inventory in one of the sponsorship categories. Let's examine how impressions are measured in each sponsorship category:

- *Venue, jersey, and event*: The most common measure is the number of fans that attend a game or competition. Most sport organizations use the number of tickets sold as the number of impressions generated. In addition, broadcast viewable signage is an important factor in the calculation. The more a sign can be seen on television or digital streams, the more potential value it has for a corporate partner.
- *Traditional media*: Television and radio ratings provided by Nielsen, Arbitron, and Rentrak are the most common sources that are used to provide the number of people who watch or

listen to sports content. Daily circulation numbers are used for newspapers.

- *Digital and mobile media*: Organizations often use page views or the number of unique visitors to count impressions. Page views count the number of total impressions consumed, while unique visitors only count distinct individuals. This means that if a person returns to a page multiple times, it only counts as one unique visit. One issue with this approach is that page views do not always mean engagement. For example, a social media post is not read by all people who like, follow, or subscribe to an account. Many partners are now focusing on engagement (i.e., how many people consume content) rather than solely examining page views or conversion rates.

The challenge with measuring impressions is that not all impressions are created equal. More specifically, conventional wisdom is that the more impressions that are generated, the greater the value of the sponsorship inventory. Super Bowl television commercials cost so much because over 110 million people watch the NFL's championship game—the highest-rated television program of the year. The Super Bowl is also consumed live, unlike many other nonsports programs, which can have time-shifted viewing (i.e., watching a program on a DVR) where viewers can fast-forward through advertisements.

Are all 110+ million viewers of equal value to companies? Oftentimes, the answer is no. For example, many companies are business-to-business enterprises rather than business-to-consumer companies. That means these companies need to target specific decision-makers that make enterprise-wide decisions. For example, Oracle is a *Fortune* 500 company that primarily sells enterprise resource planning, database software, cloud applications, and data center operations service offerings. A significant portion of people watching the Super Bowl would not be buying these products. Therefore, it is easy to make the case that spending money on the Super Bowl is an inefficient use of Oracle's marketing and advertising dollars. Instead, Oracle could target channels that focus on the people that are more likely to make a purchasing decision for their business for Oracle service offerings. Sponsorship impressions that target this demographic should be more valuable to Oracle because they are more likely to be viewed by the company's customers.

The quality, and not just the quantity, of impressions is a critical concept for sport organizations. More specifically, smaller sports teams or leagues do not need to generate hundreds of thousands or millions of impressions to create value for sponsors. The sport organizations that can effectively communicate how they reach customer demographics to their corporate partners will achieve sponsorship success.

CORPORATE PARTNERS GO LOONY FOR MINNESOTA UNITED SPONSORSHIP

Since InBev acquired Anheuser-Busch in 2013, the company has more closely examined sports sponsorship. In particular, the newly combined company wanted to see where it was getting value for its sports sponsorship dollar and reduce spending when it was not. Head of Media Connections Lucas Herscovici articulated this strategy when he said, "It's not about signage, logos and doing defensive [property] deals. It's about choosing the right partners and the right passion points to drive the convergence of media, content and experiences" (Lefton, 2015).

Minnesota United (whose mascot is the Loon) clearly understood the company's goals when it began working with the sports sponsorship and analytics company Block Six Analytics (B6A) to show AB-InBev how it was one of those right partners. The North American Soccer League team had an existing partnership with the alcoholic beverage company and felt it was delivering value. However, it did not know how to calculate and communicate this value to AB-InBev and risked losing its sponsorship without this capability.

Minnesota United accomplished these goals by using B6A's software as a service platform called the Partnership Scoreboard. First, Minnesota United used B6A's corporate asset valuation model to show how AB-InBev achieved its revenue and brand goals across different channels with a single ROI metric. This includes showing every calculation in the model and evaluating how each activation element delivers value based on the unique ways that AB-InBev conducts business. Second, Minnesota United provided AB-InBev with access to the Partnership Scoreboard's dashboard that updates every time a sponsorship activation occurs. Rather than waiting for the end of the season to see results, AB-InBev could log into the Partnership Scoreboard and see updates in real time.

The ROI outputs in the Partnership Scoreboard almost exactly matched AB-InBev's internal calculations of the sponsorship's value. Equally important was that Minnesota United could communicate clearly by using a technology that presented the information in an easy, digestible way to an important corporate partner. This provided the foundation for AB-InBev to renew its sponsorship with Minnesota United because it knew that the team valued its partnership in ways that aligned with company's brand and revenue goals.

Relative Valuation

The most common ratio used in sports sponsorship is cost per thousand impressions (CPM). CPM is also the most common relative metric used in other advertising or marketing channels. Here is the formula to calculate a CPM: CPM = cost of sponsorship/(impressions/1000). Different sponsorship categories will have different CPM rates. The CPM rates vary because of the ease of generating impressions in the channels and the value of people within those channels. Digital and mobile typically have the lowest CPMs because it is relatively easy to generate a high number of impressions while having a lower level of measured engagement in these channels. Luxury/hospitality suites are typically on the opposite end of the CPM spectrum. These CPMs are often higher than the average CPM, but these often occur with the most lucrative demographics.

Does that mean that digital and mobile channels are less valuable than other forms of sponsorship? Not necessarily. In fact, many corporate partners are shifting resources to sponsorships focused on digital, social, and mobile activations because they can obtain detailed engagement metrics. Digital media also enables advertisers to more easily reach younger consumers that can add significant long-term value to companies and are often difficult to reach in other channels. This can make digital sponsorship more valuable while still having a lower price point than traditional media. This helps to show how understanding CPM rates can provide a good framework for discussing value across different channels.

Comparable Valuation

Sport organizations typically utilize comparable valuation to value corporate sponsorships. Comparable valuation is examining the value of an asset relative to similar assets in a category. For sport organizations, this means pricing sponsorship inventory in ways that are similar to other teams in the league or geographical area. The reason sport organizations use this approach is because of fear that a corporate partner will purchase inventory from another team or league if the team's prices are higher.

There are a couple of problems with this approach. First, it is not always clear what the prices for sponsorship items should be. Sport organizations are often private enterprises that are not required to share the prices of their sponsorship inventory items with other teams or leagues. Even public high schools and universities often refrain from sharing prices. That means sport organizations often rely on estimates or corporate partners to obtain pricing information.

The second issue with focusing on comparable valuations is that organizations primarily compete on price instead of value. It implies that sports sponsorship is solely a commodity where buyers will look for the lowest price. Sport organizations potentially compromise revenue when evaluating inventory in this way. Each sports team and league will have different abilities to target specific demographics. For instance, the PGA Tour typically targets older, male fans, while the National Women's Soccer League (NWSL) focuses on a younger, female demographic. Different partners will prioritize different demographics and receive varying levels of value by working with either the PGA Tour or NWSL based on their business model and objectives.

Another factor is the marketing goals of corporate partners. Larger brands will often focus on customer acquisition and customer retention because people already know what service offerings these companies provide to consumers. Therefore, large companies typically want to find sponsorship inventory that either impacts their bottom line or creates better engagement with customers. In addition to generating revenue, smaller companies often use sports sponsorship to help increase awareness and perception of their brands. Sport organizations often have large, passionate followings in the region in which they compete. Smaller corporate partners then use sports sponsorships to communicate to a large number of new customers about their presence in the market using the sports team they follow as the vehicle.

Sport organizations are advised to use all three types of valuation models when completing sponsorship valuation. Using an inherent valuation approach enables properties to determine quality and quantity of impressions. Employing a relative valuation enables sport organizations to communicate impressions using a metric that corporate partners are already familiar with when examining advertising spends. Finally, a comparable valuation benchmarks valuations with other organizations' price points factoring in the considerations discussed in this chapter. Sport organizations do not need to assign the same weight to each valuation type. However, using a combination of each approach will ensure that a property achieves a fair market valuation.

How Do You Communicate Sponsorship?

This section provides an overview of the essential communication strategies that can help ensure not only connection but also understanding of and the ability to communicate the value demonstrated by analytics to corporate sponsors. We will discuss the importance of audience analysis, creditability, institutional rhetoric, and presentational performance. These topics are crucial to generating sales and creating effective, long-term relationships.

A first consideration is who comprises the audience and how to determine their level of understanding of the value of data in a corporate sponsorship. Who are the influencers of the decision? Who are the people who keep the process going? And who is ultimately going to make the decision? Understanding and not alienating non-decision-makers is often a stumbling block to achieving a thorough assessment of what a valuation package can deliver to the buyer. In particular, it is critical to determine a sponsor's familiarity with valuation, big data, and analytics. There are some sponsors who fully embrace the numbers and some sponsors who will only make decisions on intuition. Most sponsors, however, have some knowledge of sponsorship value but will not be fluent in the language of big data.

For example, many sponsors want to work with sport organizations because they have the ability to target their customers in unique ways. Sponsors want to take advantage of the powerful emotional connection that fans have with their favorite leagues, teams, athletes, or events. What sponsors often do not understand is how this connection can be quantified and how this relationship can impact their bottom line. Using the valuation frameworks discussed earlier in the chapter to quantify and communicate sponsorship valuation will create deep and long-lasting sponsorship relationships.

This approach demonstrates the importance of understanding the values of the target audience when completing this type of analysis. It is not always easy to appraise what an audience's most deeply held values are at different points in time. Many sponsors are looking to maximize revenue and profits by having a relationship with a sport organization. This often focuses on a sport property's ability to target specific demographics based on consumer age, gender, income, and geography. However, maximizing the bottom line may not always be the primary consideration. A sponsor may be looking to enhance its brand perception by associating the brand attributes of the sport organization with their company through a sponsorship, which is often referred to as "the halo effect." It is often necessary to personalize the information to enable the audience to clearly picture how the partnership will look and feel when it is completed.

A second and related consideration is credibility, which underlies all sponsorship communication. A hurdle to gaining trust is understanding the underlying elements of the term credibility. A foundational term is ethos, which originates in Greek antiquity and is, in essence, built on credibility. Ethos cannot be faked. It centers on the audience's perception of the communicator, and without it, meaningful connection with an audience is difficult to accomplish. Ethos, according to the philosopher and rhetorician Aristotle, can only be achieved by the audience viewing the communicator as possessing moral character, goodwill, and intelligence. In this context, corporate sponsorship interaction can only be built on past behavior, an ability to communicate transparently, sensitivity to audience needs, and following through on promises. Ethos is what sport organizations need to strive for with sponsorship. It is the communication interaction positioning that is most likely to create an environment of trust and cooperation (Kennedy, 1991).

A third important issue when communicating corporate sponsorship data is understanding the importance of institutional rhetoric. It can be thought of as a communication program, unique to a specific organization that uses it to inculcate its philosophy and values in its workers, products, and customers. It is made up of both the formal and informal communication patterns of daily and large-scale interaction. It is also made up of the informal—the dress, the vernacular, and the referential language of a specific organization. It can be thought of as a package of communication inputs that are orchestrated to form a way of positioning the organization in the world and communicating within it.

It is critical that corporate partnership presentations are delivered with an understanding of the institutional rhetoric of the buyer. Moreover, identifying those communication singularities that can be an obstacle for understanding and subsequent translation by the buyer of the data to other markets is crucial to achieving a true ability to interpret the partnership from the buyer's point of view. For example, a company that wants to develop a partnership with the New York Yankees must understand the degree to which excellence is embedded in their organization's communication, how they interpret the concept, and how to integrate that into a presentation.

Finally, the corporate sponsorship value package needs to be presented. The manner of performance could range from a formal presentation for the buyer to a more casual lunch or a phone call. An inherent problem for data delivery is clarity. Often the amount of data and the complexity of calculations obfuscate the takeaways from the data. Most sponsors want intelligence that translates into action. Clearly introducing and defining insights, terminology, and purpose of valuation as soon as possible in a presentation is critical to securing buy-in from the sponsor. Developing a common language and using narrative constructs that utilize data enable sponsors to use qualitative analysis to understand quantitative concepts. In addition, data visualization is critical to achieving these goals. Creating graphics that turn numbers into images, or infographics, makes complex calculations much easier to digest. The sooner a sponsor can understand what the results of a valuation are, how the results were obtained, and how the results can be applied, the better.

A corporate sponsorship relationship changes over time and the communicators need to recognize that not only will the value analysis need to be consistently adjusted but any new players and circumstances need to be monitored on an ongoing basis. Where audience analysis often fails is the inability to recognize that it is never static. The feedback process from the client is absolutely essential and needs to be constantly evaluated. The communication touchpoints often include interpreting basic research, engaging in interpersonal contact, and asking and answering frequent questions.

Data can be engaging, emotional, and persuasive. Skilled communicators understand that without each other, data and communication skills suffer. The sports industry demands that people effectively use data as the foundation for creating a trusting and lasting relationship with the client. Even the most obvious and ideal product for a buyer needs to be translated into language and a message that they can not only understand but also relay to their internal staff and ultimate end users.

Conclusion

One of the most famous quotes from the book *Animal Farm* is "All animals are equal, but some animals are more equal than others" (Orwell, 1954, p. 112). How does George Orwell's allegory on communism in the Soviet Union apply to sports sponsorships? All sports sponsorships can be valuable, but some sponsorships are more valuable than others.

This chapter provides the framework for determining how to understand the value of sports sponsorship. Traditional methods tend to focus on quantity over quality when it comes to sports sponsorship impressions. This chapter spotlights both the quality and quantity elements of sports sponsorships by focusing on the business of each sponsor. By completing an inherent, relative, and comparable analysis of sponsorship inventory, sport organizations will have the ability to demonstrate to sponsors how they generate value based on their revenue and brand goals.

In addition, this chapter examines the best way to communicate this information to sponsors. By understanding their audience's needs, building credibility through clear communication of data, and tailoring concepts using a sponsor's terminology, sport organizations will effectively connect with their sponsors. This approach enables buyers and sellers of sports sponsorship to use data to speak the same language and have effective conversations that promote mutual value.

Sports sponsorship is constantly changing. Sponsorship inventory is being created daily. Companies' expectations of sponsorship are dynamic with different types of companies having increasingly differentiated needs. New technologies enable sport organizations to create targeted promotions that reach specific demographics. Quantitative analysis will play a significant role in all of these areas. However, big data are incomplete without the ability to communicate the results to sponsors. The successful entrant into the sports sponsorship industry will be able to both crunch and communicate the numbers.

References

Grossman, A. (2015). Should sports leagues be worried about merger of Anheuser-Busch and Miller? *Forbes,* November 11, 2015.

IEG. (2015). Sponsorship spending report. IEG, Chicago, IL.

Kennedy, G. A. (1991). *Aristotle on Rhetoric: A Theory of Civic Discourse.* New York: Oxford University Press.

Lefton, T. (2015). A-B to sports partners: Adapt to a new world. *SportsBusiness Journal.*

Orwell, G. (1954). *Animal Farm.* New York: Harcourt, Brace.

11

Market Research Analytics and Data-Driven Innovation

C. KEITH HARRISON AND SUZANNE MALIA LAWRENCE

Contents

Introduction 173
Literature Review: Women as Sport Event Spectators................. 174
Market Research and Live Analytics.. 176
Innovation Driven by Data.. 177
Fan Engagement 179
Connecting with Women Fans in Innovative Ways 179
    Case Study: Montana State University Gridiron Girls
    Football Clinic 180
Conclusions: Beware of the Affinity Trap and Involve Various
Cultural Groups 182
References 184

> Women are females first and consumers second.

Bridget Brennan—*Why She Buys* (Brennan, 2009)

Introduction

In the book *Veeck—As in Wreck*, Bill Veeck (Veeck and Linn, 1962), the pioneer marketing innovator, captures one of the most important concepts in modern sports business and market research demographics: *women*. In the early to mid-1900s, Veeck estimated approximately 25% of the team's fan base were women (Veeck and Linn, 1962). Hence, Veeck was well before his time as he recognized paying close attention to the nuances of diverse fans and spectators has great value for a sport organization in several ways. The first way is by examining the presence of who attends the event, how often, and what these fans purchase while attending the event; the key here is that these three components are based on the fans' cultural backgrounds. Second, data in "real time," based on the three components just mentioned, allow business leaders in the sport and entertainment industry to objectively assess how revenue generation might be strategically approached, strategically implemented, and evaluated. Consider how Veeck, many decades ago, understood this philosophical approach: "Ever open-minded, Veeck understood that the presence of women at the ballpark meant that whole families were more likely to attend, increasing the club's profits. One of Veeck's early notions was to revive a momentary innovation of the 1890s, Ladies' Day, and bring it into the twentieth century" (Dickson, 2012, p. 21). Dickson (2012) continued to explain, "Beginning with the 1919 season, a few Fridays were announced as Ladies' Days. Full-page newspaper advertisements offered free tickets for women, many of whom decided to pay an additional fee to upgrade to the box seats, of which Wrigley Field had proportionally more than any other ballpark in the major leagues" (p. 21).

Therefore, the purpose of this chapter is to unpack a practical approach to collecting data at live-action sport events with a specific demographic group. "Live Analytics" have the uniqueness to gather data at the height of spectator emotion versus gathering spectator impressions of their experiences after an event, which is merely a memory. While this chapter focuses on the female demographic, many of the concepts and strategic approaches can be applied to other affinity groups. With this in mind, sport business leaders should also strategically approach other fans and spectators of sport: African Americans, Latinos, Polynesians, and Asian Americans. There are other ethnic, generational, and cultural groups that also warrant scholarly and practitioner attention in this area; however, the scope of this chapter focuses mainly on women. Prior to the presentation in regard to market research execution with females, a review of the academic literature on women fans and spectators is outlined.

Literature Review: Women as Sport Event Spectators

There is a growing body of literature on women fans of sport, especially in traditionally male-dominated sports like football. Existing research on female fans and spectators tend to focus on gender differences with respect to attendance at live sporting events (Fink et al., 2002; Gauthier and Hansen, 1993), female consumption in regard to live television broadcasts of sporting events (Clark et al., 2009; Gantz and Wenner, 1995), gender differences relating to motivations for sport spectatorship (Farrell et al., 2011; James and Ridinger, 2002), and fan affinity and avidity in regard to female consumers of sport (Clark et al., 2009; Dixon, 2002; Wann et al., 2004). Few studies have focused on a multimethod assessment in regard to the overall game day experiences of female fans and spectators (Balfour, 2012; Greenwell et al., 2002). Gosling (2007) expressed the importance of scholars conducting additional investigations of the "everyday experiences and identities of female sport fans" (p. 250).

Many previous research studies have used a qualitative approach to learn more about the experience of women at sporting events. For instance, Balfour (2012) examined the experiences of women fans at Major League Baseball (MLB) games and found women felt stereotyped in terms of the assumptions that females do not know much about sport. Also, women in the study also felt empowered by those male and female fans who respected their "knowledge of the game" and the female presence at this type of sporting event. Other scholars have examined how women are considered to be "outsiders" or "inauthentic supporters" (Pope, 2012, p. 86) and how men establish the social norms present at sporting events (Jones, 2008; Pope, 2010; Pope and Williams, 2011). Further, Pope (2013) recently made an important contribution to the literature by filling the empirical gap on women sport fans. While this work compared female fans of soccer and rugby in London, it revealed that there were two extremes of support for these two sports. These supporters ranged from "masculine" to "feminine" styles of experiencing sport. Pope (2013) also stated, "There is a need to conduct further cross-comparative studies between fans of different sports and for future research to put women's experiences on the sports research agenda" (p. 192).

Other scholars have also written about how women sport fans and spectators have been commodified (Wenner, 2013). Scholars have explained how female sport spectatorship and consumption "cannot be reduced to a set of fixed characteristics" but should rather be "viewed as a process" (Toffoletti and Mewett, 2014, p. 4). For example,

Brennan (2009) explained two common mistakes people make when creating products intended for women: (1) simply creating pink versions of existing products and (2) trying to market existing products to women without sufficiently adapting them to the specific needs of the female demographic as a targeted audience. Also, Lough and Kim (2004) examined a women's professional basketball league in South Korea that made continuous attempts to improve the spectator experience (e.g., through in-game promotions and an improved league website); however, all of these new marketing initiatives were "not based on known needs and wants because no research had been done to determine or understand the needs and wants of the fans" (p. 41).

While some sport organizations are still attempting to develop optimal marketing strategies focused on women consumers, scholars and practitioners have written throughout the past 20 years about the importance of marketing to the female demographic. Branch (1995) claimed it is imperative for sport organizations to create a marketing mix of products and services that appeal to a woman's preferences with respect to quality, price value, feelings, and emotional well-being. In terms of "untapped markets," Branch (1995) over two decades ago suggested the ability to connect with the female audience allows sport business leaders to increase profits and allows women to fully participate as respected spectators. Sutton (1994) echoed the importance of creating meaningful and authentic connections with women consumers, as "companies and sponsors seeking to target and reach the female consumer must demonstrate the ability to not only understand the lifestyles and interests of women, but to effectively communicate the image and direction of the company as compatible with that lifestyle and image" (p. 20).

Market Research and Live Analytics

According to Davenport and Kim (2013), "Analytics can be classified as qualitative or quantitative according to the process employed and the type of data that are collected and analyzed. Qualitative analysis aims to gather an in-depth understanding of the underlying reasons and motivations for a phenomenon" (p. 4). This approach aligns with why fans of any gender attend live sport events to begin with—spectators want to feel and experience the excitement in person. However, the specificity of a particular demographic group during live-action viewing is a win for the fan, spectator, and business leader looking to gain an advantage within the sports marketplace. Thus, there must be a logical approach to collecting data through intercept surveys. Recently, one of the authors of this chapter attended a National Basketball Association game in Oklahoma City; during the fourth quarter of the game, he observed researchers for the home team seeking impressions from fans walking on the concourse. In general, there is a rubric that fits a systemic approach to this type of market research.

A Live Analytics rubric to collecting data includes the following steps for the sport organization (externally or internally):

- Approval to collect data at sport event(s).
- Assembling a team to collect data (college students are a great resource for this process if university faculty engage in this type of research).
- Logistics of collecting the data should be handled more than a few hours prior to game starting time so that data collection will run smoothly. For example, all the necessary materials used to administer the surveys should be organized so that data collection and execution will be maximized (surveys, clipboards, pencils, and for electronic survey administration items should be downloaded on the device and iPads charged).
- Researchers need to be trained prior to the event so that they can collect accurate data.

Finally, once the data are collected, the data need to be analyzed and coded. After data analysis, the business development part begins by listening to the demographic group of customers being targeted. While 100% of the input and feedback provided by customers is not always given consideration for actionable items by business leaders, the process of interpreting the data from fans and spectators is a process that can benefit both the sport organization and customers at the event.

Innovation Driven by Data

What does an individual do after the data are analyzed and how does this process lead to innovation? This is an important question. There are some important steps in the process that supersedes data analysis. The first is the stakeholders must be convinced that action can be taken. Data reveal potential patterns and create opportunities to develop new trends, which maximize what customers have communicated with respect to preferences. The following are some common action steps involved in this process:

- Identifying all the stakeholders
- Documenting stakeholder needs
- Assessing and analyzing stakeholder interests and influence
- Managing stakeholder expectations
- Taking action
- Reviewing status and repeating (see Davenport and Kim, 2013, p. 27)

After the stakeholders buy into the process, implementation and innovation can occur. This is what allows the data to drive the strategy toward initiatives that hopefully coincide with existing corporate partnerships and enable the organization to prospect and seek out new sponsorship opportunities.

One case example of this innovation process is the women fans and spectators project at California State University Northridge (CSUN) involving the men's soccer, women's basketball, men's basketball, softball, and baseball teams. Data were collected during the fall 2014 semester with three teams and with CSUN's softball and baseball teams during the spring 2016 semester. It is important to note again that the data can confirm or reveal new directions that organizations should take.

The data with this particular school confirmed one corporate partnership that was inked simultaneously at the completion of the data collection during fall 2014. The data also have driven some new partnerships that CSUN's athletic director Dr. Brandon Martin is seeking to secure with his colleagues within CSUN Athletics. Once corporate partnerships are secured, then the focus can turn toward activation and fan engagement. One approach to fan engagement is to highlight the affinity group being targeted. CSUN decided to create an annual "Girls and Women" theme event at some of their home athletic games based on the positive impact that the Live Analytics data collection had on the female fan base. The next section provides a more in-depth analysis of how market research, fan engagement, and innovation are interconnected.

Fan Engagement

The engagement of avid or casual fans is of the highest priority for many teams and brands seeking to connect with the audience. This engagement begins from the time fans and spectators purchase tickets, buy apparel to attend the event, transportation to the event, parking at the event, tailgating, and last but not least social media with wireless access. Sutton and Sutton (2015) highlighted how marrying social media to the fan experience is not only respectful of the customer, but it is great for return on investment (ROI) purposes. Understanding the social media preferences of women specifically has been proven to be an effective approach for marketing, sales, and game day experience leaders in the industry. Best practices for fan engagement based on market research are driven from the social media space and allow social media to compliment a female fan or spectator preference. For example, previous research indicates that women are the key purchaser not only for themselves but also the spouse and kids. Quantifying and qualifying what women want during a sporting event informs various touch points of business that can be maximized for better game day experience and profit when researchers listen to the data.

Connecting with Women Fans in Innovative Ways

Before providing an overview on how one university approached women football followers as valued drivers of data-driven decisions and innovation, some recent work commissioned by the National Football League (NFL) is relevant to contextualize this case study. Harrison and Bukstein (2013), in their study of approximately 400 women fans from two NFL teams, determined that women during a professional football-sporting event most valued the following:

- Hygiene
- Health and healthier food options
- Kids
- Apparel choices

Figure 11.1   Montana State University Gridiron Girls football clinic.

These findings are important to this chapter's discussion about data-driven decision-making with regard to female sport fans and spectators for at least two reasons. First, it is important to gather reliable data from a demographic that is nearly 50% of the audience both at live-action events and watch parties both in their private homes and at sports bars. Second, the findings are important because some organizations make mistakes with demographic market research and the application of these data findings when developing marketing, sales, and promotion planned events. The findings earlier allow innovation to take place on the business side in terms of corporate partners strategizing to position, activate, impact, and engage a given product, signage, or other inventory.

In addition to the business side, there is the physical culture side of sport business. Women themed clinics have become more and more popular over the last decade with sport organizations. Thus, market research before and after an event comprised of women can only be positive for innovation and new business development (Figure 11.1).

Case Study: Montana State University Gridiron Girls Football Clinic

On April 1, 2016, Montana State University's football program held a women's football clinic for Bobcats women fans. This initiative was led by head football coach Jeff Choate and director of football operations

Brittney Johnson. Brittney was the primary business leader and this case study is a great example of the growing trend of female fan and spectator passion for football. Before organizing "Gridiron Girls," Brittney based the development and direction of this one-day camp in part on market research in 2014 that she assisted with professional sport teams in Boise, Idaho (Idaho Stampede basketball and Idaho Steelhead hockey), the Minnesota Vikings, and the aforementioned NFL report on women (see Harrison and Bukstein, 2013). Prior to April 1, 2016, there had never been a clinic specific for women football fans and spectators at Montana State University. Approximately 120 women paid $50 to attend this clinic in Bozeman, Montana, and the overall response was outstanding especially considering that there was no major promotion or advertising about the event.

The difference maker at Montana State was that even without specific data from Montana State women football fans, the "Football 101" clinic theory with women was not the strategic approach. "Football 101" is typically an approach that assumes that women know little to nothing about football. The focus at Montana State was on interaction and allowing the women to engage in the physical culture of football with actual members of the collegiate team at Montana State. The event took place from 6:30 to 10:30 p.m. on a Friday. From 6:30 to 7:45 p.m., the women competed with respect to who could throw the football the farthest, punt the ball the farthest, and run offensive and defensive drills with the head coach and Bobcat football players. From 7:45 to 10:00 p.m. in the stadium club facility, the women clinic attendees were allowed access to the head coach and the players to discuss how players dress head to toe and other topics related to their academic, athletic, and social identities as football players. A fashion show culminated the event with the football jerseys and other athletic apparel being the focal point of women and fashion (Figure 11.2).

Finally, there was one last innovative aspect of the Montana State women's football clinic—the gift bag that featured a T-shirt and one other small but major item. Sponsored by Scholar-Baller®, each woman received a key chain that empowers them in a small but impactful way. The key chain reads: "Thinkwoman/Montana State University Bobcats: We Know the Game." The key chain was a huge hit according to Brittney Johnson: "The women loved the key chain and some of

Figure 11.2   Participants in the Montana State University football clinic.

them even grabbed more than one for their spouses, friends or children" (personal communication, April 2, 2016).

This case study echoes some of the themes from the review of literature presented earlier in this chapter. The Gridiron Girls clinic gave the women an active voice and moved beyond the "shrink it and pink it" approach that was a stalemate with many women fans over the years. While no intercept and Live Analytics data were collected at the first-ever Bobcat women's football clinic, plans are being made to gather data from the women that attended and participated in the first event and Live Analytics will be implemented during year 2 of the clinic. Anecdotally, one woman interviewed by a local television station in Bozeman was asked how she felt about the event and stated, "this (football clinic for women) is a dream come true."

Conclusions: Beware of the Affinity Trap and Involve Various Cultural Groups

To bring this chapter full circle, we begin this section with another quote from innovator Bill Veeck (2001) on his own underestimation of the female demographic and its impact on his organization: "The number of women at Cubs games increased gradually until on

July 6, 1930, 30,476 women jammed Wrigley Field, causing late-arriving patrons with tickets to be turned away at the gate. On that day, 51,556 people packed themselves into a ballpark that normally accommodated 40,000" (Veeck and Linn, 2001, p. 21). Veeck also recalled, "The biggest mob of women I ever saw in one place in my life. We got in all we could: thousands were left outside. Regular patrons couldn't get to their seats. There was no room for the men who paid. The streets were blocked…traffic was at a standstill" (Veeck and Linn, 2001, p. 21).

To recap, research and the analytics process drive innovation and new business development. This chapter has encouraged innovation through the strategic approach of paying attention to various demographic groups. In particular, the female demographic at sport events has proven to be a great investment in the area of market research. In terms of best practices, some professional sport organizations have been successful with women fans and spectators. The Washington Redskins, Baltimore Ravens, Los Angeles Rams (formerly St. Louis), Minnesota Vikings, Orlando Magic, and San Antonio Spurs are just some of the teams that "get it" when it comes to understanding the women fan demographic. These teams have invested in market research, intercept surveys, women themed nights at games, and female affinity clubs that host social and athletic events centered on the game or physical fitness. The analytics approach of these various teams enables each organization to make decisions based on "facts only" versus a hunch or armchair assumption about what women want and how they want to be engaged as followers of sport teams.

However, sport organization leaders approaching affinity groups when it comes to gender or race must embrace the reality that not all tribal groups want to be swept with the same cultural brush about their particular fan identity. Two examples of this happened in 2015, one in MLB and one in the NFL. Both the Washington Nationals and Tampa Bay Buccaneers collected data on the female fan demographic and based on these data developed a few initiatives to connect with women fans. Both teams received backlash after having themed nights centered on wine, fashion, and social mixers. While these three things have been supported by evidence in various studies in scholarly and practitioner research (e.g., see Harrison et al., 2016), there is a major lesson to be learned about market research and analytics. "Numbers Never Lie" is a cultural cliché, but there are limitations with numbers as they tell us *what* but do not explain *why*. Thus, content is king, but positioning is queen (Harrison, 2015). Each of these two teams received negative criticism from avid women fans because the positioning of the "Ladies Night" promotional materials was too overt in the overall representation of women as fans. To empower women based on the data points was clearly the goal of the Nationals and Buccaneers, and there is nothing inherently flawed in being proactive about engaging women with a sport organization's brand. The takeaway is that maybe some focus groups that trial tested how Ladies Night promotional and print media materials were positioned before they went public might have decreased some of the negative criticisms as feedback could have been given on how some women perceived the advertisements. In the final analysis, sport teams (and college athletics programs) and brands of any type should systemically collect data on women and other types of affinity groups. The key is to implement practical initiatives that are subtle, nuanced, and authentic versus stereotypical and shallow. This is the goal of market-driven research and analytics—to drive innovation and create new categories, niches, and lanes of business to increase the ROI and return on objectives of sport properties, corporate partners, and other stakeholders.

References

Balfour, K. L. (2012). Life in the stands: The experiences of female Major League Baseball fans. (Unpublished doctoral dissertation.) University of Tennessee, Knoxville, TN.

Branch Jr., D. D. (1995). Tapping new markets: Women as sport consumers. *Sport Marketing Quarterly, 4*(4), 9–12.

Brennan, B. (2009). *Why She Buys: The New Strategy for Reaching the World's Most Powerful Consumers.* New York: Crown Business.

Clark, J. S., Apostolopoulou, A., and Gladden, J. M. (2009). Real women watch football: Gender differences in the consumption of the NFL Super Bowl broadcast. *Journal of Promotion Management, 15*(1/2), 165–183.

Davenport, T. H. and Kim, J. (2013). *Keeping Up with the Quants: Your Guide to Understanding and Using Analytics.* Boston, MA: Harvard Business Press.

Dickson, P. (2012). *Bill Veeck: Baseball's Greatest Maverick.* New York: Walker & Company.

Dixon, M. A. (2002). Gender differences in perceptions and attitudes toward the LPGA and its tour professionals: An empirical investigation. *Sport Marketing Quarterly, 11,* 44–54.

Farrell, A. O., Fink, J. S., and Fields, S. K. (2011). Women's sport spectatorship: An exploration of men's influence. *Journal of Sport Management, 25,* 190–201.

Fink, J. S., Trail, G. T., and Anderson, D. F. (2002). Environmental factors associated with spectator attendance and sport consumption behavior: Gender and team differences. *Sport Marketing Quarterly, 11*(1), 8–19.

Gantz, W. and Wenner, L. (1995). Fanship and the television sports viewing experience. *Sociology of Sport Journal, 12,* 56–74.

Gauthier, R. and Hansen, H. (1993). Female spectators: Marketing implications for professional golf events. *Sport Marketing Quarterly, 2*(4), 21–26.

Gosling, V. K. (2007). Girls allowed? The marginalization of female sport fans. In J. Gray, C. Sandvoss, and C. L. Harrington (Eds.), *Fandom: Identities and Communities in a Mediated World* (pp. 251–260). New York: University Press.

Greenwell, T. C., Fink, J. S., and Pastore, D. L. (2002). Perceptions of the service experience: Using demographic and psychographic variables to identify customer segments. *Sport Marketing Quarterly, 11*(4), 233–241.

Harrison, C. K. (2015). What cultural diversity can teach sports about engagement. *SportBusiness Journal,* October 26–November 1, 2015, pp. 15–15.

Harrison, C. K. and Bukstein, S. (2013). Occupational mobility patterns: A case study of leadership and access in the National Football League. *Sociology Mind, 3*(4), 264–267.

Harrison, C. K., Bukstein, S., McPherson Botts, G., and Lawrence, S. M. (2016). Female spectators as customers at National Football League games. *International Journal of Sports Marketing and Sponsorship, 17*(2), 172–200.

James, J. D. and Ridinger, L. L. (2002). Female and male sport fans: A comparison of sport consumption motives. *Journal of Sport Behavior, 25*(3), 260–278.

Jones, K. (2008). Female fandom: Identity, sexism, and men's professional football in England. *Sociology of Sport Journal, 25*(4), 516–537.

Lough, N. L. and Kim, A. R. (2004). Analysis of socio-motivations affecting spectator attendance at women's professional basketball games in South Korea. *Sport Marketing Quarterly, 13*(1), 35–42.

Markovits, A. S. and Albertson, E. (2012). *Sportista: Female Fandom in the United States.* Philadelphia, PA: Temple University Press.

Pope, S. (2010). Female fandom in an English 'sports city:' A sociological study of female spectating and consumption around sport. (Unpublished doctoral thesis.) University of Leicester, Leicester, U.K.

Pope, S. (2012). The meaning of sport in the lives of 'hot' and 'cool' female fans of football and rugby union. In K. Toffoletti and P. Mewett (Eds.), *Sport and Its female Fans* (pp. 81–98). London, U.K.: Routledge.

Pope, S. (2013). The love of my life: The meaning and importance of sport for female fans. *Journal of Sport and Social Issues, 37*(2), 176–195.

Pope, S. and Williams, J. (2011). Beyond irrationality and the ultras: Some notes on female English rugby union fans and the 'feminised' sports crowd. *Leisure Studies*, *30*(3), 293–308.

Sutton, B. and Sutton, D. (2015). Where to find answers about management, brand strategy. *Sport Business Journal*, December 14–20, 23.

Sutton, W. A. (1994). Communicating with women in the 1990s: The role of sport marketing. *Sport Marketing Quarterly*, *3*(2), 9–20.

Toffoletti, K. and Mewett, P. (2014). *Sport and Its Female Fans*. London, U.K.: Routledge.

Veeck, B. and Linn, E. (1962). *Veeck—As in Wreck: The Chaotic Career of Baseball's Incorrigible Maverick*. Chicago, IL: University of Chicago Press.

Veeck, B. and Linn, E. (2001). *Veeck—As in Wreck: The Autobiography of Bill Veeck*. New York: G. P. Putnam's Sons.

Wann, D. L., Waddill, P. J., and Dunham, M. D. (2004). Using sex and gender role orientation to predict level of sport fandom. *Journal of Sport Behavior*, *27*(4), 367–377.

Wenner, L. A. (2013). Reflections on communication and sport: On reading sport and narrative ethics. *Communication and Sport*, *1*(1–2), 188–199.

12

TALENT ANALYTICS

Utilizing Analytics to Evaluate Employee Performance

BRANDON MOYER

Contents

What Are Talent Analytics? 188
Sport Business Applications of Talent Analytics 190
   NBA Sales DNA Initiative 191
   The Aspire Group "WHOPPPP" Talent Analytics Model 193
How Other Industries Successfully Use Talent Analytics 194
Utilizing Talent Analytics during the Employee Hiring Process 196
The Future for Talent Analytics 198
References 199

Imagine you are the "director of sales and service" for a professional sport franchise and want to begin rewarding the "top performers" on the ticket sales staff. What is the process for evaluating the most valuable employee? Are performance evaluations solely based on total revenue generated by each salesperson or are there other metrics that can be, and should be, used? In the past, ticket sales representatives were often rewarded and evaluated based on standard metrics such as total calls, total meetings set, total seats sold, and total revenue generated. Companies are beginning to better understand the importance of investing resources into developing sophisticated metrics that can be used to analyze employee performance. In a recent study, 78% of large companies (with 10,000 or more employees) rated human resource (HR) and talent analytics as "urgent" or "important;" however, only 7% of those companies rated their organizations as having "strong" HR data analytics capabilities (Bersin et al., 2014).

Innovative companies are beginning to understand how to measure the highest level of employee productivity and engagement and reward those individuals with the resultant goal of retaining, and maintaining, top employee talent. This chapter provides a holistic overview of "talent analytics" and details how talent analytics are utilized in the sport business industry to evaluate candidates, measure employee performance, and predict future employee success. In addition, examples from other industries will be introduced in hopes of providing insight into what sport business organizations can do to more effectively and efficiently analyze the employee workforce.

What Are Talent Analytics?

The term "talent analytics" refers to an "organization's use of big data to assess talent, both at the candidate and current employee levels, and should help to shape a more productive and efficient workforce" (Furst, 2015). The six uses of talent analytics that companies leverage, from the most simple to the more sophisticated, include (1) human-capital facts, (2) analytical human resources, (3) human-capital investment analysis, (4) workforce forecast, (5) talent value model, and (6) talent supply chain (Davenport et al., 2010).

1. *Human-capital facts*: Human-capital facts are the simplest form of talent data and include metrics such as head count, labor utilization, turnover, recruiting practices, and appropriate staffing levels. Companies should carefully analyze these metrics to measure appropriate staff levels. For example, the ticket sales staff for the 2016 Golden State Warriors should not be as large as the ticket sales staff for the 2016 Philadelphia 76ers. Due to the success of the Golden State Warriors on the court, it is assumed that tickets are easier to sell and more in demand than the tickets for the 76ers. Additionally, the Golden State Warriors game day service staff will need to be larger to accommodate the average of 19,596 home game fans compared to the Philadelphia 76ers average of 14,820 home game fans. Ineffectively monitoring these metrics can result in overstaffing (which will cost the organization millions in terms of unnecessary dollar

spent) or understaffing (which can lead to lost sales and an unhappy fan base).

2. *Analytical human resources*: The concept of analytical human resources refers to the segmentation of HR data, which is used to gain powerful insights into specific departments or functions. Analytical HR data integrate individual performance data with HR process metrics such as time and cost in addition to outcome metrics such as engagement and retention. Ticket and sponsorship sales departments throughout the sport business industry rely on these automated systems to deliver real-time data on both individual sales representatives and sales departments. With these metrics, sport organizations are able to identify successful sales representatives and monitor those employees who need to improve in specific areas.

3. *Human-capital investment analysis*: Human-capital investment analysis helps to measure which actions have the greatest impact on business performance. Sysco, a leader in this area, began analyzing its workforce by looking at dimensions such as supervisor effectiveness, diversity, and quality of life. Sysco discovered that highly satisfied employees generate higher revenues, and employee satisfaction can also be linked to lower HR cost, higher employee retention, and superior customer loyalty. Sysco has been able to identify actions made by management that have the greatest impact on the company and can implement immediate improvements if satisfaction scores dip. By implementing this analysis, the company has saved nearly $50 million in hiring and training costs (see Davenport et al., 2010).

4. *Workforce forecast*: The concept of workforce forecast analyzes turnover, succession planning, and business opportunity data to identify potential shortages. In 2010, when LeBron James and Chris Bosh "took their talents to South Beach," the team quickly sold all available season tickets. This led to the Miami Heat eliminating the entire season ticket sales staff, claiming the team "no longer require[d] a season ticket sales team to sell tickets" (Talalay, 2010). While at the time this seemed to benefit the team's short-term financial health, it is unhealthy to make such drastic organizational decisions

based on an unstable player market. Implementing better workforce forecasts can help organizations make decisions with both short-term and long-term strategic business objectives in mind.

5. *Talent value model*: The talent value model addresses employee motivation to remain with a company. Uses for the talent value model include calculating what an employee values most and creating a model to accommodate those values. Sales managers offer incentives for improved performance or to boost productivity; however, if these incentives are not individualized and applicable to the sales force, the incentives may not be as effective. Offering a 3-day beach vacation package to the Miami Dolphins sales staff may not be as effective as offering the same package to the Boston Celtics sales staff, due to the geographical location of both organizations.

6. *Talent supply chain*: The talent supply chain helps companies make real-time decisions about talent-related demands. Applications of these metrics include forecasting inbound call center volume and allowing hourly staff members to leave early based on those forecasts, as well as predicting "Black Friday" sales based on previous days sales to adequately staff a retail store. For sport organizations, this application can help provide game day staff, specifically those working in a team retail store, with a better understanding of fan spending habits on game day. If 80% of the in-stadium retail merchandise is sold 2 hours before the start of the game, a team is better able to adequately staff the high traffic stores and can begin to send part-time hourly employees home within an hour after the game starts to provide cost savings. These business decisions require timely and accurate data combined with rigorous analysis.

Sport Business Applications of Talent Analytics

The following case studies pertain to the different applications of talent analytics within the sport business industry. The NBA Sales DNA initiative was designed to measure and compile data on sales executives across the league. The Aspire Group acronym

"WHOPPPP" is what The Aspire Group uses to measure candidates during the hiring process and provide employees with feedback on performance.

NBA Sales DNA Initiative

On the court and on the field, many teams incorporate the Caliper profile test to assist with candidate recruiting decisions. The Caliper profile is an instrument used for evaluating personalities, using over 25 personality traits that relate to job performance. Teams have found that by using the Caliper profile, athletes who were recommended based on personality outperformed those who were not. This same Caliper profile has also proven to be accurate when evaluating sport business candidates.

In the book *How to Hire & Develop Your Next Top Performer*, Caliper's Chairman Herb Greenberg and President Patrick Sweeney state that the internal motivation factors are what distinguish the top 20% of the sales force from others (Greenberg and Sweeney, 2013). Greenberg and Sweeney divide the sales DNA into three essential traits:

1. *Empathy*: The ability to sense a customer's needs while not sympathizing to the point of losing objectivity
2. *Ego drive*: The desire to persuade others for self-enhancement
3. *Ego strength*: The ability to take rejection and turn it into motivation

The Caliper model stresses the importance of hiring based on potential, not experience. The model also provides sales managers with instructions on how to mold employees into superstars:

- *Spend more time with your best salespeople*: This does not encourage favoritism; rather, it advises you to accept that you will not be able to change people. This recommends you study your top representatives, as this will help you hire those who resemble them. Your best representatives will appreciate the attention.
- *Don't let the empty seat haunt you*: Be patient when hiring your next sales representative. It is easy to make a rash decision and

settle for a mediocre candidate when you are short-staffed. Instead, always make sure you are recruiting top talent (whether you are hiring or not) and keep that prospect list accessible.

- *Forget about mediocre experience*: The Caliper model recommends that all things equal, hire a candidate with more experience. The model also poses the question: what good is a candidate with 5 years of mediocre experience?
- *Look inside*: Only 30% of employees are in roles that match their personality and skill set. Remember to look at executive assistants or other support roles within your organization, as these prospective candidates are easily accessible and could be your next top performer.
- *Beware of interview stars*: These are the people incredibly focused on making a great first impression. They *really* want you to like them, which may spell disaster, especially in a sales role.
- *Get a second opinion before hiring someone like you*: It is in your nature to like people who are like you, but this bias can lead to hiring for the wrong reasons. Different roles require different DNA (see Hanson, 2012).

During the 2014 MIT Sloan Sports Analytics Conference, the sales DNA model was discussed as it relates to selling corporate sponsorships. The proposed model used data to provide powerful insights into the drivers of individual sales performance and explain the variance within sales teams. The sales DNA model took individual performance metrics and combined them with survey and behavioral data. The model found correlations, which industry executives were able to use to better understand the intrinsic personality traits needed to be successful at selling sponsorships. The study found there was a variance of three to four times when comparing the high performance sales representatives to the low performance sales representatives. The study also found that extroversion, specifically assertiveness, is the personality trait most important to be successful in a sales role and that empathy is the personality trait most inversely correlated with sales performance.

Interestingly, the McKinsey Sales DNA model also showed that despite people not openly admitting that rewards drive success, the behavioral data and survey data revealed that salespeople enjoy the idea of their pay being contingent on performance (McKinsey & Company, 2014).

The Aspire Group "WHOPPPP" Talent Analytics Model

Established in 2008 by Bernie Mullin, The Aspire Group is a global sport and entertainment marketing company. The Aspire Group has partnered with over 130 sports and entertainment properties who rely on Aspire to drive revenue, attendance, and enterprise value growth through ticketing, marketing, and revenue enhancement, strategic consulting and research, and sports investment optimization. In an interview in 2011, Bernie Mullin was asked what characteristics he believes make successful sport business leaders. He responded, "At Aspire, we look for WHOPPPP in our candidates and all of our managers and staff" (Apostolopoulou, 2011):

> *W*ork ethic
> *H*onesty, integrity, character
> *O*penness to learning
> *P*assion for sport business and sales
> *P*roduction (results)
> *P*ositive attitude
> *P*otential for leadership

Once The Aspire Group attracts the best talent in the industry using the "WHOPPPP" benchmark, company leaders continue the development of employee talent with the "Raise Your Game" development program. The context for each Raise Your Game session focuses on the situation that the sales and service consultants for The Aspire Group face each day. Within the first 24 months of employment, each employee at The Aspire Group is educated, evaluated, and required to demonstrate application of the first 24 Raise Your Game sessions. The 24 Raise Your Game sessions are divided into four segments and include sessions covering a wide range of topics, such as ticket revenue yield management, motivation and values, understanding sport finance, and intelligent e-marketing. The Aspire Group believes that the demonstrated application of the Raise Your Game sessions is what prepares employees for long-term success as sport business executives.

How Other Industries Successfully Use Talent Analytics

This chapter has discussed ways in which successful sport organizations leverage different talent metrics to better understand, and measure the success of, their sales force. However, the sport business industry can learn from other industry leaders such as Google, Best Buy, Harrah's, Sysco, and other companies that understand exactly how to obtain the highest level of productivity, engagement, and retention of their best talent and then replicating that success (Davenport et al., 2010).

Harrah's Entertainment is a well-known entertainment company that employs analytics to select the customers the company believes provide the greatest potential profit. Harrah's also extends this approach to hiring decisions, using insights provided by data to put the right employees in the right jobs and creating models that help with delivering the correct number of staff members to deal with front desk, phone calls, and other service locations. Harrah's uses analytics to hold itself accountable for knowing what matters most to its staff because the company understands a content staff leads to a more productive staff. For example, Harrah's used analytics to measure the effects of its health and wellness programs on the company's bottom line. The company found that preventive-care visits have increased, lowering employee urgent-care visits and saving the company millions of dollars over the past year (Davenport et al., 2010). The following are other examples how industry leaders utilize talent analytics:

- Recently, a financial service company countered a 60% turnover rate by using predictive talent analytics to better staff its offices. This resulted in the organization being able to reduce turnover by over 30% and experience savings of over $5 million after 1 year of initiative implementation (Roberts, 2014).

- There are many companies that base hiring decisions on stellar academic records from prestigious schools. However, AT&T and Google, both leaders in the technology industry, have developed a quantitative analysis metric that indicates the ability to take initiative is a far better predictor than academic records (Davenport et al., 2010).
- Companies like Starbucks, Best Buy, and Limited Brands emphasize the importance of employee engagement. With analytics-based research, these companies can identify the value of a 0.1% increase in employee engagement, and for Best Buy, that value equates to more than $100,000 in increased operating income (Davenport et al., 2010).
- A leading medical device company experienced high attrition from its highly paid sales representatives as poor performers were not retained. Utilizing predictive talent analytics, the company shaved attrition by 1% and experienced over $30 million in savings (Roberts, 2014).

Laszlo Bock, Google's vice president of people operations, explained that the company does not "use performance data to look at the averages but to monitor the highest and lowest performers on the curve. The lowest five of performers we actively try to help as we know we have hired talented people and we want them to succeed" (Davenport et al., 2010). Google takes a unique approach to human resources, referring to the function as "people operations." The people management decisions at Google are handled by a "people analytics team," which reports directly to Google's vice president of operations. This operation produces dashboards and insightful correlations based on feedback from employee surveys. The overall goal is to substitute the use of opinions with data and metrics.

Most have heard of Google's free food, playful work environment, and 20% free time, but it is important to note these initiatives are all data driven. A few of Google's data-driven people management practices include a retention algorithm, predictive modeling, improvement of diversity, calculating the value of top performers, and a hiring algorithm. Google's retention algorithm proactively and successfully predicts which employees are going to be the most difficult to retain. Google uses these data to approach and encourage management to act before it is too late. The predictive model uses "what if" analysis to improve forecasts of upcoming people management issues and opportunities. The company's diversity initiative uses analytics to solve problems related to employee interactions and inclusiveness. For example, the people analytics team conducted analysis to identify the root causes of weak diversity recruiting, retention, and promotions. The results that were produced in hiring, retention, and promotion were dramatic and led to actionable business strategies (Sullivan, 2013).

Utilizing Talent Analytics during the Employee Hiring Process

Having a productive and effective sales force starts with attracting the best talent and candidates who fit the organization. This process starts with assessing what makes the current employees successful in their current role and using that model to hire for open positions. These models can be used to evaluate candidates, implementing data-driven decision-making as opposed to merely using intuition or "gut" to make hiring decisions. As a recruiter, using different skill-set and personality assessments can help to group candidates into different categories. When creating these models, it is important to realize that just because one or two traits correlate with success, it does not mean those are the only things to look for during the job candidate evaluation process.

Once the right people have been found for the job, it is important to follow and track employee careers to determine whether they should move through the ranks or stay where they are in terms of the position and person "fit." Taking advantage of these metrics can help company leaders make better decisions about employees and help these leaders better determine the cause of turnover and attrition. For example, an HR manager can use these data to see that an employee who starts as an inside ticket sales representative is twice as likely to stay with the company for over 3 years if this sales representative is promoted within 9 months of initial hire. Knowing this threshold can help HR managers discuss career paths with employees, which can help with retention of top talent.

CURRENT ANALYTICS ISSUE: PROTECTING AN ORGANIZATION'S ANALYTIC PROPERTY

**By Noel Paul and Stephen Winter, attorneys
at global law firm Reed Smith LLP**

Teams are increasingly using proprietary data analysis and statistical tools—what we will call "analytic property"—to gain a competitive advantage on the field and in their business operations. As demonstrated by the theft of analytic property from the Houston Astros by an employee of the St. Louis Cardinals, details of which surfaced in 2015, sport teams and their vendors or consultants are as vulnerable to the disclosure of proprietary information and technology as *Fortune* 500 companies, whether through cyber-attacks, trade-secret espionage, rogue or departing employees, or human error. There is no fail-safe method to protect analytic property, but a suite of legal tools and internal controls can reduce an organization's risk of loss.

As a starting point, organizations should ensure that employees understand the importance of maintaining the confidentiality of sensitive data and protecting the integrity of computer systems. An employee handbook can help initiate this conversation with new hires and memorialize protocols for handling analytic property and confidential data. These protocols could restrict access to analytic property and other confidential data to select employees, mandate password changes, or prohibit the use of outside storage devices. Organizations could identify their chain of command in the event of a data breach and clearly identify contact information for decision-makers and skilled information technology (IT) personnel. These basic steps cannot be emphasized enough: for example, a 2016 "Market Pulse Survey" published by SailPoint found that 20% of respondents at private companies would sell their passwords to a third party, 42% could access corporate accounts after leaving their job, 33% downloaded software without telling IT, and 70% uploaded sensitive information to the cloud (SailPoint, 2016).

Potential legal tools for protecting analytic property include nondisclosure agreements, which can be designed to prevent key employees, including employees with access to proprietary data, from using confidential information without permission. Organizations can require third-party consultants, vendors, and independent contractors to execute similar agreements. Additionally, most states permit companies to use noncompetition agreements to prevent, on a temporary basis, employees with unique or proprietary knowledge from working for competitors.

Organizations may also be able to shift their risk of financial loss if their confidential or proprietary information is disclosed. For example, organizations often can include contractual provisions in agreements with third parties (like vendors and consultants) to require those third parties to pay an organization's legal fees and other expenses if the third party is at fault for loss of information or a data breach. Organizations also may be able to purchase specialized forms of insurance to help minimize their financial losses.

The Future for Talent Analytics

From the examples provided, it is clear that some sport organizations are properly beginning to integrate talent analytics into hiring and retention decisions. However, many sport organizations have a lot to learn about the proper uses of talent analytics as it pertains to attracting, motivating, and retaining the best talent in the industry. Modeling sport organizations similar to how Google approaches its human resources would, as Google says, allow human resources to "bring the same level of rigor to people-decisions that we do to engineering decisions" (Sullivan, 2013). Using some of Google's past and current people management practices previously mentioned, such as the algorithms, modeling, and diversity practices, will help sport organizations drastically improve their HR departments. Similarly, leaders in other industries can improve talent analytics operations by emulating the overall team concept prevalent in many sport organizations. Davenport (2014) explains, "[W]hen companies do employ human resource analytics, their approaches are not as sophisticated as those of sports teams, and thus far they have been applied only to individuals. But assessing employees by investigating group performance with or without a particular person's presence could be a valuable technique" (p. 11). Sharing best practices will enable sport organizations and other innovative companies to optimize the impact of talent analytics strategies.

References

Apostolopoulou, A. (2011). Industry insider: Bernard J. Mullin. *Sport Marketing Quarterly, 20*(4), 192–196.

Bersin, J., Houston, J., and Kester, B. (2014). *Talent Analytics in Practice.* Deloitte University Press, London, U.K.

Davenport, T. (2014). What businesses can learn from sports analytics. *MIT Sloan Management Review*, 10–13.

Davenport, T., Harris, J., and Shapiro, J. (2010). Competing on talent analytics. *Harvard Business Review*. Retrieved from https://hbr.org.

Furst, J. (2015). Using talent analytics to increase your bottom line. Retrieved from http://www.business.com.

Greenberg, H. and Sweeney, P. (2013). *How to Hire & Develop Your Next Top Performer.* McGraw-Hill Companies, Inc, New York.

Hanson, D. (2012). 6 tips for hiring your next sales all-star. Retrieved from http://www.forbes.com.

McKinsey & Company. (2014). Sales DNA in sports sponsorships. *Sloan MIT Sports Analytics Conference,* New York.

Roberts, G. (2014). Making the business case for predictive talent analytics. Retrieved from http://www.digitalistmag.com.

SailPoint. (2016). Market pulse survey: Weak security practices leave organizations exposed. Retrieved from http://www.sailpoint.com.

Sullivan, J. (2013). How Google is using people analytics to completely reinvent HR. *ERE Media*. Retrieved from http://www.eremedia.com.

Talalay, S. (2010). With season tickets sold out, Heat fires season sales staff. *Sun Sentinel,* July 30, 2010.

13

DATA VISUALIZATION AND DATA-DRIVEN STORYTELLING

RYAN SLEEPER

Contents

Visualization Is the Key to Understanding Data............................201
INSIGHT: A Strategic Framework for Data Visualization 202
Data-Driven Storytelling 204
    Know Your Audience 205
    Introduce the Value of Data Visualization 206
    Keep It Simple 207
    Retell an Old Story 209
    Use Comparisons 211
    Balance Data and Design 213
Additional Insights for Finding and Sharing
Actionable Stories 213
References 218

Visualization Is the Key to Understanding Data

We live and work in a world where 2.5 quintillion bytes of data are created every day (IBM, 2015). To express the magnitude of this number, a quintillion equals 1 billion squared—or a 1 with 18 zeroes behind it. The technology available to collect and store so much data is evolving at such a pace that the figure referenced earlier is likely to be quite outdated by the time you read this chapter. To add perspective to the exponential growth of data, 90% of the world's data have been created in the last 2 years alone (IBM, 2015).

To this point in the book, our team of authors has discussed data related to ticket sales, CRM, direct marketing, digital marketing, branding, and even talent. There is a common link among all of the case studies: visualization is the tactic used to make sense of the data, discover insights, and communicate actions that will help improve their respective organization's bottom line.

It is not a coincidence that data visualization is the common thread among analytics topics, leagues, and teams. Visualization is one of the most powerful tools for data, with benefits including

- Reduced time to insight
- Increased accuracy of insights
- Improved stakeholder engagement

One of the reasons data visualization is so powerful is preattentive processing, or the human ability to rapidly process certain visual properties subconsciously. There are several visual attributes that humans are able to process before dedicating their attention to understanding the environment. These attributes include, but are not limited to, size, color, density, motion, and orientation (Healey and Enns, 2012).

To demonstrate, here is one famous example adapted from Stephen Few (2004) that uses a simple preattentive attribute to help the end user process data more efficiently.

First, count the nines in the raw data:

18703296268231594813597401486523049874125368952140368786 29302145852147

Now, count the nines again, this time with the nines encoded in bold in the sequence:

18703296268231594813597401486523049874125368952140368786 29302145852147

By taking advantage of one of the most basic preattentive attributes, color/shading, end users are more

- Efficient when counting the number of nines
- Confident that the correct number of nines were identified
- Engaged with this view as compared with the row of raw numbers

INSIGHT: A Strategic Framework for Data Visualization

In the past 7 years as a data visualization consultant and content marketer, I have personally designed and constructed hundreds of data visualizations. To this day, I have yet to build a dashboard that *every*

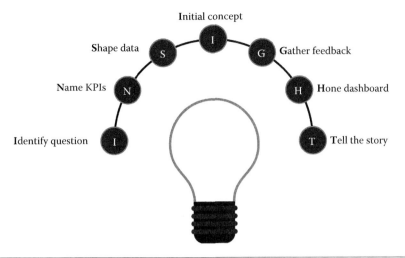

Figure 13.1 INSIGHT framework.

viewer thought was perfect. In my view, data visualization is a form of art, and with that, its value is in the eye of the beholder. Due to the limitless possibilities and variables that are involved with creating a data visualization, I have developed the "INSIGHT framework" as a tool for maximizing the chances a data visualization will be well received (Figure 13.1):

- *Identify the business question*: One of the most common pitfalls in data visualization is trying to answer too many questions in one view. By prioritizing what the data visualization will answer, you are able to keep the view simple and make it clear to the end user what stories they should be looking for in the dashboard.
- *Name the key performance indicators (KPIs)*: These KPIs should all help answer the business question that the data visualization is attempting to address and analyze.
- *Shape the data*: In order to work with the data in a data visualization software program, data should be prepared in advance in tabular form. For the most flexibility, each column header should represent a unique field, with subsequent rows representing every entry for each of those fields.
- *Initial concept*: Get an idea documented, even if it is simply a sketch of the direction you are planning to take. By not committing too much time to the initial concept, you will have the flexibility to pivot based on stakeholder input.

- *Gather feedback*: Ask end users what they think of your initial concept and if they believe it will meet their needs. This step helps instill some stakeholder ownership during the design process so key stakeholders are more likely to support the final product.
- *Hone the dashboard*: This is your opportunity to incorporate stakeholder feedback and finalize the data visualization.
- *Tell the story*: Finally, you are ready to distribute the dashboard and allow the stories in the data to begin making an impact.

Data-Driven Storytelling

Storytelling has been used in every culture as a means of engaging audiences and communicating everything from entertainment to moral values. Stories work because humans are wired to retain stories, not independent facts or statistics. In fact, after a presentation, 63% of attendees remember the stories presented, while just 5% of attendees remember the individual statistics (Heath and Heath, 2007). This is particularly relevant to data, where business insights risk being lost amidst a deluge of increasingly large sets of numbers.

Think about each number in a data set being the equivalent of a word in an English dictionary. One could argue that there are technically many great stories in a dictionary—or more precisely—the ingredients for many great stories. There are "ingredients" for stories like *Harry Potter*, *The Wizard of Oz*, and *To Kill a Mockingbird*. The challenge is that there are over one million words in the English language. The world needs translators like J.K. Rowling, L. Frank Baum, Harper Lee, and other great authors to bring those words to life. Numbers are the same way. It does not matter how skilled analysts are at collecting data or how much technology has improved to store that data, unless an organization has the translators who can find and communicate the stories within the data.

Much like stories such as *Harry Potter*, data storytelling includes three critical elements: (1) plot or story lines, (2) characters, and (3) narrative. With data, story lines can be considered the insights, KPIs and contextual metrics can be considered the characters, and the narrative is data visualization (or the style in which the insights are communicated). Data storytellers are encouraged to consider the following tips when creating a data visualization.

Know Your Audience

There are not many tactics that are going to improve the chances of your data visualization making a difference around the workplace more than the first tip: *know your audience*. In fact, the tips listed here follow a natural progression, and it is no coincidence that knowing your audience is discussed first. Before you create a single chart that you intend to share, putting some thought into who that chart will be seen by will dramatically improve your data visualization.

Knowing your audience goes a long way toward making a connection and maximizes the chances that your end user will understand and happily adopt the reports that you have created. Get it wrong, and you risk permanently damaging the chances of getting your visualizations off the ground around the office. Think about this the next time you undertake a visualization project. Here are just a few examples:

- If your dashboard is intended for a C-level audience, keep your work simple and direct. Focus on KPIs and the progression toward goals. You may also consider creating dashboards that are optimal for being saved as PDFs to improve the chances that your work is either attached to an email or printed out and handed to a C-level executive.
- If your work is intended for fellow analysts and you are using a data visualization software that allows you to create interactive dashboards, build in interactivity that allows the analysts to find their own stories in the data. Filters, dashboard actions, and parameters are some of the most useful techniques for achieving this objective.
- If your dashboards are public facing and you are attempting to make your data visualization connect with a mass audience, do not be afraid to be creative and innovative and even incorporate some graphic design elements. Believe it or not, data are thought of as "dry" to some. Leveraging some of these tactics will make your visualizations much more shareable.

Data visualization is not a one-size-fits-all practice. Knowing your audience will help you prioritize and make the most of the data-driven storytelling tips to follow.

Introduce the Value of Data Visualization

This chapter introduced the concept of preattentive processing and how it helps reduce the time to insight. To maximize the likelihood of your data visualizations being adopted, it can be important to explicitly introduce the value of data visualization to your end users. The example earlier is a good exercise for achieving this goal. The following data visualization is one more example that uses reports you likely see every day. First, take a look at Figure 13.2, which is an example of a traditional business report in Excel spreadsheet format with no conditional formatting. See how many seconds (minutes, maybe?) it takes you to determine the top three values in the table.

Next, take a look at the same data, encoded in different shades of gray scale. In this case, the higher the sales, the darker the gray. Now count how many seconds it takes you to identify the three highest values (Figure 13.3).

State	Consumer	Corporate	Home Office	Small Business
Alabama	$45,552	$20,843	$52,121	$8,191
Arizona	$27,301	$24,988	$47,291	$20,817
Arkansas	$3,422	$66,134	$11,505	$15,128
California	$229,462	$533,151	$284,838	$114,270
Colorado	$10,172	$38,715	$40,599	$42,725
Connecticut	$10,495	$15,899	$6,469	$9,439
Delaware	$3,543			
District of Columbia	$13,883	$77,912	$29,628	$97,446
Florida	$97,118	$180,177	$151,107	$75,207
Georgia	$23,659	$65,199	$68,561	$38,920
Idaho	$26,695	$28,374	$6,100	$34,474
Illinois	$94,632	$316,880	$152,589	$103,696
Indiana	$23,368	$105,152	$26,336	$39,225
Iowa	$8,548	$33,265	$42,301	$4,587
Kansas	$12,160	$54,677	$21,785	$21,964
Kentucky	$3,139	$32,534	$22,182	$2,905
Louisiana	$13,355	$34,178	$3,734	$15,344
Maine	$28,039	$23,837	$25,106	$20,139
Maryland	$49,992	$19,570	$44,077	$11,266
Massachusetts	$48,764	$111,533	$28,661	$39,494
Michigan	$93,473	$88,627	$79,004	$63,490
Minnesota	$25,044	$82,637	$60,135	$22,673
Mississippi	$9,916	$2,488	$17,883	$11,631
Missouri	$9,110	$61,384	$15,001	$28,207
Montana	$4,613	$5,293	$9,104	$10,394
Nebraska	$67	$18,131	$11,804	$10,920

Figure 13.2   Crosstab data visualization—basic.

State	Consumer	Corporate	Home Office	Small Business
Alabama	$45,552	$20,843	$52,121	$8,191
Arizona	$27,301	$24,988	$47,291	$20,817
Arkansas	$3,422	$66,134	$11,505	$15,128
California	$229,462	$533,151	$284,838	$114,270
Colorado	$10,172	$38,715	$40,599	$42,725
Connecticut	$10,495	$15,899	$6,469	$9,439
Delaware	$3,543			
District of Columbia	$13,883	$77,912	$29,628	$97,446
Florida	$97,118	$180,177	$151,107	$75,207
Georgia	$23,659	$65,199	$68,561	$38,920
Idaho	$26,695	$28,374	$6,100	$34,474
Illinois	$94,632	$316,880	$152,589	$103,696
Indiana	$23,368	$105,152	$26,336	$39,225
Iowa	$8,548	$33,265	$42,301	$4,587
Kansas	$12,160	$54,677	$21,785	$21,964
Kentucky	$3,139	$32,534	$22,182	$2,905
Louisiana	$13,355	$34,178	$3,734	$15,344
Maine	$28,039	$23,837	$25,106	$20,139
Maryland	$49,992	$19,570	$44,077	$11,266
Massachusetts	$48,764	$111,533	$28,661	$39,494
Michigan	$93,473	$88,627	$79,004	$63,490
Minnesota	$25,044	$82,637	$60,135	$22,673
Mississippi	$9,916	$2,488	$17,883	$11,631
Missouri	$9,110	$61,384	$15,001	$28,207
Montana	$4,613	$5,293	$9,104	$10,394
Nebraska	$67	$18,131	$11,804	$10,920

Figure 13.3 Crosstab data visualization—highlight table.

Much less time, right? This is the power of data visualization. The second image is called a highlight table, and as you can see, even the simplest forms of data visualization can lead to much shorter time to insight. You can easily create highlight tables in Excel or any data visualization software, and I have found they are a great way to introduce the power of data visualization. In the tips to follow, I will introduce more complex data visualizations and data-driven storytelling techniques, but many times, you have to start by helping your audience understand why data visualization plays an important role in analytics.

Keep It Simple

I didn't have time to write a short letter, so I wrote a long one instead.

—**Mark Twain**

I love this quote from Mark Twain because the author is putting a value on prioritizing content. It is said that Twain's complete bibliography remains incomplete due to the volume of his writings, and the fact that they were often completed for obscure publishers—not to mention under a variety of pen names. However, even as one of the most prolific writers of all time, the quote earlier implies that Twain believed the most effective storytelling was done by being clear and concise.

This same idea applies to data visualization and is the basis for the next data-driven storytelling tip: *keep it simple.* One of the most common mistakes I see in dashboard layout and design is attempting to create silver bullet dashboards that provide every possible answer to the business question at hand—all in a single view. One of the things I find myself saying often is "just because it is possible does not mean you should do it." Data visualization software makes it extremely easy to add filters, charts, and widgets to a dashboard, but there is a point when too many options for the end user actually detracts from your visualization, making it harder for the story in the data to emerge.

Less is almost always more when it comes to communicating your data-driven story. To help me prioritize what I share within a single view of my data visualizations, I often stick to a general rule of thumb of including no more than 12 widgets. I adopted this threshold from Google Analytics, which allows you to add a maximum of 12 widgets to a custom dashboard. The 12 widgets include charts, titles, and filters. To help illustrate this tip, let's take a look at one of my most-viewed data visualizations, which was built using four widgets: one title, two filters, and one chart (Figure 13.4).

I credit the success of this visualization to its simplicity. The visualization is simple in several different ways:

- It asks and answers a single question.
- It offers only two filters—one with two options, the other with four.
- The story is communicated using a single chart.

The story in this visualization is almost impossible not to understand—and understand very quickly—by analysts and nonanalysts alike. By keeping it simple, you maximize the effectiveness of your data-driven storytelling across the largest audience possible.

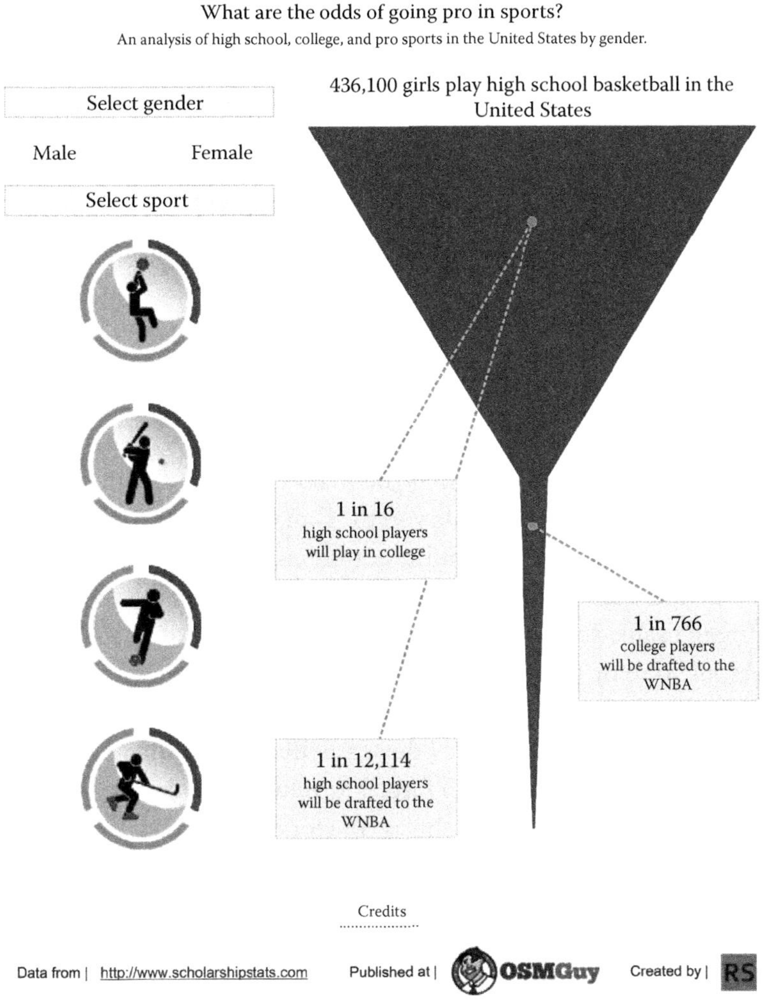

What are the odds of going pro in sports?

An analysis of high school, college, and pro sports in the United States by gender.

Figure 13.4 Odds of going pro data visualization.

Retell an Old Story

I think we have all been there—a few months after introducing a new reporting format, you may start to get the suspicion that stakeholders are not opening your weekly or monthly updates. Or perhaps they are being opened, but that fresh new reporting format that was so well received upon release is no longer being used to gain as much insight as it is capable of providing. This may be due to rarely fluctuating KPIs, a lack of understanding on how to leverage the reporting, or maybe simply a shortage of time to dedicate to finding stories in the data.

The nature of many KPIs used to answer business questions is that they are steady and/or predictable. Think about a website's bounce rate and average time on site—for better or worse—two KPIs often used to measure a company's ability to engage website visitors. Without a site redesign, these two KPIs may never fluctuate more than 5%–10% over the entire life of the website. Once you have seen these numbers two or three times, they become stale, and end users become less and less motivated to use the reporting you created for them. In the same vein, you may have KPIs that follow a seasonal pattern, and your end users know exactly what to expect from week to week or month to month; this may make them indifferent to large spikes or dips spotted in your reporting.

The good news is that data visualization provides a means for reengaging your audience by retelling your data-driven stories in new ways. Data visualization tools enable you to (1) make your dashboards more aesthetically pleasing, (2) add filters and functionality that allows end users to find their own stories in the data, and (3) make your reporting more usable so that finding insights is more intuitive for the user.

As just one of infinite possible examples of retelling an old story, I took a shot at reimagining sports standings. As a data visualization evangelist, I view data tables as the least effective way of communicating data. As a sports fan, I am forced to view tables almost exclusively to see how my team is doing; this is true for every league: NFL, NBA, Major League Baseball (MLB), NHL, and Major League Soccer (MLS), among others. Tables have been used to track league standings in European soccer leagues for over a hundred years. European soccer leagues even affectionately call their standings "The Table." To show how much more value visualizing sports standings adds compared to the traditional table, I recreated the table in North America's MLS. First, take a look at the traditional standings from MLS (for the 2014 season) (Table 13.1).

Now, take a look at the data visualization created using the same data (Figure 13.5).

In addition to Table 13.1, you now have the ability to do the following in a single view:

- Filter between Conference and Supporters' Shield standings.
- See how many games each team has played and how many games they have remaining.

Table 13.1   Major League Soccer Standings—Table

	POINTS	GAMES PLAYED	PPG	W	L	T
Eastern conference						
Kansas City	35	20	1.75	10	5	5
District of Columbia	34	19	1.79	10	5	4
Toronto	26	17	1.53	7	5	5
New York	24	20	1.2	5	6	9
New England	23	19	1.21	7	10	2
Philadelphia	23	21	1.1	5	8	8
Columbus	23	20	1.15	5	7	8
Chicago	20	19	1.05	3	5	11
Houston	19	20	0.95	5	11	4
Montreal	14	19	0.74	3	11	5
Western conference						
Seattle	38	18	2.11	12	4	2
Salt Lake	32	20	1.6	8	4	8
Colorado	30	20	1.5	8	6	6
Dallas	29	20	1.45	8	7	5
Los Angeles	27	17	1.59	7	4	6
Vancouver	27	19	1.42	6	4	9
Portland	24	20	1.2	5	6	9
Chivas	23	20	1.15	6	9	5
San Jose	20	18	1.11	5	8	5

- Hover over every single game to see the teams that played and the final score.
- Determine the number of points (wins and draws) it will take for each team to make the playoffs.
- Gain better understanding into how teams are performing relative to each other.

The same principles used to add value to this century-old story can be used to reinvigorate your reporting at work, engage your audience, and maximize the impact of your data visualization.

Use Comparisons

Comparisons are useful in data visualization because they help you avoid the dreaded question, "So what?" As powerful and simple as they are, fundamental chart types such as bar charts and line graphs are often

Major League Soccer Standings :: 2014 Season
A visualization of the MLS results table by Ryan Sleeper.

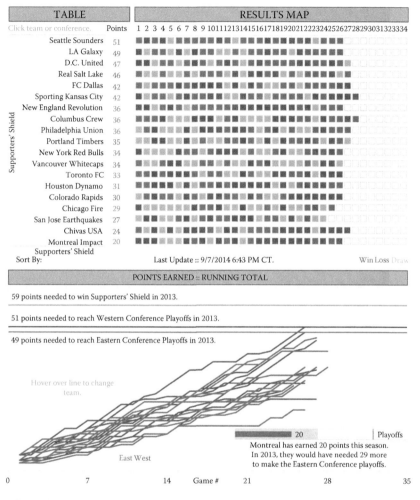

Figure 13.5 Major League Soccer standings—data visualization.

used in a vacuum. Lack of context makes it difficult for an end user to understand, engage, and eventually take action. By building comparisons into the visuals themselves, you help the stories in the data emerge, even if you are not physically present to explain those stories. There are several ways to add these types of comparisons into your work, including

- *Index scores*: Not only do these scores provide comparisons, but they also help normalize the data.

- *Sparklines*: This chart type is essentially a small set of line graphs that allow you to view high-level trends across several metrics at the same time.
- *Bullet graphs*: This chart type is a variation on the bar chart that adds context in the form of comparison points such as prior period performance and/or goals.
- *Small multiples*: This chart type is similar to a table of visualizations instead of raw numbers, which allows the end user to compare results across several different dimensions and/or measures at the same time.

For an example of small multiples, view the following visualization that featured a set of small multiple stadium maps to help illustrate how the cost of ticket prices changed throughout the 2015 MLB World Series (Figure 13.6).

Balance Data and Design

Data should always be the heart of any data visualization. Obviously, you cannot have a data visualization without data—and it is imperative that the data are accurate and honest. If I had to choose one element of a new data visualization to focus on between its data or design, I would make sure the data are right first every single time. That being said, without making some design considerations, your data visualization is doomed to falling short of its full potential. Balancing data and design is another tip that I take personally because I often hear criticism from data purists that do not see the value in complementing the data with an appealing design. My opinion on the topic stems from Seth Godin's principle of being remarkable—which means your work is good, unique, and interesting enough to cause the audience to make a remark about it. In today's age, making a remark means sharing it on social media, or in a corporate setting, it may mean passing your story along to key company decision-makers.

Additional Insights for Finding and Sharing Actionable Stories

The purpose of data visualization is to find and share actionable stories that are based in quantitative evidence. To make your insights

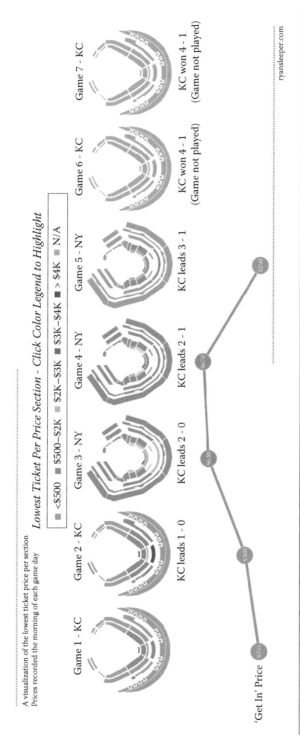

Figure 13.6 The cost of attending the 2015 world series. (Data from StubHub.)

actionable, this means sharing them with the most relevant and, many times, largest audience possible. If you fail to provide your data stories in a well-packaged design, you drastically minimize the chances of your work spreading, and thus, it is consumed and acted on by fewer people. To help illustrate, I stripped out most of the design elements in the following "viz" that compares "your salary" with the salaries of MLB players. In this dashboard, the end user can enter their own salary and compare it to the salary of any MLB player across several different hitting and pitching statistics. The data are extremely fascinating—if not depressing—but I believe it is the design that helped this become my most shared data visualization on Twitter to date.

Before (Figure 13.7)
After (Figure 13.8)

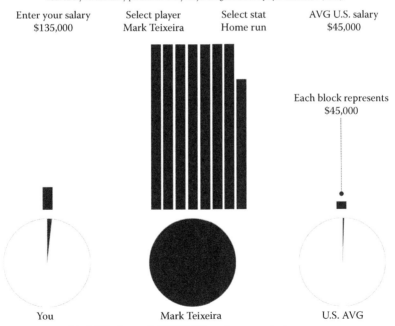

How long would it take you to earn as much as a MLB player?
Your salary vs. the salary per stat for every Major League Baseball player last season (2013).

Enter your salary	Select player	Select stat	AVG U.S. salary
$135,000	Mark Teixeira	Home run	$45,000

Each block represents
$45,000

You   Mark Teixeira   U.S. AVG

Mark Teixeira made $7,708,333 per home run last season.
At your current salary, it would take you 685 months (57.1 years) to earn that.
It would take the average worker 2056 months (171.3 years) to make that.

Figure 13.7 "Before" Major League Baseball salary viz.

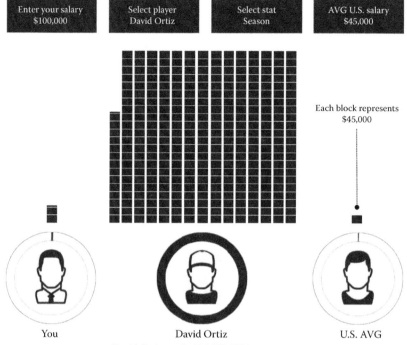

How long would it take you to earn as much as a MLB player?
Your salary vs. the salary per stat for every Major League Baseball player last season (2013).

Enter your salary	Select player	Select stat	AVG U.S. salary
$100,000	David Ortiz	Season	$45,000

Each block represents
$45,000

You   David Ortiz   U.S. AVG

David Ortiz made $14,500,000 last season.
At your current salary, it would take you 1740 months (145.0 years) to earn that.
It would take the average worker 3867 months (322.2 years) to make that.

Figure 13.8   "After" Major League Baseball salary viz.

I want to point out that the only elements in this entire design that required any Adobe Photoshop or Illustrator skills are the three icons, and even the foundation of those were built using stock Illustrator files from iStockPhoto.com. There are plenty of techniques you can use to balance data and design, even if you have never used Photoshop or Illustrator.

Design enhancements you can make immediately without any graphic design experience include the following:

- *Put some thought into your color selections*: Choose simple color palettes and "mute" them by adding some transparency.
- *Switch up the typography*: Choose some unique fonts that are easy to read and visually appealing. Make key elements different font sizes to denote your priorities in a subtle way.

- Lay out your data visualization in a way that guides the end user through your story and provides some spacing for each element.
- *Pay attention to the details*: This is perhaps the easiest way to make your data visualization stand out. Whenever end users think a data visualization looks really good, but they cannot quite explain why, it is because of the details. Clean your dashboards up by minimizing lines. Add borders to marks such as bars and shapes. Add some transparency to show overlapping values.

These are just a few of probably dozens of tiny changes you can make to your work. These details add up quickly, resulting in a polished, professional piece that will maximize the odds of your story being shared.

In an ideal scenario, the stories in your data are so compelling that the stories are self-explanatory. Unfortunately, this is rarely the case. What is worse—at times we are so close to the data and insights that we do not realize that our data visualizations need additional context in order to be properly understood. If we want our data visualizations to be understood, elicit sharing, and eventually cause action, we need to help tell the data-driven stories in our dashboards. The following are a few ways to help complement data visualization with written anecdotes:

- *Do not neglect the setup*: By adding some context in the form of a title and description to open a dashboard, you clearly communicate what your work is about. This works even better if you are able to ask a single question that the rest of your dashboard attempts to answer. This guides end users and helps them find the answer on their own, giving the discovered insights a better chance to stick with your audience.
- *Use "in-line insights" as a tactic for communicating analysis of the data*: This can be achieved by simply building a text box into your data visualizations that provides real estate to add your own thoughts about your findings and recommendations.
- *Do not underestimate the power of annotations*: Many times, the practice of data visualization is extremely dependent on context. For example, if I am analyzing web analytics data and

see a large spike in traffic, I would like to know what offline tactics may have driven the spike. I may be able to see that the spike was a result of an increase in direct traffic, but without input from advertising stakeholders, I will not be able to fully explain the trend. Perhaps our company launched a television commercial during the time frame in question. These are the pieces of context that you should add in the form of annotations.

Finally, if you have a chance to be in the room when an end user interacts with your data visualization, try to—literally—tell a story. When working to spread an idea, there is nothing quite like proposing a recommendation, through the power of data-driven storytelling, with the quantitative evidence of a data visualization to back you up.

References

Few, S. (September 4, 2004). Tapping the power of visual perception. Message posted to https://www.perceptualedge.com.

Healey, C. G. and Enns, J. T. (2012). Attention and visual memory in visualization and computer graphics. *IEEE Transactions on Visualization and Computer Graphics, 18*(7), 1170–1188.

Heath, C. and Heath, D. (2007). *Made to Stick: Why Some Ideas Survive and Others Die.* New York: Random House.

IBM. (2015). What is big data? Available at: IBM.com.

14

TEACHING A SPORT BUSINESS ANALYTICS COURSE

MICHAEL MONDELLO

Contents

Introduction 219
    Overview of Analytics in the Sport Business Industry..............220
Course Content..223
    Analytics Integration..223
    Sport Business Applications..224
    Content Delivery..225
    Class Assignments..225
    Exam 227
Concluding Thoughts 227
References 228

Introduction

Historically, most data arrived in the form of static tables. However, data today are now becoming increasingly dynamic, streaming, and augmented with information previously unavailable. Moreover, data today are more complex and available at different layers or hierarchies. Given these changes in the data analytics community, teaching a sport business analytics course presents several unique challenges warranting consideration when designing how the course will be delivered. Therefore, while certainly not exhaustive, this chapter will include personal observations, experiences, and suggestions to assist sport business/management faculty currently teaching a sport business analytics course or planning to teach a similar course in the future.

When I started teaching in the Business School at the University of South Florida (USF) in 2012, the college changed leadership with the appointment of a new dean. One major initiative the college embraced was a focus on analytics and creativity. This focus was implemented for two reasons. Companies in the sport business industry were looking for talented students trained with analytical skills. In addition, this college-wide initiative could potentially differentiate USF from other universities and help position the college as a training ground for students interested in developing an analytics-based skill set that would help lead to sustained career success after graduating from USF.

The current job market within the sport business space has expanded and evolved. Consequently, there are numerous employment opportunities for individuals trained with analytical tools. Thus, this became the focus of the sport business analytics class I teach at USF. For example, professional sport teams are now relying on analytical techniques to confirm or predict answers to questions related to ticket pricing strategies, sponsorship return on investment (ROI), and customer relationship management (CRM).

While acknowledging there are job opportunities for those individuals interested in careers involving player analytics to either build team rosters (general manager) or measure player performance (player development), the class content in my course is structured to introduce students to analytical techniques assisting the business side of the organization. Recent business trends suggest this demand in the workforce will continue to be strong as more companies recognize the value of analytically trained employees.

Overview of Analytics in the Sport Business Industry

In today's complex business environment, analytics has become an important tool for organizations. For example, as noted by Phillipps (2013) in a research study involving more than 100 surveys and in-depth interviews with senior management representing 35 companies worldwide, 96% of the respondents indicated analytics would become more important in operating their organizations in the next 3 years. This suggests organizations should continue to develop innovative strategies to successfully implement analytical techniques within a company's business model or potentially risk losing valuable market share.

According to a 2013 Chief Information Officer (CIO) survey, analytics and business intelligence was ranked as the number one technology priority. Seventy percent of the CIOs rated mobile technology as the most disruptive force for the next decade. Consequently, business schools must be responsive to these new demands to ensure the success of graduates. Moreover, McKinsey estimated the talent shortage for business analysts at nearly 1.5 million analysts by 2018 (Wilder and Ozgur, 2015).

Devoted baseball fans are probably familiar with the phrase a "five-tool" player. Recently, an interesting picture was painted when informally surveying individuals working in the sport business industry about the skill set they are looking for in hiring people for analytics jobs. Collectively, sport business leaders are looking for five specific skills and noted finding job candidates possessing all or most of these skills has been increasingly difficult. The skills for the "five-tool" analytics candidate are as follows:

1. Can they ask the right questions?
2. Do they have the research ability to gather data?
3. Do they have the technical skills to correctly model the data?
4. Once they have run the models, can they correctly interpret the results?
5. Do they have the ability to communicate the results to multiple audiences?

Industry professionals struggle to find students trained with each of these skills, particularly the ability to communicate data-driven findings. While some students have strong quantitative statistical skills, they may struggle asking the right question or being able to effectively report findings. Similarly, while other students have the ability to introduce great ideas and questions, they might have difficulty using the correct statistical technique to generate valid solutions. Consequently, this skill-set gap is a point of emphasis within the sport business analytics class I teach.

This emphasis on data has encouraged developments in CRM strategies. Technological growth within various digital and mobile platforms assists in making data collection easier and more seamless than previously possible. Concurrently, sport consumers have higher expectations for smart, relevant marketing. With increased competition within teams, rival leagues and other entertainment options, attracting and retaining consumers are especially important for the long-term viability of professional sport teams. Subsequently, understanding the consumer and furthermore establishing a deeper relationship based on individual consumer preferences are vital.

As the sport industry develops over the next few years, teams must offer individualized marketing strategies or run the risk of losing valuable clientele. Therefore, for a sport business to succeed in one-to-one marketing, these organizations must invest in CRM solutions and strategies based on accurate data. Consumers, especially sports fans, possess unique attributes and consequently should be targeted and marketed to reflect these characteristics. A strong CRM strategy can help a team acquire a complete and authentic perspective of each consumer and ultimately understand how to effectively communicate with each consumer. Within the last decade, the sport business industry has identified the importance of developing a greater understanding of consumers combined with improved capabilities of serving consumers. Previous research has consistently demonstrated the passion and loyalty sports fans have toward their favorite team(s). While sport organizations have a general sense of their fans, only a select few can realistically proclaim they possess a true 360° understanding of their customers. By engaging fans more effectively, sport organizations believe they can acquire, strengthen, and retain customer relationships. Data analytics, technological advances, and system integration will all be important factors as sport teams look to expand their customer views to 360°.

Historically, there are inherent challenges exacerbating the ability to accurately assess the financial position of North American professional sport teams, with the biggest factor being that teams have been predominately private organizations and subsequently are under no legal obligation to disclose financial information. To investigate how the adoption of sport business analytics has changed in recent years, Troilo et al. (2016) explored the implementation of business analytics in the North American professional sport industry and specifically how these tools increased revenues. Several key findings emerged. First, the adoption of analytics convinced managers their revenues were growing. Second, while the industry expected growth rates of 3%, the use of analytics correlated with growth rates twice as large at 7.2% in the year following adoption. Finally, all three primary elements of analytics (collection, analysis, and planning) correlated with increased revenue, whereas managers only associated analysis with perceived incremental revenue growth.

Course Content

Analytics Integration

One of the initial challenges instructors often face when delivering a new course is deciding the specific content to deliver. Oftentimes, a simple Internet search will return dozens of example course outlines providing a myriad of ideas and suggestions to help develop a new class. Similarly, another way to borrow ideas is to ask professional colleagues to share their best practices and course outlines. However, in developing a sport business analytics course, my personal online search failed to generate any documents providing guidance or suggestions on how the course could be structured. Furthermore, despite having a fairly extensive professional network of academic scholars, to my knowledge, nobody was delivering a sport business analytics course at the time. Consequently, I developed the initial course based on readings, other analytics courses, and personal experience.

Because the majority, if not all, of the graduate students enrolled in my class are typically being initially introduced to analytics, several scholarly articles operationalizing analytics from different perspectives are included to provide a foundational understanding. This strategy has also been successful when I teach sport finance classes. For example, before introducing students to sport finance applications, initial classes focused on finance basics including financial statement analysis, capital budgeting, valuation, time value of money, and how to raise capital. Likewise, the initial class content for the sport business analytics course introduces students to broader analytics concepts prior to examining how sport organizations can specifically benefit from this type of analysis.

Among the assigned readings is the work by Davenport and Harris (2007), which classified analytics as descriptive, predictive, or prescriptive. Descriptive analytics incorporates gathering and organizing of data and then detailing the qualities of the data. While this analysis has merit, descriptive analytics provides no information about why something happened or what may occur in the future. Next, predictive analytics incorporates previous data to assist with forecasting future trends. While predictive analytics are useful for predicting trends, one cannot assume any explicit cause/effect relationship. Therefore, prescriptive analytics including methods such as optimization and experimental design provide an additional layer of analysis by offering suggestions for implementing solutions to problems.

Some additional sources proven to be good supplemental material include articles from *MIT Sloan Management Review*, *Harvard Business Review*, and *Forbes*. There is no textbook assigned, but I anticipate this will change as more resources like this book are developed. Following the introduction of analytics, but before moving to the sport and entertainment applications, students are presented with a conceptual overview and application of two key statistical tools: Excel and multiple regression. At a minimum, the students should be comfortable with basic Excel techniques and be able to work with a data set manipulating the data into various formats and tables. Similarly, in class we use these data sets to run regression models illustrating the relationships between select independent variables and a dependent variable.

Students have their own laptop computer, which allows them the opportunity to work on these analytics tools during class time. In addition to actually developing the models, there is also an emphasis placed on correctly reading and more importantly interpreting the regression outputs. Several short videos illustrating regression concepts and techniques are included. Experience has shown even if students were previously introduced to either one or both of these statistical tools in earlier classes, much is lost because they are usually not applying these skills regularly. Finally, while other statistical tools would be appropriate to cover in a sports analytics course, given the limitation of time in the semester and the focus of the course, Excel and regression are the two primary tools emphasized.

Sport Business Applications

Similar to the ways other graduate course content is built, the material covered in the class is a result from feedback solicited from several stakeholders. First, concerted efforts are made to ask industry practitioners what skill set an ideal candidate working in analytics would possess and then address these areas in the course. Next, students themselves are asked to provide specific feedback both during and after the semester related to the concepts and techniques covered in class. Finally, asking colleagues teaching similar classes for examples on how they teach could introduce a technique/assignment that would serve all students well. Because the class has only been taught for 3 years (as of the 2015–2016 academic year), changes will be made annually with respect to content delivery and exams in the class. Each of these aspects will be discussed later in this chapter in greater detail.

Content Delivery

Following the introduction of analytics and a brief primer on Excel and regression, the class focuses on the application of analytics in helping the business side of a sport organization. Among the topics covered are CRM techniques, ticketing strategies including both variable and dynamic pricing, sponsorship ROI, social media analytics, scenario analysis (including SWOT analysis and forecasting), and database marketing. Typically, the aforementioned topics are delivered via lecture with data and examples from an actual sport organization. Experience has demonstrated that students will become far more engaged in learning the content when examples presented are actual existing organizations and not fictional. One area of sport business research continuing to remain elusive centers on how to accurately quantify the expected ROI involving corporate sponsorships. For example, both national and local brands may elect to engage as a corporate sponsor involving arena/dashboard signage, activation, program advertisements, or even naming rights of the facility. Considering some companies allocate 25% or more of their sponsorship budgets toward sport events, understanding how the return on this invested capital impacts the overall bottom line of the organization is significant (Meenaghan and O'Sullivan, 2013).

Class Assignments

Class content is focused almost exclusively on introducing analytics and techniques/topics impacting the business side of sport organizations. As previously noted, each student has his or her own laptop computer with Excel software, which creates an opportunity to work on data sets and problems. We also introduce students to how regression can help build predictive models for ticket sales. Another in-class exercise introduces the students to building a ticket demand model

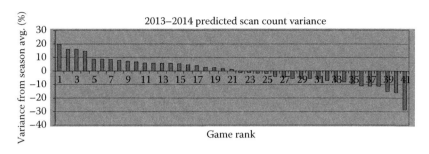

Figure 14.1   Data-driven analysis of predicted ticket demand.

using regression analysis. In this scenario, the dependent variable can be modified based on whether we are interested in forecasting single game tickets, group sales, or total gate revenue. Understanding game-by-game demand allows the sales team to create miniticket packages with evenly dispersed demand. Intuitively, teams can forecast demand based on previous trends or educated guesses, but the regression models inform us objectively of the full season schedule ranking. The two main objectives of the demand model should be to maximize top-tier game revenue in order to offer lower prices on less desirable games and to increase ticket renewal rates through ticket exchange utilization and price advantages. Figure 14.1 captures this ticket analytics information.

Finally, as the importance of customer retention continues to be a top priority for sport organizations, the ability to assign ratings to these customers based on renewal probabilities can offer excellent insights. An example of this customer retention approach and analysis is provided in Tables 14.1 and 14.2.

Table 14.1   Customer Retention Ratings and Renewal Probability

STAR RATING LOGIC		AVERAGE RENEWAL PROBABILITY	
STAR RATING	RENEWAL PROBABILITY (%) (GREATER THAN)	DECEMBER 2014	JANUARY 2015
1	0	0.3188	0.3511
2	40	0.5209	0.5285
3	60	0.7269	0.7398
4	80	0.8642	0.8628
5	90	0.9438	0.9434

Table 14.2   Customer Star Ratings and Percent of All Ticket Plans

STAR RATING	PERCENT OF ALL TICKET PLANS (%)	
	DECEMBER 2014	JANUARY 2015
1	1	0
2	1	1
3	8	6
4	24	24
5	51	53
Other	15	15
Total	100	100

Weekly homework assignments are integrated to serve as a check-point for both the students and the course instructor. Although students are allowed to work in pairs on the homework in my class, they are also strongly encouraged to work independently initially to ensure they understand the material. These homework assignments serve as examples of problems they will encounter on the exam.

Exam

Because the class I teach is delivered over 12 weeks, there is one final exam divided into two parts. The first part of the exam consists of terms/definitions and short-answer questions. The content is pulled from readings, lectures, and discussions. Philosophically, anything included on a test will be discussed previously in class. This is clearly communicated the first day when the syllabus is introduced. Once a student completes the first part of the exam, they then return to their seats and will open an e-mail from me containing a file with problems to solve. These problems are consistent with the class homework in terms of scope and difficulty. Students are only allowed to have Excel open during this second exam component. Once students finish the second part of the exam, they e-mail the completed answer file back to me.

Concluding Thoughts

The growth and scope of sport business analytics have presented a new opportunity for those teaching sport business/management classes to consider adding this course within their respective curriculums either as an elective or required course. The content could be delivered equally successfully at the undergraduate or graduate levels. There are also several ways the faculty can enhance their ability to develop a course. First, there are a myriad of sport business analytics conferences including the popular MIT Sloan Sports Analytics Conference that routinely sells out every March. On a much smaller scale, USF hosted the university's inaugural sports analytics conference in 2015, and given the enthusiasm of the attendees, the conference will become an annual event. Although data and technology can introduce additional complexity and complications to an organization, sport management programs should consider these challenges as opportunities. Academic programs adequately preparing their alumni to embrace analytics and creativity will position the program to industry decision-makers as a leader and innovator in sport business training. Furthermore, when students observe firsthand how research can be a useful tool for identifying and providing viable solutions to sport organizations, these students can then continue this practice upon entering the sport business industry after graduating.

References

Davenport, T. and Harris, J. (2007). *Competing on Analytics*. Boston, MA: Harvard Business School Press.

Meenaghan, T. and O'Sullivan, P. (2013). Metrics in sponsorship research— Is credibility an issue? *Psychology & Marketing, 30*(5), 408–416.

Phillipps, T. (2013). The analytics advantage: We're just getting started. Deloitte Touche Tohmatsu Limited, London, U.K.

Troilo, M., Bouchet, A., Urban, T. L., and Sutton, W. A. (2016). Perception, reality, and the adoption of business analytics: Evidence from North American professional sport organizations. *Omega, 59*, 72–83.

Wilder, C. R. and Ozgur, C. O. (2015). Business analytics curriculum for undergraduate majors. *INFORMS Transactions on Education, 15*(2), 180–187.

Index

A

AB-InBev, 160, 164–165
AFC Ann Arbor, 152–153, 155–156
Analytics, definition, 2–3
Analytics department
  data aggregation, 112
  efficiency and effectiveness
    postgame guest and member
      relations survey, 109, 111
    sales representative
      introduction e-mails,
      109–110
  public data
    digital advertising, 113, 115
    raising ticket prices, 112–114
    using maps, 115–120
  responsibilities, 108
  simple analysis, 111
Archtics, 57
Aspire Group
  collegiate athletics ticket sales, 70
  FRMCs, 70–71
  marketing and revenue
    enhancement, 70
  sports investment
    optimization, 70

strategic consulting and
  research, 70, 74
TiMSS, 70
  acquire new fans, 72
  8-point philosophy, 71–72
  Georgia Tech FRMC, 73–87
  grow casual fans, 72
  plan, 71, 87–88
  retain avid fans, 72
  road map, 71
  tactics, 73
The Aspire Group "WHOPPPP,"
  193–194
Average resale price (ARP),
  42–46, 50

B

Bar-coded tickets, 91
Brand equity
  Aaker's model, 93
  component elements, 90
  CRM, 101–102
  economic value, 91
  fan engagement, 94
  fan equity, 93–96
  guiding theory, 95–96

marketing premium metrics,
    94–95
NFL teams, 99–101
social media equity, 94, 96

C

California State University
    Northridge (CSUN), 178
Caliper profile, 191
"Cameron Crazies," 135
Chief Information Officer (CIO)
    survey, 220–221
Class assignments
    business impact, 225
    customer retention ratings and
        renewal probability, 226
    customer star ratings and ticket
        plan percentage, 226–227
    homework assignments, 227
    ticket analytics information, 226
    ticket demand model, regression
        analysis, 225–226
CLV, *see* Customer lifetime value
Concessionaire Delaware North
    Sportservice, 17
Content delivery, 225
Cost per thousand impressions
    (CPM), 165–166
CRM, *see* Customer relationship
    management
Customer lifetime value (CLV)
    MLB team, 97–99
    season ticket buyer behavior, 91–93
    season ticket holder management,
        90–91
    six-figure levels, 90
Customer relationship management
    (CRM), 3
    accountability and efficiency, 68
    Archtics, 57
    authentic and meaningful
        relationships, 62

brand equity, 101–102
database, 60–61
definition, 55
description, 56
development, 221
ExactTarget, 57
and fan engagement, 11–14
Fan Interactive case study,
    67–68
goal, 61
information tracking, 57–60
Marketo, 57
Microsoft Access, 56
Microsoft Dynamics CRM,
    56–57, 65–67
Oracle Eloqua, 57
Salesforce.com, 56
software, 55
targeted campaigns, 62–65

D

Data collection, 4
Data, definition, 2
Data-driven analytics process, 3
Data-driven business decision, 2
Data-driven storytelling
    balance data and design, 213
    comparisons, avoid dreaded
        question, 211–213
    crosstab data visualization,
        206–207
    data collection and storage, 204
    know your audience, 205
    odds of going pro data
        visualization, 208–209
    retell an old story, 209–211
    traditional business report, 206
    Twain's bibliography, 207–208
Data manipulation, 224
Data visualization
    actionable story sharing
        and findings

Adobe Photoshop/
  Illustrator, 216
"After" Major League Baseball
  salary, 215–216
"Before" Major League
  Baseball salary, 215
design elements, 215
design enhancements, 216–217
quantitative evidence, 213, 218
self-explanatory, 217
written anecdotes, 217–218
benefits, 202
data-driven storytelling
  balance data and design, 213
  comparisons, avoid dreaded
    question, 211–213
  crosstab data visualization,
    206–207
  data collection and
    storage, 204
  know your audience, 205
  odds of going pro data
    visualization, 208–209
  retell an old story, 209–211
  traditional business
    report, 206
  Twain's bibliography,
    207–208
preattentive processing,
  202, 206
strategic framework, 202–204
Descriptive analytics, 223
Digital and mobile media,
  160, 163
Digital marketing
  digital advertising and
    retargeting, 145–146
  fan acquisition, 150–153
  online interaction, 153
  robust digital analytics
    acquisition data, 154
    audience data, 153–154
    behavioral data, 154

conversion, 154–155
customer relationship
  management, 155
ticket sales, 146–148
videos, 148–150
Digital ticketing, 24
Direct marketing
advertising, 121–122
e-mail subject line direct
  marketing test, 123–125
margin of error calculation, 123
vs. mass marketing, 119
methods of, 119
parts of, 121
sales creative direct marketing
  test, 125–129
test and learn, 122
#DukeMBBStats data visualization
  platform
awareness, 136
built-in social media
  functionality, 133
"Cameron Crazies," 135
core function, 133
cross-marketing, 134
effort, 134–135
"For Duke, by Duke" mantra, 132
GoDuke.com, 133, 136
performance-related stats and
  analytics, 137
player tracking analytics, 132
revenue-generating
  initiatives, 134
unique label, 134
Dynamic pricing, 9, 43, 102

E

Economic downturn, 161
E-mail subject line direct marketing
  test, 123–125
Employee hiring process, 196
Ethos, 168–169

F

FanCap app, 13
Fan engagement
  brand equity, 94
  CRM, 11–14
  female demographic, 179
Fan Interactive case study, 67–68
Fan profiles, 137–142
Fan Relationship Management
  Centers (FRMCs), 70–71
Father's Day themed direct
  marketing test, 125–129
Feedback gathering, 204
Feedback process, 170
Female demographic
  data driven analysis, 177–179
  fan engagement, 179
  Ladies' Day, 174
  market research and live
    analytics, 176–177
  Montana State University
    Gridiron Girls Football
    Clinic, 180–182
  "Numbers Never Lie," 184
  reliable data gathering, 180
  scholarly and practitioner
    research, 183–184
  strategic approach, 183
  women as sport event spectators,
    174–176
"Football 101" approach, 181

G

Game-day revenue categories, 2
Gate revenues, 69
Georgia Tech FRMC
  acquire new fans, 81–82
  customers retention, 77–79
  data capture techniques, 82–84
  growing fans, 79–81
  key lead categories, 86

long-term relationship, 85
performance analytics, 87–88
personalized communication
  strategy, 84–85
postgame surveys, 75
postseason surveys, 75–76
robust research strategy, 76
Get-in price (GIP), 42, 50

H

The halo effect, 168
Harrah's Entertainment, 194
HR data segmentation, 189

I

In-line insights, 217
INSIGHT framework, 202–204
Intellectual property, 160
Iron Duke, 139–140

J

Johnson, Brittney, 180–181

K

Key performance indicators (KPIs),
  7, 137, 203, 205, 210

L

Logical approach, 177

M

Magic Money, 30–32
Major League Baseball (MLB)
  team, 37, 41, 55, 62, 97–99
Mass marketing, 119
McKinsey Sales DNA model, 193

Median listing price (MLP), 42, 46, 48–50

Microsoft Dynamics CRM, 56–57, 65–67

Minnesota United Sponsorship, 164–165

N

National Football League (NFL) teams, 9, 37, 47–49, 58, 97, 99–101, 115, 160, 179, 210

National Women's Soccer League (NWSL), 166

NHL All-Star Game, 17

O

Oracle, 163–164

Orlando Magic organization, 7
digital ticketing, 24
Fast Break Pass
All-Star Pass, 29
buyers, 27–28
Buzzer Beater Pass, 29
casual fan research insights, 25–26
Experience technology, 26
Fall Fast Break Pass, 26
Fall Fast Break Plus Pass, 26
Fall Pass, 29
Fall Plus Pass, 29
goal of, 25
Half-Season Pass, 28
randomized seat assignments, 27
sales, 29
2015-2016 season, 27–28
Season Pass, 28
Slam Dunk Pass, 29
Weekday Pass, 28
Weekend Pass, 28

season ticket members
advantages, 31–32
Loyal Blue research insights, 29–30
Magic Money, 30–31
Not Going feature, 30
targeted fan intercept surveys, 17
VenueNext's platform, 31

P

Partnership Scoreboard, 164

Point-of-sale software systems, 4

Predictive analytics, 223

Prescriptive analytics, 223–224

Primary and secondary ticket markets
before and after SEO, 35
ARP, 42–46, 50
brokers, 37, 43–44
dynamic pricing, 43
e-retailing sites, 36
GIP, 42, 50
MLP, 42, 46, 48–50
revenue generation management, 36
sales barometer, 37
sales representatives, 36
season ticket holders, 37
SVG/total inventory, 42, 50
"The Fight of the Century" case study, 45–47
ticket flooding, 41–42
ticket reselling
Black Friday sales, 40
digital advertising resources, 36
Golden State, 38
StubHub, Inc., 38, 40
ticket barcode cancellation policy, 38
Ticketmaster, 38–39
U.S. Supreme Court decision, 39

Tom Brady and Ticket Markets
   case study, 47–50
Winnipeg Jets, 44

Q

Qualitative analysis, 176

R

Raise Your Game session, 193–194
Regression analysis, 225–226
Return on investment (ROI), 16–17,
   73, 85, 87, 147–148, 158,
   165, 179, 225
Return on objectives (ROO), 16–17,
   73, 87

S

Sales creative direct marketing test,
   125–129
Salesforce.com, 56
Sales representative tracking, 54
Search engine optimization (SEO),
   35, 37, 150
Seat listing average (SVG), 42, 50
Sponsorship inventory, 162, 166
Sport business analytics course
   CIO survey, 220–221
   college-wide initiative, 220
   course content
      analytics integration, 223–224
      class assignments, 225–227
      content delivery, 225
      exam, 227
      sport business applications,
         224–225
   CRM development, 221
   customer relationships, 222
   incremental revenue growth, 222
   job market, 220
   McKinsey estimation, 221

North American professional
   sports team, 222
skill set, "five-tool" analytics
   candidate, 221
strategic development, 220–221
USF, 220
Sport Business Industry
   business analytics application areas
      corporate partnership
         acquisition, valuation, and
         evaluation, 15–17
      CRM, 11–12
      digital marketing, 14–15
      fan engagement, 12–14
      market research, 17
      social media, 14–15
      ticket pricing and sales
         inventory, 7–11
   collaboration, 20
   communication, 19–20
   consumer brand loyalty
      strategies, 7
   digital marketing tactics, 7
   KPIs, 7
   legal resale market, 7
   revenue management, 6
   strategic plan, 19
   yield management, 6
Sports sponsorship
   big data, 158
   communication strategy, 167–170
   definition, 159
   dynamic ticket pricing, 158
   inventory items, 159–160
   properties, 160–162
   ROI spend, 158
   sport organizations value asset
      comparable valuation, 166–167
      inherent valuation, 162–165
      relative valuation, 165–166
Statistical tools, 224
StubHub, 10, 24, 38, 40, 49, 97
Super Bowl XLIX, 46–49, 163

T

Talent analytics
    analytical human resources, 189
    AT&T and Google, 195
    confidential data, 197
    definition, 188–190
    employee engagement, 195
    employee hiring process, 196
    future aspects, 198–199
    Google's retention algorithm, 195
    Harrah's Entertainment, 194
    human-capital facts, 188–189
    human-capital investment
        analysis, 189
    organization risk, 197–198
    people operations, 195
    performance evaluations, 187
    sport business applications
        The Aspire Group
            "WHOPPPP," 193–194
        NBA sales DNA initiative,
            191–193
    talent supply chain, 190
    talent value model, 190
    "what if" analysis, 196
    workforce forecast, 189–190

Teaching, sport business course,
    see Sport business analytics
    course
"The Fight of the Century" case
    study, 45–47
The Ticket Wars, 38
Ticket demand models,
    8, 225–226
Ticket marketing, sales, and service
    (TiMSS), 70
    acquire new fans, 72
    Georgia Tech FRMC, 73–87
    grow casual fans, 72
    plan, 71, 87–88
    8-point philosophy, 71–72
    retain avid fans, 72
    road map, 71
    tactics, 73
Ticketmaster, 10, 38–39, 46, 57
Ticket sales, 69–70
TiMSS, *see* Ticket marketing, sales,
    and service
Tom Brady and Ticket Markets case
    study, 47–50
Traditional media, 159–160,
    162–163